Really Managing Health Care

Valerie Iles

Open University Press
Buckingham · Philadelphia

Open University Press
Celtic Court
22 Ballmoor
Buckingham
MK18 1XW

and
1900 Frost Road, Suite 101
Bristol, PA 19007, USA

First Published 1997

A catalogue record of this book is available from the British Library

ISBN   0 335 19414 1 (pbk)   ISBN   0 335 19415 X (hbk)

Library of Congress Cataloging-in-Publication Data
Iles, Valerie, 1952–
    Really managing health care / Valerie Iles.
      p.   cm. — (Health services management)
    Includes bibliographical references and index.
    ISBN 0–335–19414–1 (pb.). — ISBN 0–335–19415–X (hb.)
    1. Health services administration—Great Britain. I. Title.
  II. Series.
  RA395.G6I44   1996
  362.1′068—dc20   96–17866
                                                       CIP

Typeset by Graphicraft Typesetters Ltd, Hong Kong
Printed in Great Britain by St Edmundsbury Press Ltd,
Bury St Edmunds, Suffolk

To Eleanor Charlotte Iles Smith

Contents

Acknowledgements

In the 6 years since I joined City University and founded the Health Management Group, I have been involved in much teaching about how to manage health care, but even more so learning. I am very grateful to my colleagues and course members for all that they have taught me, the feedback they have given me and the ideas that they have stimulated. In particular I would like to thank Derek Cramp for his never-ending capacity to supply further references, new links and interesting discussion. Humphrey Bourne, John Garlick, Iain Kidson, Geoff Meads, Linda Smith and Julia Vaughan Smith have all been more helpful than I have told them. Simon Wiseman and the general practitioners of Camden and Islington have also had a considerable influence on the shape of this book. Mandy Ansell, Nancy Craven, Toni Rowe and Rosie Stephens were among those who read early drafts and provided valuable suggestions. Peter Coe, Bryan Harrison, Peter Reading and Jim Stewart were also very generous with their time. None of them, however, can be held responsible for my interpretation of the facts or concepts they provided; any criticisms must be directed at me.

In many ways, this book arises out of the two elements of our degree programmes that differentiate them from others – our emphasis on understanding the clinical dimension, and on personal development and growth. However, the person who first prompted my realization of just what is going so badly wrong with management in health care was my partner, Colin Smith. As a thoroughly effective managing director in manufacturing industry, his behaviour is very different from that which I observe in senior managers in health care.

In the dim and distant days of the Resource Management Initiative, when there were still four Thames Regions, South-East Thames commissioned an excellent training course from Price Waterhouse Consultants' Organizational

Development Team, which started me thinking about what my MBA, from the London Business School, had not taught me. Their approach has now become so embedded in my subconscious that I cannot identify particular concepts to credit, but no doubt they will recognize many.

As an employer, City University has allowed me to experience many of the emotions and learn many of the lessons described in Chapter 3, so it is cordially dedicated to them. Without Chris Heginbotham, who commissioned the book and encouraged me throughout, the book would never have been written. Last but by no means least, Laurey King has worked absolute miracles on the word processor.

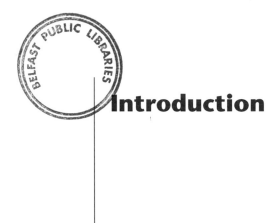

Introduction

Hardly anyone is managing health care. There are increasing numbers of managers in health care, but that is not the same thing. There is a lot of counting going on. A lot of collecting, analysing and shuffling of numbers and other data items. A lot of people making their presence felt. But influencing outcomes? Maximizing the enthusiasm and commitment of healthcare professionals around shared goals? In other words, *really managing*?

Why is this? Why is it that the growing numbers of people who believe they are managing are not doing so? Joe Batten, in his book *Tough Minded Leadership*,[1] gives us a clue. He draws a distinction between the 'simple hard' and the 'complicated easy'. The former could be something as simple, and as hard, as acting with integrity. The latter? Analysing the impact of a change in case-mix on budget projections, or redesigning organizational structures.

Today's healthcare managers are concentrating on the complicated easy at the expense of the simple hard. This is understandable. The increasing specialization of health care has led to a culture in which there is an unspoken assumption that if we could just find the expert with the correct answer, we would be able to solve any problem. While this belief may be well founded for many clinical problems where the constituent elements are cells, in management problems those constituent parts are people and the richness of personality ensures that there is no single correct solution, however complicated. Whenever we interact with other people, we cannot succeed unless we heed the simple hard.

Much of the complicated easy is, of course, necessary. Without it, managers – even *real managers* – do not have the tools with which to manage. However, without the simple hard the complicated easy does not work. Worse, it can actually impede the individuals and organizations it is supposed to be rendering more effective, and be perceived as unnecessary bureaucracy and constraint.

This is a book about the simple hard. It introduces a range of management concepts which are conceptually simple. So simple that in practice they often fail to receive the attention they warrant. So simple that it is possible to complete an MBA without having referred to some of them. I hope that it will prove useful, practical, challenging and transforming. Undoubtedly, it will prove (particularly to those whose intellect is only tickled by the complicated easy) irritating, simplistic, misguided and just plain wrong. If you find you are becoming annoyed, please turn to Chapter 6 before parting company.

The first three chapters look at different aspects of 'really managing people'. Chapters 1 and 2, 'Working through others' and 'Working with others', should be of interest to all. Chapter 3, 'Working for others', will be of most interest to those working for sizeable organizations, as will Chapter 7, 'Really managing organizations'. Those who have studied management will be able to skip Chapter 5, 'Really managing money'. Chapters 4 and 6, 'Really managing change' and 'Really managing yourself', are again aimed at everyone.

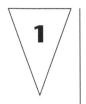

Really managing people: working through others

As soon as we ask someone else to do something, rather than undertaking it ourselves, we become managers. We rely on someone else to perform that task in the way we would do if we had the time (and the skill, the knowledge and the patience perhaps). Most of us, then, spend much of our time, in many aspects of our lives, managing other people; even though we may not call ourselves or think of ourselves as managers. Our own effectiveness, and our enjoyment of work and home lives, are strongly influenced by whether the people we rely on complete tasks to our satisfaction. Yet many of us are poor at managing others. Although highly skilled in the activities which we ourselves undertake, we fail to observe some simple rules about the management process, which, if implemented, would make us, and the people around us, more productive and more satisfied.

At its simplest, there are three fundamental rules to be followed when working through other people.

Three basic rules for managing people

1 Agree with them precisely what it is you expect them to achieve.
2 Ensure that both you and they are confident that they have the skills and resources to achieve it.
3 Give them feedback on whether they are achieving it.

Rule 1: Agree expectations

Unless people know what we want of them, they are unlikely to achieve it. Not all of it anyway. Some may complete the technical task asked of them, but have offended colleagues with their brusqueness along the way. Others may tackle the task so thoroughly and carefully that they miss important deadlines. Yet others may launch themselves with enthusiasm in a direction we know from experience is unlikely to be fruitful.

We need to agree with them just what it is we expect them to achieve and how. In different circumstances the means by which agreement is reached will differ. If you engage a cleaner in your home, you probably *tell* her what you want her to do. When it comes to your expectations of someone who is highly educated and possesses many complex skills which you do not (as is the case when managing many healthcare professionals HCPs),[1] much more *discussion* will be necessary. Here you will focus more on outcomes and leave the individual to determine how to reach them.

This seems obvious. But think about your own career. How many times has anyone sat down with you and spelled out exactly what they are expecting of you? Most people I ask, when teaching, say 'never' or 'once', and that was usually a 'holiday job' when a student. We are very bad, in health care, at saying what we expect of people. We rely on the professional tag people wear. We employ a district nurse and expect her to be a district nurse. When our notions of what that means do not coincide with hers, we blame her.

Recently, the use of job descriptions has greatly improved and as a result they have become a useful basis for a discussion of this kind. They are not, however, a substitute for it. Such descriptions cannot convey the 'how', only the 'what'. They form the basis of a legal contract but not a psychological one. Reaching agreement requires both parties to express their views and respond to those of the other. Interpreting expression and emphasis is an important aspect of this exchange and thus talking together, face to face, is really the only way to observe rule 1. What is more, it will be necessary to have conversations at regular intervals to check that both parties are still in agreement. As we are exposed daily to different influences our views change, so will those of the people we are managing and these changes may well need to be reflected in our expectations of them.

Rule 2: Ensure skills and resources

Once others know what we expect of them, we must ensure that both parties are confident that they can achieve it, that they have the knowledge, skills and resources required. This is not as straightforward as asking them. Some people will give an overconfident assertion that they do. Others, negotiating for more resources, may insist that they do not. Some may feel unsure of their abilities, although your judgement is that they will be fine. Both you and they may have underestimated what is required.

To be able to diagnose which, if any, of these situations applies, you will need to spend time with your staff, observing the skills they use, the reasoning they employ, the way they deploy their resources (including their time). When you are unable to assess their skills yourself (because they are clinical or technical skills outside your own area of expertise), you will need to seek specialist advice. This must, of course, be discussed with the staff member involved. Often when I say this, senior managers object, saying, 'but I have to trust my staff'; some even say 'management is about learning to trust your staff'. Both statements are absolutely correct, but they support rather than oppose the concept of managers accurately assessing the capabilities of their staff. Without such an assessment, you do not have trust, you have hope.

The situations described above will need to be handled in different ways if you are to implement rule 2 successfully.

When a member of staff has overestimated his knowledge or skills, then together you should review your expectations of him and consider some relevant training. It is important that you decide whether the person concerned exaggerated his abilities to you knowingly out of insecurity, or unknowingly due to a lack of insight. You will then be able to develop the kind of relationship in which he feels able to admit areas of weakness, or find ways of constructively challenging his view of himself.

In the contrasting situation where a member of staff is not as confident of his own abilities as you are, he will need to draw confidence from you. You must find ways of convincing him, reassuring him of your support, of reducing the risk for him, perhaps by putting that support in writing. Soon other members of staff whom you have similarly encouraged will be able to give credence to your case.

If it becomes clear as a result of careful observation and analysis of relevant data that your staff are 'shroud waving', you are in for a different kind of negotiation. The imposition of what you deem an appropriate level of resources will simply not work. Only the most mature of individuals or teams would not try to vindicate their position and fail to achieve your performance targets.

Personal credibility is the key here. Most shroud waving takes place when there is lack of faith in the motives or judgement of the resource allocator. There is no short cut: you will have to demonstrate integrity, a concern for your staff and their needs, and an understanding of the operational details. You will also have to convince them that your aims encompass their own. Of course if you do not have integrity, aims which encompass theirs, genuine concern for them and a knowledge of that detail then . . . perhaps they are right and you are wrong!

In some cases, the skills and resources required only become apparent as the nature of the task is revealed. When this happens and both you and your staff underestimated the requirements, you must sit down together and reach a new agreement on expectations. If you do not match your expectations to the skills and resources held by your team, then you will have only yourself to blame if they fail to perform.

Rule 3:   Feedback

Once people know what is expected of them, and have the skills and resources to achieve it, they need to receive regular feedback on whether they are doing so. This will enable them to increase their effort in one or more areas if this is necessary. Once we know they can do something, whether they do it depends on the choices they make about the effort they put in.

The way feedback is given and received will depend on the circumstances. For example, it may be in the form of anonymized data comparing the performance of different members of staff, as is the case with clinical audit. Or, it may require a face-to-face meeting between you and the member of staff in question. It will be helpful to clarify just how such feedback will be communicated when agreeing on expectations.

The importance of feedback cannot be overstated; it is by receiving feedback from others, either expressed or observed, that we improve our skills, develop and grow. We therefore owe it to the people we work with, especially those for whom we are managerially responsible, to give them the feedback that will enable them to progress. Criticism, however, may be so wounding that, far from enabling the recipient to change one of their behaviours and grow, it robs them of the confidence to attempt any change, and indeed can exacerbate the problem. The way in which the feedback is given is what makes the difference. The fact that feedback can have such an adverse impact requires us to prepare carefully before communicating it. The following points should be borne in mind.

1 It is unlikely that everything that the individual (R for recipient) is doing is wrong. Most often you will be happy with many aspects of their work, just unhappy about one or two. In order to change her behaviour, R must feel able to do so; she must be confident that she can do so, and this confidence must be drawn both from herself and from you. A 'criticism sandwich' enables this to happen. Start the discussion with praise about something she is doing that you genuinely think is good. Only then introduce the negative feedback as described below. Finish with further praise. This has several advantages, not least that you keep the negative aspects of her work in perspective. Remember the proportions of a sandwich: the filling is usually no thicker than the slices of bread. R should leave the discussion feeling that its purpose was praise or a review of progress, and that by making efforts in the direction agreed any problems will be overcome.[2]

To increase further the likelihood of your feedback being effective, there is a recipe for the sandwich filling, an approach espoused by Joe Batten. He sums it up as 'ask, listen, expect'.[3] Before you tell R what you think of her performance, *ask* her what she thinks of it. Keep refining your questions until you get to the crux of the problem, and then ask her what is causing the problem and what she can do about it. Listen (really *listen*) to what she has to say, helping her to think it through if that is what is needed (often it is not), and then make clear that you are *expecting* her to resolve the problem.

If an individual does not have the insight (or perhaps the confidence in their standing with you) for this to work, then you must provide the sandwich filling yourself.

2 You do not have the right, the ability or any interest in changing R's personality. You are concerned with her behaviour. So talk about what she does, not what she is: 'You have arrived late three times this week', not 'You are lazy'. Describe things that you have seen, heard or measured.

3 People are complex and individual and you cannot be sure of knowing the reasons why R is behaving the way she is. Restrict your comments to the behaviour and don't jump to conclusions about the causes: 'It is taking you much longer than your colleagues to do *x*', not 'You're far too tired to do your work properly'.

4 Hardly anyone is completely lacking in some behaviours or has others that must be eradicated completely. The problem is that they are more aggressive, less patient, more acquiescent, less assertive, etc., than you want them to be. So say so. Describe their behaviour in terms of more or less.

5 Keep your description neutral. This behaviour is a problem in this situation; in other situations it may be appropriate. Do not place a value on it of (good *vs* bad, right *vs* wrong), just describe it.

6 It is difficult to change our behaviour unless we know precisely what it is we have to change. So be specific. Give exact details of the time and place when an example of the behaviour occurred, preferably while it is still fresh in both memories. Only give as much information as R needs however, or can use. Don't give a catalogue of crimes if it is not helpful.

7 Different people find different methods helpful when it comes to learning how to change their behaviour. You may have found one particular course, technique, book, etc., helpful. Others may not have. Give R information, share ideas with her but do not give her advice. Let R choose; she knows how she learns better than you do.

8 Choose the time and place carefully. Even good feedback given at the wrong time or in a place where R is uncomfortable will not be effective. It is highly unlikely that she will feel comfortable when anyone else is present, so if you are planning a 'put down' in front of others, re-examine your motives.

9 Remember that the purpose of giving feedback is to enable R to change a behaviour and become more skilful. It is not to make *you* feel better. Bear in mind that although R may find it painful, the feedback is for her benefit. Feedback is often badly given because we all hate doing it, and rush through it trying to get it over as quickly as possible. Development of one's staff is one of the most important responsibilities of a manager and thus feedback is an essential element. Don't avoid it.

Prepare for it, perhaps even role-play it with a colleague or friend until you become skilled at it.

10 Do not be deflected from your purpose (the benefit of R) by a defensive or hostile response. Master your irritation (with yourself and with R) or, if you are unable to do this, move on to the second slice of bread (a positive statement) and schedule a further meeting to discuss the 'filling'. Continuing when you are angry will only exacerbate the problem. With practice, however, you will be able to master your anger to the benefit of all concerned.

A further point about feedback: people receive it even if you do not give it. They infer from your silence, they observe your body language, they overhear comments you make to other people. Sometimes they gain a fair reflection of your views; often just the opposite; more often still they are just confused. Feedback is one of the many areas of management when 'doing nothing' is just not possible. By not actively doing or saying anything, you are doing something. How much better it is to make that something really effective.

Clearly, if you are to be in a position to give feedback you must know how someone is performing. Again there is no short-cut here. You must spend time with that person, with their results, with their staff, with their clients, taking a genuine, constructive interest. There is no substitute for what Tom Peters calls 'management by walking about' (MBWA).[4] This is another concept that causes indignation among senior health managers. 'Surely', they say, 'I must only communicate with my staff through the organizational hierarchy; otherwise I am undermining the authority of my team'. They would be correct if you were to use your time with frontline staff or patients to impart news of decisions you had not told their line managers about; or if you were to gossip with them about individuals not present; or if, when they told you of a problem they had with their manager, you were not to support that manager in their absence, while also making sure you understood the perspective of the complainants.

In this, as in so much of management, the results of your actions will depend on your intentions and your integrity. If you set out to snoop, to find evidence with which to confront or to blame, then you will undermine yourself and your team. If your intention is to evaluate performance so that you can praise, offer support where needed, and keep in touch with your organization and its clients – and you have the integrity not to get ensnared in the traps that will be set for you – then the results will be entirely positive.

The other retort I hear is, 'That's all very well in theory [for you people in universities they mean!], but in the real world I'm far too busy with *my* work to spend time walking about'. What such people fail to see is that this is their work, the most important aspect of it. (Chapter 7 considers this in more detail.)

In health care, particularly where it borders social care, much of the frontline workload is undertaken off-site. In all aspects of health care, it involves autonomous practitioners working alone with clients. How does MBWA apply here? There can be no spontaneous decision to 'drop in and see how things are going' when we are talking about confidential discussions between a patient and professional, or when dropping in means catching up with a community psychiatric nurse on her rounds. And yet it is essential that performance is monitored here also. Staff in these areas also have the right to feedback that will help them to develop and grow.

Some of the models developed in other arenas may be helpful. Sales people operate entirely off-site and sales managers spend one day a month (or every two months, or every quarter, depending on the company and industry sector) with each individual team member, observing interactions with some clients, and discussing others. This is often seen by the sales rep as an opportunity to shine, and also as an opportunity to bring the skills of the manager to bear with a client they have found difficult. In social work, too, there is a well-used system of supervision in which social workers discuss with their team leader their current caseload. Again this is seen as valuable, often vital, support. Teachers, working alone most of the time, produce detailed lesson plans for their own benefit, but also as a basis for constructive discussion with departmental heads.

Many HCPs reading this will be irritated at the suggestion that this kind of supervision and discussion does not already take place in the field of health care. But think carefully, do you see your head of department, your consultant, your chief executive as a resource to be used by you? If you hold one of these posts, does your team view your role as assisting them to function effectively? Do you have the systems in place to offer them this kind of support? Just how often do you spend time discussing cases in detail with them? For each member of your team, count the number of times you have discussed their caseload in the last 6 months. Do you require your team to do this with their staff? Is your attitude to your staff that of resource and supporter, or that of policeman?

Applying the three rules in different settings

The three rules apply whenever we are managing other people. The ways in which we apply them, in particular the time horizon and the level of technical detail, will differ however.

When managing care assistants, it may be appropriate to discuss expectations of specific activities. When planning an outing with a group of clients with learning difficulties, the care assistants' manager may remind them of the purpose of the activity, discuss with them their responsibilities, and review their ideas and the support they need. On their return, they should be thoroughly debriefed to discover whether the aims were met. This may be necessary each time such an activity takes place. With a member of a Trust Board, some of the time horizons will be much longer – a year or 3 years – and the emphasis will be on approach rather than on details.

The three rules also apply when managing teams and are especially important when individual team members are accountable to different managers. Here the rules must be applied to the team. Therefore, team members must be clear about what is expected of them as a team, and they must be confident that they have the necessary skills and resources. And the team members, as a team, must receive feedback on whether they are being successful. However, teams can be likened to very immature, unpredictable individuals and implementing the three rules may be time-consuming and emotionally draining. Perhaps for this reason the majority of multidisciplinary teams are left unmanaged. Suboptimal outcomes and waste of staff time are the predictable results. There is often confusion over the most basic parameters, such as the role of the team. Some members believe it to be a source of advice for a team leader, often a consultant or GP; others perceive it as a decision-making group with all members having an equal say. When these beliefs co-exist in the same group, conflict is inevitable. Teams will naturally evolve and change in focus, as will the roles of their members; however, this is an argument for a regular review of roles and responsibilities, not for a shirking of that debate.

Because discussion with the group as a whole (in an attempt to reach agreement on roles and expectations or to communicate feedback on performance) is such hard work, it is often avoided by those with responsibility for the team. Instead, individuals perceived to be sympathetic to a particular way of thinking are lobbied and expected to sell this view to the rest of the team. This almost never works and has the result that the team will view the manager as being cowardly, in addition to being wrong.

Three simple rules for managing people. Simple and obvious. But we don't observe them. We don't implement them because to do so takes time, emotional energy and courage. In other words, they are simple but hard. We prefer to spend our time doing things that are more complicated but which demand of us only our intellect, such as introducing new systems or structures. We gravitate towards the complicated easy. And yet if we do not observe the simple hard, then we are bound to fail when it comes to the complicated easy.

Unless we implement these three simple rules we are not managing, not *really* managing. Unless we do so we can take no responsibility for the actions of others because we have little influence over those actions. We restrict our role to that of observer, presider, in certain circumstances that of administrator, business or general manager, not that of *real* manager.

You may by now have accepted the logic of the three rules, but be deceiving yourself that 'my staff *know* what they're supposed to be doing and how well they're doing it'. If, however, you are seriously considering ways in which you can introduce them, then you are probably having misgivings about the responses of your various staff members. They may be hostile, defensive, superior or apathetic. Understanding what makes different people respond in the way they do will help you engender much more favourable reactions. In the next section, we look at what makes different people 'tick'.

One last point about the three rules. Do not feel aggrieved if your line manager is not observing them with you. Not only because this is the norm, but because it gives you the opportunity to shape your role as you would like it. In this case, you can approach him with a set of expectations to which you ask him to agree. Almost invariably he will. You then explore with him your skills and resources and feedback mechanisms. Have you noticed who is now managing who?

Differences that cause difficulties

Call to mind the members of your team. As you do so, note how you feel about them. Consider the maxim 'the greatest gift you can give to anyone is consistently to expect their best'. Are you able to do that for your team members? Do you feel pleased with them, proud of them, impressed by them? Or do you find that difficult because they disappoint you, irritate you, make you feel angry, frustrated or despairing? In this section, we look at some of the reasons why they succeed in infuriating you.

Because our personalities are so rich and complex, we, naturally, differ from each other in many ways. This often adds to our enjoyment of each other, but equally often these differences can cause difficulties, misunderstandings, misinterpretations and distrust. By looking at some of these differences and at the problems they can cause, we can begin to understand how irritations and conflicts arise and thus become better able to avoid or deal with them.

Different motivation profiles

Much research has been undertaken by psychologists and others into what motivates us to expend our energy. Perhaps the most widely known motivation theorist is Abraham Maslow, who suggested in his book *Motivation and Personality*,[5] that there is a hierarchy of human needs and that only when the needs on the lowest layer of the hierarchy are met do we seek to meet the needs of the next layer. The needs he identified are shown in Figure 1.1.

Recently, workers in the field have identified sets of needs, goals or drivers that are similar but not identical to those proposed by Maslow, and which do not remain static; rather, they differ between individuals and between cultures, as well as over time. These researchers suggest that each of these drivers is important to us all to some degree, but that we differ in their *relative* importance. In other words, if we are deprived of any one of these drivers, we will be motivated to regain it; however, some are more important than others to each individual. John Hunt identifies eight such goal categories,[6] which overlap with those of Maslow as indicated:

1 *Comfort.* In addition to Maslow's physiological needs of food, drink, shelter and clothing, this category includes pleasant working conditions

Figure 1.1   Maslow's hierarchy of human needs

and sufficient money to provide a comfortable lifestyle. People who have a strong comfort driver will be motivated by performance-related financial reward.

2 *Structure.*   These map onto Maslow's safety and security needs, but relate as much to an individual's desire for certainty as to their concern about physical or financial security. People with strong structure goals will thrive in bureaucracies and environments where there are numerous clearly defined roles and their own role is precisely delineated.

3 *Relationships.*   Maslow called this category 'social needs'. It reflects the degree to which individuals seek to form lasting relationships and with whom. For many people, this is one of the most important goals. They seek collaborative rather than competitive working relationships and mourn the loss of close colleagues if their organizations are restructured and teams are disbanded.

4 *Recognition and status.*   Whereas Maslow proposed one category of 'self-esteem' needs, Hunt divides them into two: (1) recognition and status and (2) power. As recognition and power often come together (the title and the car go with the decision-making job), they can be confused. People with high recognition needs often gravitate towards academic roles and the professions, so we can expect to find many in health care. Managed sensitively, these people are easy to motivate, since they respond best to sincere praise from individuals they rate.

5 *Power.*   The degree to which someone seeks to influence and control people, events and situations. Most people who make it to the top of organizations are motivated most strongly by power. Again, it is also a strong driver in many of those who choose one of the professions.

6, 7 and 8 *Autonomy, creativity and growth.*   These three together form Maslow's self-actualization needs, but describe them more precisely. The three do not necessarily occur together, although they may do so.

The relative importance that we place on these goals or drivers can be thought of as forming a 'motivation profile'. When we try to interact with someone with a different motivation profile, we must expect not to see things in the same way. For example, my two most significant goals may be recognition and self-actualization, whereas yours may be power and structure. If, in addition, structure is (within limits) unimportant to me and self-actualization is unimportant to you, then we may well see each other in a negative light. You may perceive me as being too ready to take risks, as pursuing ill-considered schemes that are not sufficiently thought through, and in pursuit of my own ambition: 'selfish' you might say. I, on the other hand, may see you as averse to risk when you pour scorn on my ideas, and scheming when you exert your influence through other people and do not claim the credit yourself: 'cowardly' I might think. The more you try and de-risk my projects by building in contingency planning, re-quiring from me more and more detail, or the more I try and sell you the grandiose upside and how much it will do for your reputation, the more and more we will irritate each other.

Take a moment now to visualize your most difficult member of staff, the one who simply cannot see sense. As dispassionately as you can, identify the drivers that you think are most important to them. Now look at the 'demotivating factors' for those goals in Table 1.1. How many of them are you invoking? You may unwittingly (or not) have been provoking this individual into their worst behaviour. Adopting some of the actions listed under 'motivating factors' will probably transform your difficult staff mem-ber into a valuable asset.

The important point to remember is that if you are trying to motivate someone else, you must consider what it is that motivates them and not what would motivate you in similar circumstances. It is such a simple mis-take to make: We like someone; we assume they are like us; we are dis-appointed if they do not respond enthusiastically to what we perceive an exciting opportunity; we like them a little less; and soon our relationship is into a downward spiral of disappointment and irritation. If we start by thinking about them, and what enthuses them and what irritates them (with-out making judgements, just recognizing differences), we can avoid this.

Sometimes we encounter the opposite problem: we are motivated by the same thing and find ourselves locked in competition. This is especially likely if we are both seeking recognition; the more you try and grab all the limelight, the more hostile I become and the less inclined I am to give you any credit. If one of us can be honest about our need for recognition or status, then we may be able to devise ways of working together that will allow us both to gain. So ingrained, however, is the notion that 'showing off' is something to be despised, that such honesty will require courage.

It is worth reminding ourselves, in this situation, that there is nothing inherently right or wrong about being driven by any of these goals. It is not 'better' to have a strong autonomy goal than a strong relationships one, high creative needs than a strong driver towards structure and secur-ity. Being sensitive to the goals of the individuals around us allows us to be more persuasive. It requires, of course, that we invest time in getting to

Table 1.1   The motivating and demotivating factors associated with different preferences

Goal	Motivating factors	Demotivating factors
Comfort	Pleasant working environment: view, window, fixtures and fittings, temperature Salary sufficient to provide a comfortable lifestyle outside work	Scruffy, dirty, cold, uncomfortable, dull working environment Salary insufficient to provide the comfortable lifestyle that is desired
Security	Told exactly what to do and how to do it Predictable career path Financial rewards reliable Environment physically secure	Vague instructions relating to outcomes Next step uncertain Risk to income Risk of physical harm
Relationships	Opportunities to meet other people, to chat, to get to know other people and work in a team Culture where staff care for each other	Working on own, competing with others Culture where the task is all-important and people's feelings do not matter
Recognition	Sincere praise, credit given where it is due, thanks, public recognition, advice sought, name associated with project/paper/etc., the good opinion of others Personal satisfaction with a job well done. Knowledge that a genuine contribution has been made	Others taking credit for work, downplaying of role, being 'brought down to size', squashing of ideas or enthusiasm Annoyance with self over a job not well done. Egg on face
Power	Decisions to make, reports to write, opportunity to give advice, decisions implemented, advice taken and actioned (even if not acknowledged), things 'shaping up nicely' even if own name not associated with changes being made	No opportunity to influence events
Self-actualization: Growth Creativity Autonomy	New projects, new ideas, developing new skills, expectations expressed in outcomes	The same old thing, new patterns of work involve the same old skills, being told exactly what to do and how to do it

know them and the ways they respond. Really managing people cannot be done from behind a closed office door, it demands considerable face-to-face contact.

Different team roles

You are discussing an idea at your regular departmental meeting and your staff respond as they always do. Liz comes to a decision very quickly and argues her case forcefully. John also forms his views early on and marshals support to oppose Liz. Sarah tries to make sure that everyone has their say and Charles expresses concern when Liz is so abrupt with Ian that she causes offence. Ian wants to know what the deadline is and who will be writing the report, while Alison is picking holes in everyone's arguments and forcing them to think more rigorously.

If this is how your team operates, then you are very lucky (or clever, or both). R.M. Belbin has demonstrated that if a team is to work success-fully, nine roles need to be undertaken by the members of the team over its working life.[7] As most teams do not contain nine members, individuals may have to play more than one role; indeed, some people are sufficiently flexible to be able to play any one of several roles according to what is required. Most of us, however, have a preference for one or two roles and rarely take on others whatever team we are in. The nine roles are:

- *Coordinator*: coordinators guide the group, define priorities, allocate tasks and roles.
- *Shaper*: shapers are task-oriented, push the team to achieve the task, pulling together the ideas of members and keeping them focused.
- *Implementer*: implementers concentrate on practicalities, making sure that the outcome of the meeting is a series of manageable, feasible processes.
- *Team worker*: team workers look after relationships in the group. Their concern is process rather than task, the welfare of individuals rather than of ideas.
- *Plant*: plants, on the other hand, are ideas people. They originate their own ideas and can be devastatingly critical of counter-arguments, but evangelical once convinced.
- *Resource investigator*: resource investigators are also ideas people but they trade in them rather than generate them. They spot good ideas, hear of relevant information available elsewhere, link ideas together, prompt further thinking by discussing widely.
- *Monitor-evaluator*: monitor-evaluators are much less easily enthused. They carefully and critically analyse all arguments put forward.
- *Completer-finisher*: completer-finishers make sure that the group meets deadlines, completes all the tasks and in the right order. They are, in MBA groups anyway, exceedingly rare!
- *Specialist*: in many circumstances, expert advice is needed and, without access to a specialist able to provide it, a project will founder.

While the adoption of all these roles by members of your departmental team will make it very productive, it does not guarantee that relationships between individual members will be harmonious. A coordinator/shaper individual can find a monitor-evaluator/completer-finisher infuriating and vice versa, and other combinations can be just as explosive. If you are conscious of your own preferred team role, then you will be able to guard against the irritation that could be caused by another, by reminding yourself of the value of these differences – the checks and balances, the synergy. Awareness of the roles of others will help you to help them value those differences too.

If your team lacks one of those roles then consider delegating it. In the same way that you delegate tasks to different members, ask someone to adopt a particular role. They may not find it easy, but it will improve the performance of your team.

Different learning styles

You attend a course that has given you a lot of fascinating information, the skills you need to utilize that information and the enthusiasm to have a go. A colleague on the programme, however, does not see it that way at all. He cannot find anything good to say about it at all, except for the food! You wonder whether he was really ready for a programme pitched at this level. Although you may be right, it is just as likely that it was the style of the programme, rather than its level, that caused your colleague difficulty. We learn in different ways and from different activities. Psychologists Peter Honey and Alan Mumford have identified four distinct learning styles, which they term 'activist', 'reflector', 'theorist' and 'pragmatist'.[8]

Activists are open-minded enthusiasts who will try anything once. They thrive on new experiences and change, particularly when left to sink or swim, and become bored with repetition and routine. They learn most when involved in games and role-play and when they have a high profile. They also learn from bouncing ideas off other people. Activists learn least on their own, and when they are told exactly what to do and how to do it. They hate lectures, reading and learning *about* things.

Theorists are analytical, objective, logical and rational. They try to fit any new fact into their wider theory. Theorists learn a lot from teaching others. They need to know exactly what they are doing and why. They respond to well-argued ideas (about anything, relevant or not) and love lectures, papers, books and discussions. Theorists learn least when they cannot explore concepts in depth, when they will question the methodology, or when forced to act without sufficiently convincing reasons. Theorists hate learning with activists.

Reflectors are thoughtful observers who like to consider all the options, all the implications, before committing themselves. They are good listeners who take the views of others into account. Reflectors learn most from observing and considering, from thinking before being required to act, by reviewing what they have learned from an exercise or situation and from being given time to reach decisions. Reflectors learn least when forced to take a high profile, when they cannot plan, or when they do not have the information to choose a course of action themselves.

Pragmatists are experimenters, practical people who try out new ideas and accept any that work. They like solving problems and looking for relevant new ideas. Pragmatists learn most when concepts are relevant to them, when they yield practical results and when they can be implemented immediately. They love relevant simulations and action plans. Pragmatists learn least from 'ivory tower' theories and when there are no opportunities for implementation.

It does not take a great deal of imagination to see that what is an exciting learning opportunity to an activist can appear alarming or superficial to a reflector. The explanation that satisfies the theorist may well send the pragmatist to sleep. When planning how to develop your staff, offer them developmental opportunities in keeping with their learning style. Better still, identify with them the learning outcomes and let them choose their own learning programme.

Different relationship styles

No discussion of personality could ignore the work of C.G. Jung, the influential Swiss psychologist whose book *Psychological Types* was published in 1921.[9] Jung suggested that differences in personality are due to the way in which people prefer to use their minds. He suggested that when the mind is active, it is engaging in one of two occupations: perceiving (receiving information) or judging (organizing that information and forming conclusions). He further stated that there are two ways in which we can perceive (sensing and intuition) and two in which we can judge (thinking and feeling). He observed that although everyone uses all four of these processes, individuals have a preference for judging or perceiving and for one kind of perceiving and one kind of judging. We apply these processes to both our internal and external worlds, but again we have a preference for one or the other (introversion or extroversion).

Thus there are four scales on which we will have a preference for one end or the other:

Perceiving	Judging
Sensing	Intuition
Thinking	Feeling
Extroversion	Introversion

These four scales give rise to 16 combinations of preferences and hence personality types. Naturally people who are perceivers may misunderstand, misinterpret or misjudge those who are judgers; sensers, those who prefer to intuit; thinkers, feelers; and extroverts, introverts. So some combinations of personality type will be more relaxed and some more stimulating, and

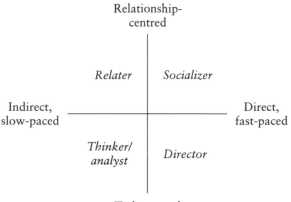

Figure 1.2   Relationship styles (Alessandra and Cathcart[10])

some will be very challenging. Clearly, an understanding of why problems arise can help to defuse them.

A number of tools for identifying these 16 personality types have been devised, of which the most well-known are the Myers-Briggs Type Indicator and the 16PF. Both of these have been extensively researched by their originators and are available through licensed practitioners. Where relationships appear to be intractably damaging, detailed diagnostic work of this kind can be helpful.

Jung's work has been drawn on by many workers, and when considering the ways in which people relate to one another, it is often enough to conceptualize personalities more simply, as do Alessandra and Cathcart.[10] They concentrate on two aspects: whether we prefer to relate to people or to tasks, and whether we think in a detailed, slow-paced way or in a more holistic, fast-paced one. By placing our preferences on each of two axes, we fall into one of four boxes, each a different relationship style (see Figure 1.2).

Socializers are enthusiastic, persuasive, motivating and creative. They enjoy being in the spotlight, and are very good at starting projects. They also have a short attention span, they take on too much, they are impatient, and do not like detail. They hate being bored and working alone. *Directors* get things done, take control, make decisions, see what needs doing and make sure it happens. They are also impatient and inflexible, they do not listen, they compete rather than collaborate, and hate people who waste their time. *Relaters* are good listeners, they are supportive of others, build trust and aim to collaborate not compete. They take time to plan interactions with others and hate friction. They are very sensitive to other people's opinion; they are not assertive and can be bullied. *Thinker/ analysts* are accurate, independent, organized and take pride in their work. They enjoy detail, are thorough and are pleased to think of themselves as perfectionists. They will insist on a detailed brief. They are surprised that others do not always see perfectionism as a virtue. They cannot be hurried, are critical of mistakes and hate surprises.

Again it is easy to see how a socializer and a thinker/analyser can rub each other up the wrong way, just as a relater and a director may do. Equally, it should be clear what can be done about it once you are aware of the cause of the tension. If your protagonist is more indirect than you are, then slow down, spell out more of the detail and elaborate on the thinking behind it. Rather than dropping in to see them, make an appointment. If they are less concerned with relationships than you, don't tell them about your family, your feelings or your health, but concentrate on the task. Similarly, if they are more direct than you, try to enthuse about the potential outcomes and check whether you really need all that detail before you can proceed. If they like talking about their family, ask about them, ask how they feel yesterday's meeting went, compliment their choice of office furniture. Remember that together you will come up with ideas, solutions, projects and services that are much better (more secure, more innovative) than either of you could have achieved alone.

People pollution

These are only a few of the many ways of looking at personalities. However, the essential point to remember is that there is nothing inherently right or wrong about any of the drivers, behaviours or preferences we have looked at, just differences, and those differences can irritate or they can enrich.

Environmental health officers observe that noise pollution only occurs when two factors are present: (1) noise and (2) hostility to the noise. In other words, we all put up with a lot of decibels when we perceive them to be pleasant. The same is true of people. We get 'people pollution' problems when there are differences *and* when we choose to perceive those differences negatively. Understanding the differences is often the first step to mastering our feelings of irritation. The very fact that such differences exist is likely to cause conflict, but such conflict can be constructive and creative or destructive and damaging. Your role as a manager is to ensure it is the former.

Max de Pree, in *The Art of Leadership*,[11] suggests that the role of leaders is to 'liberate people to achieve what is required of them in the most humane way possible'. Liberation requires implementation of the three rules outlined at the beginning of this chapter in such a way that you take account of all the differences between you and your individual team members, so that you are able to build honest, trusting relationships based on mutual respect. If that seems unlikely, impossibly difficult or even unattractive, read on.

2 Really managing people: working with others

Nowadays we are all specialists. Nobody reading this book grows all their own food, educates their own children, weaves the cloth for their clothes, makes all the music they listen to, writes all the books they read, and diagnoses and treats all the ailments from which they could suffer. As a society, we have become more and more specialized over the centuries, and the rate of specialization has quickened. One of the features of specialization is that specialist individuals or groups rely on the existence or output of other specialists if they are to achieve their own objectives. This is termed 'interdependency'. In other words, in our working lives we have all come to know more and more about less and less. This has resulted in the development of large, complex organizations, almost unknown before the Second World War, as the production of goods and services has required the involvement of greater numbers of interdependent specialists.

Specialization has brought great clinical advances but also problems of communication, a lack of shared understanding and fragmentation of responsibility. If specialist tasks A, B, C, D and E are all necessary for a successful outcome, success requires that responsibility for each of these tasks is taken, but by whom? If task C is inadequately completed but this could be remedied by an enlargement of task B or E, then who is responsible for a poor outcome? In an interdependent situation, who takes responsibility for people taking their responsibility? Very often in health care, the answer is 'no-one'. If we recognize this, then we will realize that it is not enough for each of us to take our own responsibilities, but that we must also take some responsibility across the boundary into interdependent specialties.

Sharing responsibility

Sharing responsibility is always potentially problematic. If two people share responsibility for a complex task, we could describe their joint responsibilities in the form of a cake (see Figure 2.1a).

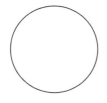

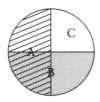

Figure 2.1a   Figure 2.1b

If each person separately takes half of the responsibility then we run the risk that person A covers half the cake (cross-hatched area) and person B covers a different half (dotted area). This leaves an area (C) for which no-one takes responsibility (Figure 2.1b).

Figure 2.1c   Figure 2.1d

One solution would be for A and B to agree on the responsibility each is taking (see Figure 2.1c). Of course, they will not now be *sharing* responsibility, *unless* they agree to keep the whole cake in mind (the complete successful outcome) and to act across the boundary if they perceive it to be necessary. This is what our responsibilities need to be if we are part of an interdependent system. If our responsibility cake has six contributors (see Figure 2.1d), then each must agree the boundaries but each must also be prepared to act sensitively across boundaries if it is thought to be necessary. Just as importantly, each should respond charitably and not defensively when others cross their boundary.

The issue of how to take responsibility across disciplines is a critical one in health care. So many of the problems that arise do so at the boundaries between disciplines and they do so because each profession self-righteously blames the other and also vigorously defends its boundaries. Given the ability and commitment of those entering the professions, how does this ill-feeling between complementary *tribes* arise? There are a number of contributory factors, which we will now consider in turn.

Causes of tribalism

Group-think

There is a tendency in any group in which members share norms, values and deeply held beliefs to engage in a phenomenon known as 'group-think'. This was first described by Janis, who observed the behaviour in groups in which some disastrous decisions had been made by very able and well-intentioned individuals.[1] In particular, he looked at the ways in which the US Administration took decisions in relation to the Cuban missile crisis and the escalation of the Vietnam War. He noted the following characteristics:

- Group members are intensely loyal to the group and to its policies, even if some of the consequences of the policies disturb the conscience of each member.
- Members do not criticize the reasoning nor behaviour of fellow members. In Janis' words, the group is 'soft-headed'. This is because members believe unquestioningly in the inherent morality of their ingroup.
- Members are, however, 'hard-hearted' when it comes to members of out-groups. They hold negative, stereotyped views of these outgroups and their leaders.
- Individual members doubt and suppress their own reasoning when it conflicts with the thinking of the group.
- If a member does question the validity of arguments expressed, then other group members apply direct, albeit subtle, pressure to conform. Most censorship, however, is self-enacted.

As you can see (by thinking for a moment about your own reaction to members of other disciplines), very many of these behaviours are exhibited within the healthcare professions and their sub-specialties.

Janis makes some recommendations to help avoid the development (or worst excesses) of group-think. These could usefully be pinned to the wall of the offices of any of the royal colleges and other professional bodies (including those for managers). They include:

1 Group leaders must validate the importance of critical evaluation of all views.
2 Leaders should require each member to discuss group deliberations with associates in other groups.
3 The group should invite outside experts to challenge the views of core members.
4 Members should be encouraged to play devil's advocate.
5 Whenever the group's deliberations involve relations with a rival organization, they should devote time to finding out as much as possible about their rivals and consider alternative ways of interpreting what the group perceives to be hostile actions.

Group-think arises when groups share beliefs and values and when they perceive other groups not to share them. If you were to ask 18-year-olds entering any of the healthcare professions, their professed concern would be with caring for others. How is it then, if they are all concerned with patient outcome, that professions perceive their beliefs and values to differ? To understand this we need to consider the ways in which they approach clinical problems.

The hierarchy of clinical descriptions

Let us consider how clinical conditions are described. The patient may feel tired and thirsty; his family may experience this as 'Dad's always too tired to play football'; his doctor having performed a urine test will talk of blood sugar levels and diagnose diabetes. We already have three different ways of describing one clinical condition. We can expand this further, to a hierarchy of descriptions in which each lower tier is at the next level of detail:[2]

level +2   patient's community
level +1   patient's family
level 0   patient as a whole
level −1   major body part (e.g. chest, abdomen, head)
level −2   physiological system (e.g. cardiovascular system, respiratory system)
level −3   system part or organ (e.g. heart, major vessels, lungs)
level −4   organ part or tissue (e.g. myocardium, bone marrow)
level −5   cell (e.g. epithelial cell, fibroblast, lymphocyte)
level −6   cell part (e.g. cell membrane, organelles, nucleus)
level −7   macromolecule (e.g. enzyme, structural protein, nucleic acid)
level −8   micromolecule (e.g. glucose, ascorbic acid)
level −9   atoms or ions (e.g. sodium ion)

In this 'hierarchy of natural descriptions', entities (or 'nominals') at one level combine together to form an entity at the next level up. So the nominals at one level become attributes at the next. However, they are not the only attributes at the higher level, as others emerge with the combination. The following 'knowledge network' expresses the hierarchy as nominals and attributes, with the emergent attributes in *italics*:[3]

Social, economic, political structures
+2   (tribe//family$_1$, family$_2$, ... *social rules* ...)
+1   (family//father, mother, children ... *customs* ...)
level 0   (human//animal, ... *highly developed consciousness, complex language, complex tools* ...)
−1   (animal//skeleton, organ$_1$, ... muscle$_1$, ... *integument*, ... , *complex behaviour*)
−2   (organ/tissue//cell$_1$, cell$_2$, ... *connective tissue* ...)
−3   (cell//nucleus, organelle$_1$, ... *reproduction* ...)
−4   (organelle//membrane$_1$, ... *ordered chemical synthesis*, ... *compartmentation*, ...)

-5 (membrane//structural protein$_1$, enzyme$_1$, ... *lipid layers, ... permeability, ... enzyme arrangement* ...)

-6 (protein//tyrosine$_1$, alanine$_1$, ... *tertiary structure* ...)

-7 (amino acid//H-atom$_1$, O-atom$_1$, ... *vibrational states, ... covalent bonds* ...)

-8 (H-atom//proton, electron, ... *excited states* ...)

-9 (proton//mass$_p$, charge$_p$, magnetic moment$_p$, ...)

quarks, elementary particles.

By looking closely at the above, we can see a number of features which pertain to hierarchies of this kind. First, we can focus our attention on only one level (and those immediately above and below it) at a time. We can track between them, and experience of a particular hierarchy increases the speed at which we can do this. We are able to trace the path from H-atoms to a cabinet reshuffle, from the effect of medication on blood electrolytes to the relief of a patient's discomfort, but we are only focusing on one level at a time. This feature is what allows someone to say that 'there is no such thing as society, only the individuals that comprise it'. The anger evoked when Margaret Thatcher expressed these sentiments arose from a belief, on the part of others, that important attributes emerge when individuals are combined into society.

Second, as we ascend the levels, individuality increases and uniformity decreases. One electron looks very much like any other electron and is readily distinguished from a neutron or proton. However, classifying both a chihuahua and a great dane as dogs and distinguishing between the class of dogs and that of wolves is much less straightforward. At the higher levels classes and terms are more ambiguous, more fuzzy, and open to different interpretations.

Third, at each level we need a different level of language. If we use a lower-level language at a higher level, it is overdescriptive and tedious without adding anything. Describing the heart in terms of all of its constituent cells takes a long time and is not necessary. Conversely, the use of a higher-level language at a lower level results in confusion or nonsense because it is overrich; it tries to ascribe attributes that do not emerge until higher levels to lower-level items (e.g. colour has no meaning at the molecular level; neither does sentience at the level of cells or of organs).

Fourth, numbers are often useful at lower levels (blood electrolyte levels, for example). They enable expression of a degree of abnormality and a measure of whether things are getting better or worse. At higher levels, quantitation is more difficult. Where high-level descriptions are converted to numbers (e.g. activities for daily living scores), they should be used with great care, since they are attempting to represent a rich, ambiguous, fuzzy, multifaceted reality. Just as words need to be used differently at different levels, so do numbers. We cannot manipulate numbers referring to high levels in the same way as those at lower levels.

Fifth, different professions tend to have expertise at different levels; indeed, many of the healthcare professions emerged as knowledge of the different layers developed. For example, although there are exceptions, typically psychologists and occupational therapists will focus on levels 0, +1 and +2 and nurses on levels −1, −2 and −3. Within professions, different disciplines also focus on different levels, so although the medical profession as a whole includes those with expertise at levels −1 to −9 (and the length of the medical training results from this), hospital-based consultants concentrate on levels lower than their colleagues in general practice.

Sixth, no level is right or wrong, or better or worse than any other level. Defining a problem completely involves consideration of *all* the levels affected. In a multidisciplinary situation, the 'clout' is often held by those operating at the lowest levels, but while the impact of lower-level malfunction on higher levels renders this understandable, each level requires expert consideration in its own right. Interestingly, where no lower-level malfunctions have been identified, for example in many mental health problems, the dynamics between the various professions involved are different. We can expect these relationships to change as the current research which correlates certain neuroendocrine pictures with particular mental health diagnoses gathers pace and starts to identify the mechanisms linking the intervening levels.

Seventh, we do not need to understand everything about every level to be able to understand explanations of the links between them.

Finally, patients sometimes hold invented hierarchies which differ from those understood by their clinicians. These are rarely explored,[4] yet impede insight into the patient's condition, compliance and satisfaction with outcomes.

There are a number of implications that arise from this hierarchy and its properties. First, if healthcare organizations are concerned with health (rather than only illness), then they have to address between them all of these levels. *But* individual HCPs can focus on only one level at a time and our organizational systems should not expect them to do otherwise. Somehow our systems need to encourage HCPs to fight a valiant battle at electrolyte level where appropriate, while still providing for the needs of patients as sociable humans and family members. These needs include dignity and meaning, and thus, at a particular time, the need for 'a good death'. At the moment they are failing to do so. This is one of the most significant challenges to healthcare organizations and we shall consider it again in Chapter 7.

Second, HCPs will naturally find communication problematic, since they use different levels of language. We need not berate each other for that, but we may need to ensure interpretation is available! We must also recognize our interdependence and the virtue of patients receiving specialist expertise, rather than amateur intervention, for each of the levels which are malfunctioning. This will be easier if those concerned remember that it is not necessary to understand everything about every level to be able to follow explanations which track from lower to higher levels. Greater exploitation of such 'tracking' would enable multidisciplinary teams to work effectively, with each member being aware of the reasoning behind an opinion. If the team then gave the responsibility for taking decisions where there are conflicting opinions to the professional most skilled at the level manifesting the greatest problems, then we might move towards a system in which multidisciplinary teams are truly teams.

Clarifying the familiarity required with each of the hierarchical levels also enables decisions to be made about how best to staff a service, which professions will be most able to contribute and what knowledge bases are necessary.

It is sometimes not realized that it is the hierarchical levels of which professions have knowledge which determine the uses to which they put their skills. These skills, particularly of those individuals intervening at higher levels, may appear nonsensically disparate to an outsider. An occupational therapist in mental health may appear to be very different from an occupational therapist working with young, physically disabled clients. However, they both share a core knowledge base and reasoning process, and this fact needs to be appreciated when decisions on skills mix are taken.

Third, if it is only at the lower levels that we can be definitive, then we need different research methods at lower and higher levels. The researcher's 'gold standard' of the randomized controlled trial, preferably double-blind – better still, double-blind and crossover – requires that the control group is matched precisely (i.e. that all the features of the entities in those groups are matched, leaving as the only variable the subject of the study). However, as we ascend the hierarchy, it becomes more and more difficult to match perfectly because of the increasing complexity and ambiguity. Whereas at lower levels we can ask a question and get a definitive answer ('yes' or 'no', or in '$x\%$ of cases . . .'), at higher levels the answers have to be qualified ('In *these* circumstances this is what we found'; 'If your circumstances are similar, then you may find the same'). Higher levels, then, require qualitative research, research which rarely yields definitive answers applicable in all settings, but qualified answers conditional on context. In other words, 'to even the most complicated of problems there is one simple, easy-to-understand, wrong answer'!

Qualitative research may be conducted as rigorously, independently and objectively as good quantitative research, or it too may suffer from poor design and execution. The fact that the results of even excellent qualitative research are qualified, as we have shown, has led to it being written off as woolly and inferior by, in particular, the medical profession. This is unfortunate for two reasons: first, doctors' behaviours and judgements are not informed by such research and, second, the quality of the design and execution of such research is not subjected to the rigorous criticism at which the profession excels. This allows too much sloppy qualitative research (quasijournalism in some cases) to be undertaken and disseminated.

A lack of awareness of the properties and implications of this hierarchy of clinical descriptions contributes greatly to the tensions between professions and to the existence of group-think.

The spectrum of views of disease

Just as different professions, or professionals in different care settings, concentrate on different levels of the hierarchy, so too do they gravitate towards different points on a spectrum of views of disease. Traditionally, there have been two contrasting views of disease, each with a long and influential history.[5] The first is that a disease is an isolatable entity having a life of its own; in other words, a disease is regarded as something that is pretty much the same whether it is experienced by one patient or another. This is the ontologic view and has been attributed to Plato. We adopt this view whenever we talk of the 'course of a disease', or when we describe a disease entirely in terms of its attributes and without any reference to patients. The second is that a disease is the change seen in a patient when not in good health. Here the sick patient is the focus of attention. This has been called the 'biographical' view of disease and can be recognized in the work of Hippocrates, famous for his highly detailed case histories. Over the centuries, both views have held sway. However, as we have come to understand more and more about humans and the diseases we experience, neither view alone is satisfactory in all circumstances.

In practice, there is a spectrum of views of disease, with a few individuals operating at each end, but most HCPs somewhere in-between:

Ontologic view of disease		Biographical view of disease
Health economists and epidemiologists	————————	Psychotherapists

The position of a HCP on the spectrum tends to depend on how well defined the disease is and on how well they know the individual patient. A general practitioner, for example, will operate further towards the biographical end of the spectrum than a hospital specialist. Similarly, doctors will tend to view patients more ontologically than nurses. The potential for strife, when the professionals involved have different concerns and feel that those concerns are not being addressed by others, is obvious.

Degree of structure in the clinical problem

There is a third cause of disharmony between different disciplines within professions, which arises out of the degree of structure inherent in the clinical problem with which they are presented. Blois represents this as a funnel (see Figure 2.2).[6] When a patient first meets the clinician, the latter needs the maximum cognitive span, since the patient's concerns could turn out to be anything or nothing, one of thousands of diseases or none at all. The

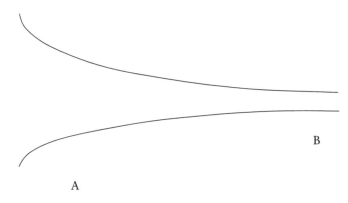

Figure 2.2   Breadth of cognitive span required of a clinician during a patient encounter

process that follows (of conversation, history-taking, physical examination, perhaps lab tests or special examinations, differential diagnosis) introduces more and more structure into the problem. At point A, the problem could be anything; at point B, the possibilities have been progressively reduced and the alternatives are now few.

People working at different parts of the funnel can sometimes undervalue each others' skills, yet the expertise required to funnel down from point A to point B is no less, just different from that required to offer specialist assessment and management once point B has been reached. The reverse is also true. Many of the communication problems that arise between primary and secondary or tertiary care workers appear to have at their root an undervaluing of the skills of the professionals on the other side of the boundary. Recognizing that different roles require different skills, rather than greater or less skill, is essential if 'seamless care' is ever to become more than just a slogan.

Philosophical stance

It is uncommon today for HCPs to have studied philosophy, and yet as individuals and professional tribes we adopt a particular philosophical stance, often unthinkingly. Indeed, that stance is part of the 'tacit knowledge' which Thomas Kuhn argues is never taught explicitly. He argues that the paradigm or framework within which we operate is invisible to us, because it is the way we structure our thinking and therefore not something we can think about. Kuhn states that 'scientists . . . never learn concepts, laws and theories in the abstract. Instead they gradually learn to think like their teachers'.[7]

When our philosophical position leads us to reason one way, while that of someone else produces a different rationale, we may be incensed and uncomprehending. It is helpful, therefore, to be aware of philosophical alternatives and thus be able to recognize not only our own beliefs but those of others. For example, one classification of ethical theories divides them into those which are motivist, consequence and deontological.[8] *Motivist* theories argue that the rightness or wrongness of an action depends upon the motive from which the act is done. *Consequence* theories deny that motive is the determinant and instead consider that it is only the effects of an action that matter. *Deontological* theories propose that the rightness or wrongness of an act depends neither upon the motive nor upon the consequences, but solely upon the kind of action it is.

The utilitarianism of Jeremy Bentham and John Stuart Mill (which espouses actions that cause the greatest good for the greatest number) is clearly a consequence theory. The work of Immanuel Kant contrasts with this and is both motivist and deontological. Kant drew a distinction between a 'categorical imperative' and a 'hypothetical imperative', rejecting the latter. The hypothetical imperative is concerned only with 'prudential action' or consequences. The categorical imperative requires that 'every action must be judged in the light of how it would appear if it were to be a universal code of behaviour'.[9] In other words, the categorical imperative is a rule which *must* be followed if one wants to behave morally. If lying were universal then society could not function, therefore one must never lie. Another expression of the categorical imperative states, 'So act as to treat humanity, whether in thine own person or in that of any other, in every case as an end withal, never as a means only'.[10]

It is clear then, that when individual utilitarians, unaware that they hold a view to which there are alternatives, disagree with others who ascribe to a number of rules which must never be broken, communication between them will be almost impossible, as they will be on different wavelengths. For them to begin to understand the logic and the emotional response of the other, they must explore the two sets of underlying beliefs.

Taking responsibility

It is a feature of the history of mankind that we have always organized into ingroups and outgroups,[11] so perhaps we should not berate both ourselves and others too severely when, as HCPs, we do so. Understanding the causes of our communication failures can help us to ensure that relationships between our own ingroup and others' outgroups do not degenerate into hostility. This, in turn, will help us to take responsibility across professional boundaries and to accept charitably the attempts of others to do so, for the benefit of patients. Fundamentally, however, our ability and desire to take responsibility for others is dependent on our ability to take responsibility for ourselves. It is only when we decide to choose how we behave, rather than reacting to our circumstances, that we can choose to exercise care for others.

In his book *The Road Less Travelled*, M. Scott Peck, an American psychiatrist and psychotherapist, provides a definition of love: 'I define love as: The will to extend one's self for the purpose of nurturing one's own or another's spiritual growth'.[12] This definition makes reference not to feelings but to intent. Peck goes further and suggests that love (genuine love which he differentiates from romantically temporary love) necessarily involves the lover in work and courage. 'If an act is not one of work or courage then it is not an act of love. There are no exceptions.'[13]

If we consider love to be a more intense and narrowly applied form of the concept of care, then we could use similar definitions for the kind of care which as HCPs we owe to our patients, our colleagues and our staff: 'Care is the will to extend one's self for the purpose of nurturing another's personal growth' and 'if an act is not one of work or courage then it is not an act of care. There are no exceptions.' Combining these two statements we can define care as 'the will to engage in acts of work or courage for the purpose of nurturing another's personal growth'.

This accords with a description by Seedhouse of the role of the doctor.[14] I have amended it to apply to all HCPs: 'The HCP will work to enable the development of potentials which will enhance the life of clients. The HCP will work to identify obstacles in the way of the development of those potentials and choose to help with those they are best equipped to assist with.'

Most HCPs would not argue with the notion that care involves work. This work includes all the years of study and apprenticeship required to develop the knowledge and skills which HCPs bring to bear with their clients; it encompasses the direct care tasks undertaken by HCPs; but it also includes, for example, the effort required to communicate effectively with other disciplines and the time it takes to ensure that resources are deployed to best effect. Courage? You need it whenever you have to give bad news; when you argue for a treatment option you believe to be in the patient's best interest against opposition from other HCPs; when you reflect honestly and openly on your professional practice and especially when you admit to mistakes.

Thinking about our role as carers in this way gives us, among other things, some criteria for many of the decisions we are called to make that are not strictly clinical or technical. For example, if you are concerned that a colleague's clinical performance is not adequate, what should you do about it? If your colleague's patients are to be cared for, then 'the role of the HCP is to remove any obstacles in the way of the development of their potentials'.

Is your colleague failing to dismantle those obstacles (clinical conditions) due to her performance? Or is she dismantling them but in a different but equally effective (or ineffective!) way from yours? This may require scrutiny of research evidence. If the former is the case, then your consideration moves outwards from her patients to encompass the clinician. How can you care for this individual? You must engage in acts of work or courage to enable that individual to grow. This will almost certainly mean informing her of your concerns.

Peck also suggests that whenever we have information and are considering withholding it, we reflect on the following guidelines:

- Never speak a falsehood, i.e. we may choose to withhold the truth but not to tell a lie.
- Remember that in each instance in which truth is withheld a moral decision is required.
- The decision to withhold truth should never be based on personal needs (power, to be liked, avoidance of discomfort . . .).
- It must be based entirely upon the needs of the person or people from whom the truth is being withheld.
- Note that the assessment of another's needs is so complex that it can only be executed wisely when one operates with genuine care for the other.
- The primary factor in the assessment of another's needs is the assessment of that person's capacity to utilise the truth for his or her own growth.[15]
- Our tendancy is to under rather than over estimate this capacity.

Peck also points out that we should approach this task with humility, checking and rechecking the validity and reality of the truth as we perceive it.

The view is sometimes expressed, particularly within the medical profession, that our concern for her patients can conflict with the need to demonstrate respect for the clinician.[16] However, if we respect a clinician, we respect her integrity, her concern for her patients and her ability to use the information given to her constructively. Of course, she may choose not to do so. She may respond defensively or angrily, particularly if we have expressed it ineffectively (usually through a lack of genuine care for her, or out of an undue concern for ourselves). But if you have prepared your presentation carefully, remembering to address your colleague's goals, preferences and styles (see Chapter 1), rather than your own, and with genuinely constructive intent, then this is less likely. Even so, it will require courage on your part as well as on hers.

Prevention is better than cure and setting up a system for constructively monitoring the performance of all the interdependent specialists in an organization will help avoid situations of this kind developing. Whose responsibility is it to do so? Ultimately, those with executive management responsibility for the organization, but they can only do so if all concerned respond constructively, and not defensively, when they try. The constructive response to a suggestion, particularly from someone outside our specialism, is essential if the interdependent organization is to succeed. Unfortunately, it is not always a feature of behaviour within healthcare organizations. As it is so important, it is worth thinking through the feelings that inhibit its appearance.

People are so complex that we can find characteristics in everyone that we can like, respect or admire. We may choose to concentrate on those characteristics when we call an individual to mind, naturally we do that for our friends or colleagues with whom we have rapport. With others, however, we tend to do the opposite and choose to dwell on characteristics we dislike, particularly if they are in any way a threat to us. That we can to a large extent choose how we feel about another person can be of great assistance as we go about our professional duties, interacting with a large number of other people and disciplines. Choosing to see the best in our professional colleagues, and choosing to respond generously instead of jealously to their proposals, makes our working lives not only more enjoyable and less stressful but also more productive and fruitful. It is when we can extend respect to others that we can develop the open, honest, trusting relationships that are both satisfying and synergistic.

Being aware of our feelings is the key here: When that suggestion was made, how did I feel? Why did I feel that way? If when we examine our feelings honestly we find that they include fear or mistrust, or both, then we have an agenda for action that is more helpful for all concerned (including ourselves), rather than an expression of defensive anger, however logically argued. On that agenda will be: (1) tackling our fear and (2) developing and using an open mind about the motives of the person making the suggestion.

Tackling fear (and fear is often at the root of our negative emotions, such as anger and resentment) again requires honesty and clear thinking: What precisely am I afraid of? What is the very worst that could happen? Why does that matter to me? How does this fit with what I want to achieve with my life?

Handling conflict situations

There are occasions when two individuals working together have different views which bring them into conflict. How each individual chooses to behave in such a conflict situation depends on two things: how much they want to meet their own needs (have their own view carry the day) and how much they want the other party to have their needs met.[17] Their wishes on these two counts give rise to five possible kinds of behaviour (see Figure 2.3).

We will all experience situations in which it will be appropriate to act in each of these ways. Whether we decide to race someone else for a parking space, or graciously allow them to have it, will be influenced by whether we are in pressing need of speed and by whether we know and like the other driver. There is no right or wrong about any of the five behaviours, they are simply appropriate or inappropriate in particular circumstances. And they can, of course, all be undertaken with as much grace as the situation permits. However, if you think about people you know, you will be aware of some individuals who have got 'stuck' in one of these behaviours. Whatever the situation, they insist on winning (competition), or always give in (accommodation), or simply will not turn up to meetings to discuss it (withdrawal). Some are hooked on 'deals' and will always come up with an offer: 'If you give up x, I can give you y' (compromise). More rarely do people get stuck in the collaboration box, and since for many situations this is the most appropriate behaviour, this causes less of a problem, but where swift decisive action is required these people may hesitate.

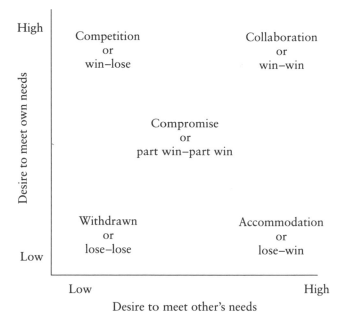

Figure 2.3   The five behaviours available to parties involved in a conflict

Recognizing that you can choose the behaviour you adopt in a conflict situation is the first step towards more successful negotiations. The second step is identifying your own needs and those of the other party. Selecting the appropriate behaviour is the third step. Engaging in the negotiation, and persuading your 'adversary' to behave productively, is only the fourth step and not (a trap it is so easy to fall into) the first. If the dispute is of major importance to both of you, and you have made the effort to fully understand the other person's needs and concerns, then you will probably select collaboration as the most appropriate behaviour. But what can you do if the other person is 'stuck' in one of the other behaviour boxes?

The two axes in Figure 2.3 suggest the ways in which you can persuade them to collaborate. If the other person is in competition mode, you are unlikely to be able to move her down the vertical axis. You must try to persuade her along the horizontal one by getting her to see your needs. You will have to sell her your needs, your problems, the difficulties you have with her proposed solution. Then you can ask her to devise a solution that meets your needs as well as her own. If there is an underlying trust between you, this will not be difficult. If there is a history of some animosity, it may be more so. However, new sales reps are taught as part of their training that the oldest sales trick in the book is, 'I have a problem, can you help'. People like being asked for help; we like being asked to solve other people's problems. If you can convince someone of the validity of your problems, the most cantankerous opponent is likely to want to help solve them.

If negotiating with someone who routinely chooses to accomodate his opponents' views (lose–win in Figure 2.3), you may initially rejoice. However, on reflection, you may consider the issue to be of too great importance to the people he represents for any such agreement to be sustainable. Inviting him to give his own views before you make your's known can be helpful. In a task-oriented culture, it is tempting to write people like this off as a soft touch. Individuals concerned with maintaining relationships are essential in all organizations, and valuing this rather than deriding it enables the other skills, knowledge and insights of those individuals to contribute to the development of really workable solutions.

Colleagues who simply opt out of discussion about an issue are often encountered in healthcare professions. Here you need to persuade them of the importance to them and to you (and hence to them again, since you are interdependent) of the matter at hand. The reason for their reluctance must influence how you choose to do this. If, for example, they feel that 'people spend far too much time talking and nothing ever changes anyway', you will have to examine recent history. Are they right? Do you have the systems in place to implement any decision reached? If so, demonstrate this. If they consider that whatever anyone else decides they will proceed unaffected, then you will need to disabuse them of this, but persuasively rather than vituperatively! If they dislike conflict and want to avoid heated discussions, you must recognize this as a valid need and seek to meet it. Compromisers, who are often interested in doing the deal rather than the outcome, require similar consideration. They will need to be convinced that all needs must be met.

If it proves impossible to get the other party to collaborate, then you may need to disengage completely. This requires careful thought, because unless there is turbulence of some sort, then your 'no-deal' position probably means the retention of the *status quo*, which may be your opponent's wish. The healthcare environment is becoming more turbulent, however, along with every other sector of society, and this no-deal veto is becoming less of a threat to effective decision-making than it has been in the past.

Resisting unreasonable demands

Major issues will invariably require the kind of planning described above. But on a day-to-day basis, we often find ourselves in a position where a colleague, a boss, a patient or a member of our staff makes what we perceive as an unreasonable demand. Sometimes this will be habitual. They may, for example, insist on taking their holidays in August every year, preventing you from doing so. They may expect you to take an unfair share of the workload. They may insist on study leave that increases the load on others in your team, or on treatment you believe to be inappropriate for their clinical condition. These are often inherently win–lose situations where one of you will be dissatisfied with the outcome. Resentment is a recipe for unproductive working relationships, and there must be a fair balance between give and take to avoid this brewing. You must therefore find ways of resisting these unreasonable demands to make sure that this balance is kept, always bearing in mind that your judgement about the balance may be suspect! There are three techniques that can be of assistance here.

First, once you have decided the position you wish to take, then calmly state it. If the response is anything other than agreement, then keep restating it in a pleasant, repetitive voice. Ignore any side issues that are raised by the other person, for if you engage with them in an argument about their reasons (or yours), you introduce the risk of losing it. Just keep repeating what you want to say. You may choose to offer a workable compromise, but only do so once you are confident that the other person has heard you and accepts your view as valid; otherwise if she feels she can brow-beat you, you are creating further problems for yourself in the future. This technique is often called 'broken record'.[18]

Second, whenever someone makes a demand or request of you, stop and note your immediate reaction. Take time to observe how you are feeling and decide whether you consider the request reasonable or not. Remember that you do not have to make an instant decision, as you can always ask for further information. If you decide not to accede to the request, then say 'no'. Just 'no'.[19] Practise saying 'no' without excessive apology or excuses – there is a difference between an explanation and an excuse. Ask yourself whether you are explaining because of your own anxiety or because you genuinely want the other person to understand your reasons. Remember that when you say 'no' you are refusing the request, not rejecting the person. Very many HCPs hate saying 'no', and when in training sessions we use role-play for this kind of situation, they will flounder, imply a negative reaction, apologize and generally go 'all round the houses' rather than say that one word. As a result, the people making requests of them receive such confused messages that they remain unaware of the stress they are causing. Take time to prepare a simple, unambiguous response, deliver it and then keep quiet.

The third technique, selling your problem, will be familiar from the previous section. When asked to do something you do not want to do, work out *why* you do not want to do it. What problem would be caused by doing it. Then instead of advancing your solution, state the problem and invite the other person to solve the problem. Keep restating the problem (using broken record) until it has been solved to your satisfaction.

Listening

In this chapter, I have referred a number of times to the importance of identifying someone else's needs, but this is harder to do than at first might seem. Putting ourselves in the other person's shoes can shed some light but, as we saw in Chapter 1, we all see the world in very different ways. Asking the other person is the obvious solution, but the efficacy of this will depend on our ability to listen. When I suggest that this is a skill that needs to be developed, HCPs always protest that they spend all their day listening, and indeed many of you do – but a different kind of listening. At work most of us listen purposefully. We look for themes or key facts that enable us to diagnose a problem and suggest a solution. All the time we are listening we are actively processing the information with a view to making a response. In our social lives, we adopt a similar listening pattern, although sometimes with different intent.

As Roger Gaunt, in his book *Personal and Group Development for Managers*, says:[20]

> To listen well is to begin to manage well. Yet somehow the essence of listening eludes me. For it has to do with a transparent openness to the speaker that is only achieved at cost. 'I so easily only hear the resonances within myself when you speak. I don't listen to you at all, but only to the memories within myself that your words activate. I so deeply want confirmation of myself that I hardly hear you at all.' Yet when a person does grow sufficiently to give unconditional attention to another, then there exist the conditions of significant change. *Development* may then take place.

If we are to understand another person well enough to empathize with their needs in the complexity and richness in which they exist, then we need to listen in a different way. We need to focus our attention entirely on the other person, letting go of our sense of purpose, not doing anything with the information we are given other than absorbing it: not judging it, not organizing it, but experiencing it, feeling it. This 'bracketing'[21] of ourselves with the person we are listening to engenders empathy and insight in a way that no other kind of listening can. It is an essential element of any really close relationship, at work or at home. It requires (but also nurtures) a genuine interest in the other's position, a considerable amount of work in the form of concentration, and self-discipline in overcoming the urge to switch back into our more normal listening mode. It is not something we can sustain for a very long period of time, but it is an important component of working successfully with others.

Synergy

By reflecting on the content of this chapter, it becomes clear that the keys to working well with others are self-discipline and generosity. The *discipline* to take the time and trouble to understand the needs of colleagues, to choose to behave towards them in a constructive way; the *generosity* to interpret their motives and behaviours positively. Both discipline and generosity can be easier to sustain if you are clear about what it is you are trying to achieve or contribute. For most HCPs, because of the degree of specialization discussed earlier, achievement of one's own goals requires the involvement of others. Keeping the goal in mind (and in heart as well) will put more energy behind your attempts to build good relationships with others.

The real payoff in working with others comes when you gain more from the collaboration than is necessary because of your interdependency, when you gain more from joining forces than together you put in, when the whole is greater than the sum of the parts, when there is synergy. Synergy often occurs where it is least expected. In 'know-how' industries like health care, it usually takes the form of cognitive leaps and there can be no leap if there is not a novel situation in which a particular way of thinking can be applied. Such situations cannot be predicted. The development of synergy therefore requires an openness to new ideas and technologies, to approaches from other individuals or departments. It also requires a generosity with your own ideas that runs counter to the culture in many academic settings. Here, too, a definition of your own personal goals will be helpful, as will an appreciation that people who work well with others can achieve so much more than those who insist on working alone.

This runs counter to many of our formative influences in education, where working alone was the norm and it was the task completed that was assessed. It takes a huge shift in attitude to accept that the choices about how we work with others deserve as much attention as the choices we make about the tasks we undertake ourselves; that these 'process' issues are tasks in themselves and have a valid claim to our working time.

3 Really managing people: working for others

Almost all of us work for someone else, even if we are self-employed. There are very few people who have the resources to be able to take decisions and implement them without having to convince someone else of their validity. For the rest of us, taking any action which requires additional money, people or premises requires us to gain the approval of resource allocators either within the organization or outside it – boards of directors, bank managers or major customers. In other words, we depend upon the approval of others to be able to achieve our own personal goals. This is not interdependency of the kind discussed in Chapter 2, where different specialists rely on each other to undertake tasks which, together, form a complete service for the patient. This is straight dependency.

As we saw in Chapter 1, people differ in their response to dependency. Some like it, some tolerate it, many (those with strong power or autonomy goals) hate it. Since it is often individuals in that latter category who rise to leading positions in the healthcare professions, it is not surprising that there is often tension between senior clinicians and management boards. Individuals choosing primary care as a career, and the relative autonomy of independent contractors status, also fall into this category, and the fireworks between them and their local contract holders are often spectacular.

This chapter is intended for people who dislike dependency, people who find it difficult to achieve their own goals within their current organization or contractual arrangement; people committed to effective care of their patients who find their resource allocators unsympathetic to, and ignorant of, the needs of patients, and how they can best be met; people who find that working in their current post induces anger, frustration and demotivation; and people who experience a conflict between their role with patients, where they are a specialist carer with a credibility that inspires confidence and trust, and their role in the organization or system where they feel undervalued. If you are in such a position, there are a number of questions you will find it helpful to answer.

1 Are my aims congruent with those of my organization?

Every organization has a different set of aims (sometimes expressed as a mission statement, although many mission statements consist of a set of 'apple pie and motherhood' statements that are not specific to the organization and hence not helpful here). The aims or mission of an organization derive from the concerns and emotions of key opinion-formers and decision-makers within the system. If you have worked in your organization for some time, you will know what many of the key opinion-formers care about. Those individuals you do not know well, you will need to get to know better. Find a vehicle for discussion with them and use the listening skills described in the last chapter to try and really understand what their interests and values are. If you feel unattracted to the prospect of wasting your time with these people, remember that you do not have to like them, you do not have to admire them – you only need to obtain information that you can then analyse to get the best deal for your patients. They will not, of course, provide you with the information you need if you express antipathy in word, deed or body language, so you will need to prepare yourself in advance. Somehow you must bring to this meeting an open mind, an ability to concentrate on what is being said and to take it at face value, without interpreting it in the light of past events and the anger these have induced. Only in this way will you be able to empathize sufficiently well to succeed in obtaining the information you need.

When you have identified the priorities and perspectives of the organizational decision-makers, you will be able to compare these with your own – once you have clarified what your own are. To do this you will need to write down a statement of your aims, an individual mission statement. You will, undoubtedly, be tempted to think this unnecessary, that you know what your aims are. Resist the temptation. Write them down. Write a statement of purpose and then a set of primary aims.

Clearly, any incongruity of aims is going to cause problems. If you believe the greatest contribution you can make is through research and your organization is interested only in efficient service delivery using existing technologies, then both you and they will be unhappy. Although this example may seem improbable, it can and does arise, as both individual and organizational aims change over time. Perhaps more common is the case where your wish to offer specialist care to a particular group of patients conflicts with the organization's wish to meet the more generalist needs of a wider group. If there is a genuine disparity between your aims and those of the organization, then you are ready to move on to Question 3. If there is not, the next question becomes relevant.

2   Are my values in harmony with those of my organization?

Values are the beliefs that drive our actions. The beliefs that are shared by members of an organization make up its culture. Another way of describing an organization's culture is 'the way we do things round here'. Is the way they do things round here the way you want to do them?

Values are rarely expressed in writing, and when they are, they are often the values of the small group of people writing them rather than of the organization as a whole. So to identify them you will have to establish the values of the key opinion-formers and decision-makers whose aims you needed to understand to answer Question 1. Some of the relevant beliefs of these opinion-formers will concern patients, customers, the services offered, the organization, their staff, their colleagues, themselves and their work, and the future. Identifying their beliefs will assist you in assessing their level of confidence and maturity. The more genuinely confident individuals are about their own abilities, the more generous are their beliefs about others and the more able they are to work effectively with others, to give credit where it is due, to encourage, respect and develop others by offering them opportunities and assistance.

In his book *The Seven Habits of Highly Effective People*, Stephen Covey describes what he calls a 'maturity continuum'.[1] At one end of this continuum is a mode of behaviour he labels *dependency* (see Figure 3.1). In this mode, individuals believe that their feelings, their behaviours and, to a large extent, their fortunes, are entirely caused by factors outside their control. These factors could be genetic, psychosocial (their upbringing) or environmental (the situation in which they find themselves). Dependent individuals are essentially reactive. The language of the reactive person is peppered with phrases like: 'There's nothing I can do . . .', 'He makes me so angry . . .', 'They won't allow me to do that . . .', 'If only . . .'. Covey draws a distinction between this reactivity and proactivity, which he defines as 'more than merely taking initiative, it means taking responsibility for our own lives'. Proactivity is rooted in the concept that we choose our thoughts, feelings and behaviours, they are not dictated to us by circumstances or conditioning but are within our control. In other words 'between stimulus and response we have the freedom to choose'.

Dependency _____ Independency _____ Interdependency

Figure 3.1   Maturity continuum

Independency is the midpoint on the maturity continuum, when individuals decide to take responsibility for themselves. The language used by reactive and proactive individuals can be contrasted as follows:[2]

Reactive language	*Proactive language*
There's nothing I can do.	Let's look at our alternatives.
That's just the way I am.	I can choose a different approach.

He makes me so mad.	I control my own feelings.
They won't allow that.	I can create an effective presentation.
I have to do that.	I will choose an appropriate response.
I can't.	I choose.
I must.	I prefer.
If only.	I will.

Further still to the right, at the other end of the continuum, is a state of *interdependency* where individuals recognize that they can achieve very much more if they take responsibility not only for their own life but also for collaborating effectively with others.

The position of individuals on this continuum strongly influences the degree to which they possess a genuine self-confidence, with dependency commonly co-existing with lack of self-esteem. The values held by individuals with a firm sense of inner security will differ from those of their less mature colleagues and they will be more likely to live by them. Insecure individuals are more concerned about how others see them than they are in making valid judgements about how to help others optimize their contribution. Their devastating wit, scapegoating of others, constant criticism of peers involved in the same arena, will shape an organization in which they are influential. The values they espouse may well sound attractive (although they are likely to talk of rights and respect rather than of contribution and growth), but their behaviour is often at odds with them. Such individuals will find it very difficult to accept any criticism, preferring to shoot the messenger rather than reflect on the message. Their mature counterparts treat criticism as an opportunity to learn and grow. They find it inappropriate to shoot the messenger because they take the trouble to understand their point of view even if they disagree with it. Empathy is not in the nature of the insecure individual, who is too concerned with their own needs to get close to other people's.

Diagnosing an individual's maturity or genuine self-confidence is not always straightforward, because we are sometimes misled by arrogance or complacency. Both of these are features of insecurity rather than confidence but can be confused with it. Confident individuals take pride in their own achievements, as do arrogant individuals. Their attitudes to the achievement of others differ, however: the former delighting in them, taking an interest, making recommendations, etc.; the latter belittling, criticizing, finding fault. Similarly, confident individuals are sure enough of their integrity to want regularly to test their view of reality, their understanding of themselves, their responses and the filters through which they see the world. This may look like self-doubt and the preserve of the insecure – far from it. Its opposite is complacency and the belief that there is only one way of seeing the world. People who care more about whether you like them or admire them than they do about what they can do to help you achieve your objectives (and in so doing achieve theirs), are ineffective managers. Working for them is going to be a miserable experience, unless you yourself are very mature.

Being big when working with or for little people is not easy. All too often we find ourselves responding in a way that disappoints us, makes us feel diminished: when we join in hostile gossip, for example, or when we 'give as good as we get' to critical colleagues at a meeting. Sometimes, if we cannot rely on our temper or our tongue, the mature course of action is to avoid the meeting, avoid the coffee room. Acting with integrity in an organization without discipline and generosity, where gossip is not discouraged, where meetings are not kept to task, where individuals are scapegoated, where constructive criticism meets defensive anger, requires great strength of purpose.

Your role as a *real* manager is to develop the maturity of your part of the organization by developing the confidence of the people in it. Max de Pree describes maturity in an organization as 'a sense of self-worth, a sense of belonging, a sense of expectancy, a sense of responsibility, a sense of accountability, and a sense of equality'.[3] Are you going to be able to do that in this organization?

3   Are there other ways of achieving your aims?

If you have been honest in describing your purpose and primary aims, you can now generate a list of alternative means of achieving them: moving to another trust/practice/authority; joining a different kind of organization (a charity, a university, the independent sector); combining your existing role with another (writing, lecturing, setting up your own business), etc. Think these alternatives through realistically, avoiding the opposing temptations of being dismissive without sound evidence and of assuming the grass to be greener behind another fence. Subject your alternative organizations to the same kind of analysis as you have your own.

4   Do I want to stay?

When you have appraised all the available options, you will be able to decide whether or not you wish to stay where you are. You may find that, even though your goals and values do not coincide with those of your current organization, those of the alternatives are even more dissimilar. If this is the case, you will decide to stay, knowing the disadvantages but prepared to work to overcome them. With this positive intent, the skills that you develop to do so will undoubtedly increase your own maturity and that of your staff. It is an opportunity for the real personal growth that springs out of difficult, challenging circumstances.

You may find, when you get closer to the decision-makers, that your aims and values are similar and that you are happy to stay where you are. You may, however, come to realize that you are not in the best place for you to achieve your objectives and that you must, in your own interests and that of the organization, devote energy and time to moving on. This is a very different situation to that where, infuriated by another setback, you march in to your resource allocator protagonist and hand in your resignation. It is a constructive response to the situation rather than a destructive one. The difference between them may not be apparent to the organization you leave, but it will be to you and to the organization you join. In the latter case, you will find there the same old problems you thought you had left behind; you will have taken them with you.

Staying on

If you fall into the category of people to whom this chapter is addressed, the considered decision to remain where you are is an important step, but only the first step. The next is to reflect on your purpose and primary aims and identify precisely what or who in your organization or system is preventing you from achieving them. Very often the problem lies in interactions with the gatekeeping departments. By these I mean departments such as finance or personnel whose approval is required before decisions can be implemented.

Often there are individuals in these departments who are genuinely interested in supporting you. Equally often they are staffed by people who believe their concerns are of paramount importance to the organization, without appreciating the balance that is essential – necessity without sufficiency. Budget containment is necessary, as is observance of employment law, but they are not sufficient. Often our problems in dealing with these departments arise because we adopt a similarly unbalanced attitude. The development of clinical practice, the introduction of an additional and beneficial service, the adoption of a new approach whose clinical value has recently been demonstrated, these are all essential, but they too are not sufficient. They must not be allowed to jeopardize the financial viability of the organization or expose the organization to risk of employment litigation.

Internalizing the importance of this balance will help you in your dealings with gatekeeping departments. Overt recognition of it ('We realize that the financial aspects of this are critical. Would you help us to think them through') and a request for help at an early stage can often prevent problems from arising. Where there is a history that makes such conversation difficult or unproductive, or where you find the arguments for your proposals so compelling that you flare at the prospect of having to justify them again, at a cost to you of considerable time, then you may find it worthwhile asking a colleague to write the business case for you. A couple of briefing sessions to a peer who understands your reasoning and concern but who is not directly involved, and thus who is not as passionate as you, can be time well invested. Naturally, you would reciprocate the favour. Once our emotions are disengaged, insurmountable problems often become interesting puzzles, so the time spent on them is enjoyable rather than infuriating. Even if you decide to write the case yourself, testing out the arguments with someone slightly removed from it often enables you to make them more convincing. It would be very sad if clinicians were not passionate about their practice and their patients, but this essential emotional commitment is bound to make dealings with gatekeeper functions fraught. All concerned need to realize this and find ways around it rather than personalizing the situation.

When presenting a business case you are basically answering the following question: 'I can invest my resources (money, staff, time, premises) anywhere, so why should I choose this particular project?' The case should therefore specify how investment in this project will help the decision-maker meet *their* objectives. It should spell out the benefits to be reaped from the investment: for example, better clinical outcomes resulting in more contracts; reductions in future costs and how these will be delivered. It must also detail the full costs. If the case can be supported on these grounds, then approval will rest on whether you are judged capable of delivering the benefits. The case should therefore also describe your strengths and how this project exploits them, how this project fits within the strategic direction of your service and your track record in managing investments of this sort.

If, despite your investment of time and energy, your case is not approved, how do you respond? One way is to express your anger to all concerned – to the decision-maker(s), your staff, your patients – explaining indignantly to them all that your ability to care for your patients is being hampered by others. This is perhaps one of the most common reactions, yet what impact does it have? Your staff are further demotivated and less able to provide the care or support your patients need. Your patients lose faith in your ability to meet their needs and have to cope with anger and frustration as well as their clinical condition.

Another way is to ask for the reasons why your case failed, and why other cases have been supported. Work on the assumption that all concerned are reasonable people, that if the evidence convinces you, it can convince them if you present it in a way that meets their needs. Invite them to discuss with you their reservations, hear them out, reflect on them and address them. If, for example, they feel that you already have sufficient resources within the department to develop this project, invite them to discuss how they have come to that conclusion. If their view is based on faulty information, then correct it; if not, then consider whether there may be some justice in their position.

As a general rule, whenever you are tempted to blame someone else, stop for a moment and reflect on whether there is anything you have done or are doing that is exacerbating the problem, or whether you are actively trying to resolve it. As Eldridge Cleaver stated: 'if you are not part of the solution you are part of the problem'.[4] All of us, if we are honest with ourselves, will find many instances every day when we have been part of the problem rather than the solution, when we have acted little rather than big, when we could have been effective rather than angry. Dwelling on these mistakes does not help at all, but neither does ignoring them. Recognizing them and learning from them is the way forward. It is very difficult to do this unless we learn to lose our anger. While we are angry with someone we are less effective. The impact is on us. It does not touch them, does not harm them, does not reduce their effectiveness – only our own. We can choose our feelings about people, we can choose to see their virtues and disregard their vices. Even when this is difficult, we can choose not to let them get the better of us by making us angry. Here again generosity and self-discipline are required. Keeping in mind our purpose will once again help.

Perhaps as important as anything else is our recognition of our own role in influencing the mission and values of our organization. As far as the organization is concerned, are we part of the problem or part of the solution?

4 ▽ Really managing change

The increasing specialization of society has had another major impact on our lives – the rate of change grows faster and faster. As the wag said, 'change isn't what it used to be'.

Evolutionary history teaches us that all organisms must adapt with their environment or die, and that organisms developing a feature that helps them to succeed in their environment prosper, at the expense of those who do not. The lesson for organizations (big or small) is that change is essential when there are changes in their environment. They are also necessary if a change in the organization will help it to be more successful, even if there has been no change in the environment. In other words, necessary change can be prompted externally or internally. It must, however, always take account of both of these (environment and the resources of the organization itself) and of what the organization deems success to be.

The thought processes necessary when considering intervening in a service or organization are comparable with those when intervening clinically with a patient, and require similar evaluation of condition, prognosis, options, costs, benefits and risks. Just as *primum non nocere* (at least do no harm) is an important value in medicine and the clinical professions, so it is when managing healthcare organizations. It must never be forgotten that all interventions in organizations incur costs and risks and the anticipated benefits should always outweigh them.

All too often changes are introduced by enthusiastic management teams without adequate analysis and evaluation of the costs, benefits and risks associated with different options. In any change which affects job security, one of the greatest costs of that change is its impact on the ability of staff to respect and care for others, while they feel under threat themselves. Since this is at the root of all health care, it should be jeopardized with great caution. This is not to suggest that jobs should never disappear or that organizations should never be restructured. An organization that is *really* being managed will, however, be constantly making small changes as circumstances permit and radical change (without radical change in its environment) will be seen as a manifestation of failure.

One of the reasons that inappropriate changes are implemented is that the people introducing them do not adequately understand the organization they are 'managing'. More strife has perhaps arisen at the imposition of unidimensional solutions to complex, ill-defined, multifaceted, incompletely understood problems, than from any other cause. It is widely – and falsely – assumed that one of the roles of a manager is to solve problems; indeed, problem-solving is one of the competences identified in the Management Charter Initiative. On the contrary, the role of the manager is to *sell* problems not *solve* them. Their role is to help everyone (including themselves) to understand the problems and to work with them to find a solution. This requires a lot of listening, noticing, testing out ideas, being prepared to rethink, getting others to rethink, increasing everyone's awareness. This is an active, engaging role in which consultation papers have little or no place. Solutions are generally to be found on the frontline, because that is where the information is richest and the commitment to outcomes greatest. The role of the *real* manager is to harness this information and commitment to a constructive use, rather than antagonizing and deflecting it by introducing changes perceived as unnecessary or dangerous.

Diagnosing an organization's ailments requires a bringing together of information about its own resources and competences, about its environment and about its purpose. The most common framework for doing so is the widely used 'SWOT analysis' (Strengths, Weaknesses, Opportunities and Threats). Having seen many SWOTs for organizations, departments, services and practices over the last few years, I have become convinced that the vast majority are hardly worth the paper they are written on, and they certainly do not justify the valuable clinical and managerial time spent thinking about them. They usually consist of more or less relevant facts organized under four headings. Perhaps fortunately, most of them go no further – there is often no conclusion, no indication of how strategic decisions are informed as a result of this 'analysis'.

The purpose of a strategic analysis is to diagnose the key issues that the organization needs to address. So just as patient management requires, in addition to a diagnosis, the consideration of treatment options, appraisal of those options and the devising of a programme of care, so decisions about services also require option appraisal and the devising of a programme of change.

The strategic analysis is conceptually very simple and its value depends on the calibre of the analyst – her insight, understanding, experience, judgement and creativity. In this way, it is very similar to the clinical diagnostic process. Bayes' theorum,[1] for example, is a conceptually simple approach to identifying the probability of a particular diagnosis given the finding of

a sign or symptom. Its successful application depends on a good understanding of probabilities and prior probabilities, which requires experience,
insight and judgement. The analogy goes further: just as a clinician will be
expertly useful with patients in their own specialty and dangerously wrong
in another (largely as a result of mis-estimating prior probabilities), the same
is true of managers. The crucial insight and understanding on which judgement and creativity should be based are not reliably present in managers
imported from unrelated industries.

In this chapter, I will take you through the stages required for a rigorous strategic analysis. If you apply them with care, honesty and clarity of
thought, then you will derive a set of change priorities, some of which will
surprise you. If none of them do so – in other words, if you come up with
a set of conclusions that you could have produced without indulging in any
analysis – you will have failed to think clearly or honestly or hard enough.
Used properly, this is a most valuable tool to have at your disposal.

Strategic analysis

The strategic options open to any organization depend on three elements:
the goals of the organization, its resources and competences, and the environment in which it operates. The first three phases of your deliberations
consider these.

Phase 1:   Vision

The first step in your analysis is to state explicitly what is the contribution that your service can make; that is, what is its mission. If you are
jaundiced about mission statements, find another phrase to describe this
stage (vision, direction, contribution) and forget all the lengthy, worthy
but irrelevant mission statements you have seen. Yours can be three words
long if those words sum up what it is you and your team care about. It
is for your own benefit and not for public consumption. You may choose
to make parts of it public, but if you set out with that intention you will
end up with the kind of multipurpose manifesto statement which makes
our eyes glaze. A good mission statement captures the emotions of all the
key players, of all the people who influence performance by making choices
about how they spend their time. This does not mean that all of these
people have to be involved in drawing it up. That can be highly effective,
but it can result in a bland, politically correct, inoffensive, meaningless
hotchpotch. One perceptive individual, closely in tune with other members
of the department, can often come up with something more pertinent that
strikes a chord, although the others may not have expressed it that way
themselves.

The mission statements of even apparently similar organizations or services can differ markedly, because they reflect the aspirations and feelings
of individuals within them. An outsider might be tempted to think, for

example, that the aims of general practitioners in inner London would be fairly undifferentiated. The following list of genuine statements illustrates how diverse they can be:

- Being, and being recognized to be, a leading edge practice.
- Being a friendly practice, part of the community, where patients are almost friends.
- Meeting the healthcare needs of a very deprived population without burnout.
- Being primary carers; adopting a holistic perspective; concerned with health rather than only health care.
- Making a reasonable living for the partners in an enjoyable and interesting way.
- Working towards the best possible health for patients; not only treating them but persuading them to take responsibility for their own health. At the same time, developing partners and staff to the full.

The reason for articulating a mission/vision statement is simply that you cannot decide how best to get there until you know where you are trying to go. Often, indeed *usually*, when the members of a clinical team come together to discuss a mission statement, they find that individual members have different views of what their contribution could/should be. Gaining agreement on direction is a very valuable outcome, especially where differences were previously unrecognized or unacknowledged.

The statement is often most useful when split into two sections: *purpose* (What are we here for?) and *primary aims* (What are the key things we must do in order to achieve that?). Neither purpose nor primary aims will include the ongoing clinical tasks of assessment, diagnosis, treatment, etc. These are, of course, fundamental, but can be thought of as forming a lower, more detailed level. Your purpose should *not* include the words 'to provide'. It should state what it is you want to achieve as a result of that provision. Primary aims will almost certainly include reference to your means of resourcing your activities. This could be in the form of:

- Persuading the purchasers of the value of treatment x or the priority of clinical condition y.
- Ensuring that the attractiveness of your service is known to (and being sold by) the people negotiating contracts on your behalf.
- Developing and maintaining systems to monitor your performance against the criteria specified by purchasers.

Typically, you will have some difficulty deciding what is a primary aim and what is your purpose, and in distinguishing between these and ongoing tasks and objectives. In many cases, people return to their mission statement after the next stages in the analysis. Usually, they find that what they thought was their purpose turns out to be a primary aim. Thinking of this analysis as an iterative process may prevent feelings of frustration or disillusionment.

Table 4.1 Examples of helpful and unhelpful mission statements

Mission statement of a training and development department	*Example of an unhelpful mission**
Purpose: To support the delivery of the long-term business plans of the Trust by ensuring a sustained supply of skilled professionals and support staff, in a rapidly changing environment	The Trust will provide to its patients services of the highest quality which are sensitive to the needs of individuals
Primary aims:	The Trust respects and values the contributions made by its staff
1 Analyse manpower requirements of Trust in a number of feasible scenarios	The Trust aims to respect choices made by its clients and to treat all staff and clients with fairness and dignity
2 Collaborate with other employers and with other training providers to ensure opportunities for career progression and development	
3 Research, design, evaluate and implement education, training and development initiatives to supply shortfall	
4 Involve users in collaborative learning with staff	
5 Promote cost-effective use of internal and external training resources	
6 Maintain organizational support and funding for department	

* Fictional (but does it look familiar?)

The first time you undertake such an analysis, you may choose to side-step the next phase and move straight to phase 3. Phase 2, however, does encourage your thinking to be more rigorous, so it is worth including when you are more familiar with the rest of the process.

Phase 2: Analysis of resources and competences

Tom Peters and Robert Waterman describe seven elements of an organization and suggest that only when all seven elements are in harmony, supporting and being supported by each other, can the organization be considered 'organized'.[2] It can still be heading in the wrong direction if no attention has been paid to the external environment, but it will be heading there very efficiently! These seven elements are: strategy, structure, systems, style, staff, skills and culture. In this phase, you consider these in turn and reflect on any harmony or dissonance.

Strategy

The actions that an organization plans in response to, or anticipation of, changes in the external environment, customer needs and the strategies of competitors. You will need to consider all the services offered, your clients and your customers. When you have listed the services and clients, try and describe the ways in which your services differ from those of other departments/Trusts/practices in the same clinical arena. What needs of the clients are you meeting? Does this differ from your competitors? How? Have you asked your customers (the people or agencies who actually fund your services) what it is that they are looking for?

Michael Porter, one of the founding fathers of business strategy as an academic discipline, suggests that fundamentally there are only two competitive strategies: differentiation and cost leadership.[3] Which do your services fall into? If the former, in exactly what ways are they differentiated? Can you demonstrate superior clinical outcomes or greater reassurance for patients? If not, then how efficient are you? How good are you at utilizing your resources to the full? Are you able to offer a similar service at a similar or lower price?

Structure

The means by which organizations divide up tasks and how they integrate and coordinate them. At its most basic: who is accountable to whom for what? In small companies or departments with a simple product range, there need be no organizational structure as such. Everyone who needs to talk to someone else can do so; they all have access to new product or market information as it becomes available. All members of staff can have input into decisions made by the 'boss', who will probably be working alongside them.

Larger organizations have to be divided into sub-groups in order for them to be 'manageable'. In other words, for people within the organization to have access to the people they most need to talk to, to receive new product or market information quickly, and to be able to inform resource allocation decisions with an appropriate level of frontline detail. The most appropriate basis for subdividing the organization will depend on circumstances.

It is helpful here to differentiate between 'line' and 'staff' functions. Line functions are those immediately concerned with production or service provision or with managing that activity. Staff functions are those which advise line managers and/or provide services to them. Examples of staff functions are personnel, accounting, legal services, planning and information technology. On the whole, there are two options for the management structure of staff functions: either they are managed centrally, or staff report to the line managers to whom they provide a service.

It is the line staff, more numerous and more intimately connected with the customer, about which there is more discussion. There is an overall tension in large organizations between the wish to keep the span of control, for individual managers, reasonable and the wish to keep the number of layers in the hierarchy as few as possible. At its starkest, this either results in a tall, thin organizational structure or a short, fat or 'flat' one. In general, tall, thin structures are appropriate when:

- There is a stable workforce. It takes a long time to work your way up such a hierarchy, but if you are going to work for the same company for 40 years, you may need such promotions as an incentive.
- The market for your product is stable/unchanging. When it is not important that information about market changes reach the top quickly.
- There is a high degree of specialization. When it is genuinely difficult for managers to manage teams outside their own speciality.

In times of rapid change and a transient workforce, the flatter organization (characterized by many Japanese companies) is fleeter of foot and more responsive, but may require a larger number of generalists or people with a wider range of skills.

There are a limited number of ways of subdividing people with 'line' functions within organizations, and only two of these are feasible in health care. They can be subdivided according to their technical skill base or according to the product on which they are working. These are known as 'functional' and 'divisional' structures. For example, they can be divided into nursing, medicine and physiotherapy, with each group managed by a nurse, a doctor and a physiotherapist, respectively. This is a functional structure. Alternatively, they can be divided into care groups where nurses, doctors and physiotherapists all work with a particular group of patients (e.g. the elderly) and are managed by a care-group manager whose role (as a manager) does not contain a clinical or technical component. This is a divisional structure. There is a third generic structure which is a mixture of the two: a matrix structure. Here people are grouped both according to their technical function and to their product, and have two managers – the head of the technical function and the product manager. An example in the NHS would be of a physiotherapist working within elderly care being accountable both to the head of physiotherapy services and to the elderly care manager.

All of these structures have inherent advantages and disadvantages. There is no such thing as a structure perfectly suited to its circumstances. The choice of structure reflects prevailing opinion about which kinds of information flows are the most important.

The advantages of a functional structure include easy access to clinical/technical expertise, state-of-the-art clinical/technical changes being rapidly communicated, and an emphasis on high clinical/technical standards. The disadvantages include slow formal communication between frontline staff from different disciplines (because requests must make their way up one hierarchy, down another and back again), group-think leading to friction between professional groups, and professional 'preciousness' – a confusion of the good of the profession with the good of the patient. The advantages and disadvantages of the divisional structure are the converse.

What is the structure in your organization? Are you experiencing the advantages and disadvantages described above? Does your structure support your strategy? What information flows will successful implementation of your strategy require? If, for example, your strategy is to offer services that are differentiated in terms of superior clinical quality and yet your structure is a divisional one with frontline staff having little access to professional advice and support, then your structure does not support your strategy. You must find a satisfactory way of providing this clinical/technical advice.

Systems
All of the procedures, both formal and informal, that make the organization 'work': budgeting, training, auditing, communicating, referral, assessment, discharge. The list of systems that any healthcare organization requires to support its strategy and its staff is very long. It is in the careful devising of systems that the disadvantages inherent in the organizational structure can be mitigated. Unfortunately, the converse is also true: the advantages can be minimized by carelessly designed processes. Organizational structures allow information to flow; management processes (systems) ensure it does (or not).

List the systems that are critical to achievement of your strategy. Do they differ from those which play a dominant role in your organization? Suppose your strategy is to differentiate your services by offering superior communication with patients and referrers, and you support that with a divisional structure. What systems would you need to have in place to be able to deliver that strategy? Your success may be limited if you have unidisciplinary patient records and no means of monitoring enquiry response times.

Staff
How many of which kind of staff work in your organization? Without their active support the strategy will not be realized. How motivated are they to work energetically in support of the organization's strategy?

Skills
The kinds of skills required in healthcare organizations fall into four categories: clinical/technical; interpersonal; managerial and research/reflection. Do you have the people with the right skills to support your strategy? If so, are they in the right place (structure) and supported by the right systems? It would be difficult to deliver a strategy of low-cost provision of commodity services if your staff includes a number of highly skilled (and expensive) clinicians who specialize in complex tertiary cases. Do you need to reconsider your strategy?

Style
The way senior staff come across to the rest of the organization. How do they behave? What do they value? Note that what they say is of little importance, it is what they *do*, what they reward, that determines the

organization's style. A low-cost strategy must be supported by an emphasis on low costs at all levels in the organization. Similarly if the service is to be differentiated on a particular feature, senior staff must lead by example and constantly manifest their concern for that feature.

Shared values or beliefs
'Culture' would be a more appropriate term, but of course does not begin with an S! What people believe significantly influences the way they behave, so these beliefs must be in harmony with the other six elements.

Typically, management textbooks are fascinated by, but in awe of, culture, describing it as indefinable, difficult to change, profoundly influential. It is possible to feel too defeatist about this and breaking it down into its constituent parts can help prevent that. The beliefs that are shared normally relate to clients, customers, services, colleagues, bosses, ourselves, the organization and the future. It is quite feasible to ascertain what these are and, having done so, to intervene to change the beliefs if they are incorrect. Culture change certainly does take a long time if it is allowed simply to follow changes happening in the other 6 Ss, but does not have to if it receives effective attention in its own right.

The real eye-opener of the 7S checklist is when you mentally link every S to every other to form a 'wheel' (see Figure 4.1). When you do so for your service, where does the harmony arise? What about the dissonance? Do your systems support your strategy? Do they motivate your staff, maintain and develop the right skills? Does the structure take account of the people in the organization? Do the systems of communication support that structure? Is the style appropriate for the staff and for the strategy? Does everybody buy this strategy? If they do not, or if they thwart the systems, or the structure does not take account of pockets of different cultures, then your organization is not working, not as it could and should. In most cases, a structure, a system, an individual is not good or bad, right or wrong, strong or weak in their own right, only in relation to the other Ss.

It is worth stressing again that the structure of an organization is only one of seven characteristics that must support each other. From the amount of restructuring that has taken place in the NHS in recent years, one might be led to think that this is the most important of those characteristics. But it is not. As Gaunt says, and most of us would wearily agree with him when faced with yet another reorganization, 'What is really needed is not an alteration of the formal structure but a new spirit within'.[4]

When you have identified the harmonies and dissonances between the Ss, you are in a position to list the strengths and weaknesses of your department/practice/Trust in achieving its mission.

Phase 3:   *Analysis of the external environment*

Now you need to turn your attention to the environment in which you are operating. The external environment for you and your team will certainly

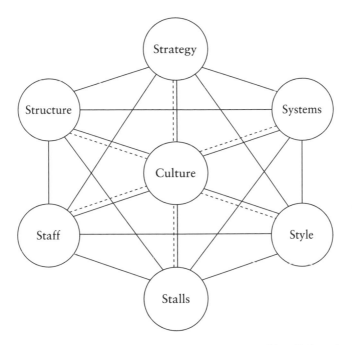

Figure 4.1 Each of the 7Ss must support and be supported by all the others

include everything external to your organization, but also any other parts of your organization over which you have no control.

Using the 7S checklist helps us to avoid overlooking essential factors within the organization. Similarly considering the external environment under four headings which produce the acronym PEST allows us to scrutinize its most salient features. PEST stands for Political, Economic, Sociological and Technological factors.

- *Political*: some big P factors (including legislation by politicians) but small p issues are usually just as, if not more, relevant.
- *Economic*: include macroeconomic trends if they are going to affect you; remember the more local financial position and the priorities and perspectives of purse-holders.
- *Social*: these factors could relate to anything that will affect your services – divorce rates and the impact on children; the changing attitudes of consumers to service providers, appointments, etc.; also demographic changes.
- *Technological*: any technological advances in a relevant sphere (not just clinical).

At this stage you can keep the ideas free and flowing without worrying too much about relevance (that comes in the next phase). When you have described the external context of your practice, you are then in a position to identify any factors which may help you to achieve your mission (opportunities) and those which may hinder it (threats).

Phase 4:   SWOT – identifying helpful and unhelpful factors internal and external to the service

In the next phase, you bring together the internal and external analyses and relate them to your mission. In other words, you list your strengths, weaknesses, opportunities and threats. If it is genuinely to contribute to your thinking, then you will need to observe the following guidelines.

1   Always specify the reference point
Are your strengths, weaknesses, opportunities and threats stated in relation to:

- your ability to achieve your mission?
- your competitors in another Trust?
- your competitors within your own Trust?

2   Be precise about your strengths and weaknesses
Try asking three questions about each feature you list:

- So what? What can we do as a result of this? keep on asking this until you reach a statement about either costs or outcomes or both. If you cannot discern an impact on either of these, it is not a strength nor a weakness.
- Are we better or worse at this than anyone else is?
- Why? Just as you went on asking the 'so what' question, keep on asking the 'why' question until you reach the real underlying cause. What is causing this feature? Why does it occur?

You will undoubtedly find that many factors are both a strength and a weakness. Be specific: exactly what is the strength and what is its cause; exactly what is the weakness and what is causing it. Note the following examples:

Example: A midwifery unit
Strength: Range and diversity of services offered
So what?   Meets diverse client demands and makes service attractive to both clients and purchasers
Cause: Imaginative responses by individuals x and y to outspoken advocacy service

Example: An outpatients' department (OPD)
Strength: Service standards in obstetrics and gynaecology
So what?   Meets or exceeds the demands of the Patients' Charter and keeps purchasers happy
Cause: Commitment from consultants who are heavily involved in monitoring performance

Example: An outpatients' department
Strength: Generally high level of patient satisfaction
So what? Keeps purchasers happy
Cause: Good customer care skills of OPD manager.

It will be clear from the above examples that the real strength is to be found in the *cause* of the feature first identified or observed. The same is true for weaknesses. The following is an example of woolly thinking:

Weakness: Strategic direction unclear
So what? Low morale
Cause: Poor management skills

Weakness: Waiting times for admission getting longer
So what? Increased number of complaints
Cause: Inability to keep up with demand

In the first case, it is not at all clear that lack of strategic direction is a weakness; morale is such a fuzzy and unmeasurable concept, that it can always be claimed to be high or low. In the latter, neither the results nor, more importantly, the cause of the weakness (increasing waiting times) are identified. A further round of so what? and why? is needed. Is the inability due to over-contracting or under-delivery? These are different weaknesses. Similarly in the following scenario:

Example: An outpatients' department
Weakness: Long waiting times
So what? Does not meet the demands of the Patients' Charter and purchasers are unhappy
Cause: Consultants arriving late for clinics in some specialties

A further 'why?' needs to be asked. Why are they arriving late? *That* is the weakness in the system.

3 Be precise about the opportunities and threats facing you

Remember that these are external factors over which you have no control; do not confuse opportunities with options (things you can do). The reason you are undertaking the analysis is to identify the options available to you, so they have no place here. Again check your thinking by asking 'so what?' about each of the factors you list. What impact could this have on your organization? If none, then it may be an interesting fact but not relevant here. When you are sure that it is indeed an opportunity or threat, ask yourself what the organization would have to do to respond to it. You will again find that some factors can be thought of both as opportunities and threats; again you need to think carefully about exactly what aspects fall under the two headings.

Example: Opportunities for a training department

1 Community care
So what?   Need for change agents and facilitators
Therefore we must?   Position ourselves so that we become the natural provider

2 GP fundholding
So what?   Trust staff need new skills
Therefore we must?   Analyse skills required and develop training programmes

Example: Threats identified by a Trust wishing to close a hospital

1 Concern of local community
So what?   May lobby to prevent closure
Therefore we must?   Keep community informed about our reasoning and keep abreast of local opinion

2 Interference of local MPs
So what?   May take position based on own political needs
Therefore we must?   Assess political needs and give MPs information that will help them to meet their needs as well as those of the Trust

Example: A Trust is losing business to a neighbour

Threat: Purchasers favour neighbouring provider
So what?   Survival threatened
Therefore we must?   Improve relationship with purchaser and discover their concerns; improve our ability to deliver service levels required

---

If you care about your service and are knowledgeable about it, and are prepared to stand back from it sufficiently to think very clearly about it, this stage will be interesting and satisfying. It will almost certainly take one person at least half a day, probably more. Two people will take longer! It is unlikely that you will be able to persuade an entire department or practice to be objective enough to complete this satisfactorily, so it is usually more effective if one or two people undertake the analysis and then present and discuss it with the rest of the team.

Phase 5: Teasing out critical issues

The next stage is the most critical and requires the greatest insight and judgement. This is when you identify the key issues that the service/department must address. There are no rules about how to tease these out. You will need to scan your four 'boxes' – strengths, weaknesses, opportunities and threats – and keep in mind your mission.

As you do so, there may be one or two factors which occur in just one of the boxes that are so important, represent such a huge risk, such a terrific opportunity, that you cannot ignore them. (For example, the threat previously mentioned of the loss of business to a neighbouring service provider.) These will certainly be part of your list of critical issues. They will be in the minority though. For the most part, critical issues are those which have different strands or aspects mentioned under several of the headings. Usually, these strands are to be found in the 'causes' section of the strengths and weaknesses boxes and the 'organizational response' section of the opportunities and threats boxes.

If you have completed the preceding stages honestly and thoroughly, then this stage does not take long. Typically, though, this is where an inability to stand back becomes apparent. When your list of critical issues is a diatribe against another group or a wishlist (or both), think again! To help you to check your thinking here, write down a definition of each issue using Rudyard Kipling's 'six good men and true' (what, when, how, why, where and who). What is the issue? For whom is this an issue? Where, when and how do they experience it? Why has the issue arisen?

Example: A community-based palliative care service whose mission is to enable people dying of terminal diseases to have a pain-free, dignified death

Strengths include: quality service provided for patients and carers *and* for professional clients (district nurses and other terminal care teams)

Weaknesses: paternalistic approach combined with 24 hour accessibility of service undermines the professionals we say we want to support

Opportunities: neighbouring local team struggling with their workload, providing less good service than ours

Threats: some primary care teams and GP fundholders antagonized by perceived arrogance in the past; others do not know of our role as an expert resource and support for them

One of the issues here will be that the stated strategy of being a resource to other professionals offering palliative care is not being acted upon

Other strengths, weaknesses, opportunities and threats indicate that there is a growing divergence of culture between groups believing terminal care to be a vocation and those who see it as a professional service. The critical issue can therefore be described more precisely as:

What:	service failing in its mission because professionals who could be offering a better service do not receive expert support to enable them to do so
Who:	patients and professionals experience it; staff, divided into vocationalists (V) and professionalists (P), perpetuate it
How:	Vs and Ps differ in their approach; systems support direct intervention rather than support for other professionals to intervene
When:	when making choices about how to respond to a call for help from a patient
Where:	N/A
Why:	Vs and Ps differ in their beliefs about the best way to achieve the mission and the service is allowing these conflicting beliefs to coexist

Phase 6:   Setting objectives

The next stage is one of the most enjoyable. You imagine what your world would look like if the issue were not an issue. What does it look like, feel like, what happens in it if that issue has been completely resolved? Now capture the flavour of that world, in one or two sentences, as an objective for your change programme to achieve. One description for each issue. The more accurately you can describe the resolution (or absence) of this issue, the more useful your objectives become.

Phase 7:   Appraising options

When you have a list of objectives, you may be tempted to think that you have a programme for action, but there are many ways in which these objectives can be met and you will need to choose between them. Taking each objective in turn, list all the possible actions which could contribute to its achievement. Some of these will be realistic and feasible, some will be fantastic. The fantastic may prompt further feasible suggestions, so they can usefully be left on the list until discussion is exhausted. When there is a list of practical suggestions linked to each of the objectives, look carefully through them. Do any similar suggestions occur under different objectives? Are there any groupings of suggestions that make sense? List these themes with the relevant suggestions underneath them.

Example:	Outpatients' department
Issue:	
Who:	Issue for OPD manager
What:	Many of the resources on which OPD performance depends are outside the influence of the department and its manager
When:	Constant
Where:	Off-site, i.e. arises out of the department
How:	Non-OPD staff are not according OPD the priority it requires
Why:	Not all staff are committed to the achievement of the OPD mission

Objective: Patients under the out-patient care of the Trust receive a service that recognizes that their time is valuable, and that meets their clinical needs in a courteous and efficient manner

Options:
1 Investigate reasons for lateness of certain consultants
2 Raise profile of OPD within Trust
3 Develop service level agreements with contributing firms and departments
4 Sell OPD problem to consultants and engage them in redesigning the system
5 Review role of OPD manager

After the options for all the other critical issues are listed, one of the *themes* that becomes apparent is:

Reorientation of OPD: instead of clinical teams contributing to OPD and its mission, the OPD should contribute to clinical teams and their missions

The options include:
• review the role of the OPD manager
• contributing firms and departments to take more managerial responsibility
• sell OPD to consultants and engage them in redesigning system
• OPD manager to report to consultants on performance measures for their patients so that:
• consultants can account to purchasers for non-adherence to performance standards
• OPD staff to be involved in decision-making meetings of clinical teams.

You will probably identify three or four such themes and these are your change priorities.

As we saw earlier in this chapter, in any organization the '7 Ss' should support each other. Thus since the changes that you are proposing will affect one or more of the Ss, you will need to consider whether this necessitates change in any of the other six. Your proposed changes may well be remedying a dissonant S to bring it into harmony with the others. But any change in an S that is in tune with any of the others will require changes in those too. Introducing a new system (of almost any kind) will inevitably require training (skills), changes in job description (staff), perhaps in remuneration (also staff), may well change slightly the areas of accountability (structure), require a change in attitude (culture) or working practices (systems). When a proposed change requires significant change in *all* the other Ss, you may wish to consider again its feasibility.

Phase 8: Further preparation

At each of the last two stages you will again have been tempted to recognize a list of actions to be undertaken. There are, however, two further valuable stages before you reach your action plan. The first of these is called a 'force field analysis'. It is based on the work of Kurt Lewin, in which he suggests that when implementing any change there are a number of factors which work with us to help us achieve the change (he calls these 'drivers') and a number which impede the change ('restrainers').[5] Listing both drivers and restrainers for each of the themes listed in the last stage enables you to consider ways in which you can enhance the drivers and diminish the restrainers. If you are to successfully introduce the change themes, then clearly you need to tackle these first.

Force field analysis

Drivers	Restrainers
The forces which will help us	The forces which will hinder us
achieve our change objectives are:	in achieving our change objectives are:

1 →)←
2 →)←
3 →)←
4 →)←
5 →)←
6 →)←
7 →)←
8 →)←

Ways in which I can enhance the drivers:
1
2
3
4

Ways in which I can diminish the restrainers:
1
2
3
4

A stakeholder analysis is also essential. For this you must list all the people who have a 'stake' or interest in this change programme, together with an indication of how important it is that they support the changes. Three categories are sufficient: those who must actively support the changes, those who must acquiesce, and those whose support is not at all necessary (whose views can be ignored). These individuals can also be categorized according to whether they are strongly in support of the changes (lions), strongly opposed to them (mules), or will go along with the opinion-formers (sheep).

A scan of the grid produced soon makes it clear just who are the people you need to spend time and energy convincing:

Stakeholders	Must support	Must acquiesce	Can be ignored
A			Lion
B		Sheep	
C	Mule		
D		Lion	
E	Sheep		
F			Mule

If you have a mule whose active support is essential and you do not persuade them of the virtues of the change (using the material from Chapters 1 to 3), then the change programme will fail, and the fault will lie not with the mule but with you. It will, of course, be much more agreeable to spend your time with the inoffensive, non-threatening individual whose views can be ignored and who strongly supports you!

Phase 9: Implementing the changes

Always remember that as a result of your analysis, and the thinking around it, you will see things differently from your staff. Where you can, take them through your analysis. Occasionally, this will not be practicable, but even here (perhaps especially here) it is essential that you sell the problem(s) before you try and sell your solution and its benefits.

Once you have identified the changes to be made (and note that there are eight planning stages before implementation), you will need to decide who is to take responsibility for the change programme. This is a responsibility you delegate, so you need to observe the three rules of Chapter 1. You must agree with the individual(s) exactly what it is you expect them to achieve. You must both be sure that they have the skills and resources to achieve it, and exactly what those resources are. Can they, for example, rely on your being available for discussion? Do they have a budget? Dedicated secretarial support? And, third, you must make sure they know how they are doing (feedback from you, progress monitoring charts, etc.).

The role of the change manager will now be to:

- allocate tasks and deadlines
- monitor progress
- reward successful progress and invoke sanctions for lack of it (as agreed with individuals in advance)
- devise and implement contingency plans
- liaise

- listen
- enthuse about the benefits to the individuals involved (using material in Chapters 1 to 3).

Phase 10:   Evaluating the change

One of the most valuable elements of any change programme is that which is so often neglected – evaluation of the change. This stage offers the opportunity for learning that is rich and real. Without it, this learning is lost to both individuals and the organization. Certainly you and your change manager should reflect on the following questions. The learning will be even richer if the discussion can be made wider:

Reviewing the change:
- Did the change achieve its objectives?
- How closely did the actuality mirror the plan?
- How did it differ?
- Why?
- How do the stakeholders feel about the change?
- Is there anything more you need to do to achieve the objectives or to influence the feelings of the stakeholders?

Learning for next time:
- What would you do differently another time?
- Why?
- How?

Any change means the disappearance of something and the introduction of something else. This disappearance, or loss, is in one sense a bereavement and the reactions to bereavement are well documented. The stages of denial, anger, grief, resignation and, finally, acceptance and moving forward can often be seen in individuals or groups exposed to change. Recognizing this can help you to sense when it is the timing, rather than the shape, of your implementation programme that needs to be altered in response to the feedback of your staff.

Successful and unsuccessful change

Received wisdom has it that with any change there are winners and losers. When that change involves a restructuring of the organization, there are indeed people or departments who end up with more or less positional power than they had before. As a result, restructuring has become an easy option for ineffectual managers to deal with staff they find difficult – by making them redundant rather than developing them or sacking them (both of which require more effort and integrity).

The idea that there have to be winners and losers, however, is a dangerous one, in that it can lead to a callous shrugging of the shoulders over the fate of individuals or services. While it is unlikely that everyone will 'win' by the same amount, it is certainly feasible and desirable to aim for everyone to win something. This cannot be positional power for everybody, but as we saw in Chapter 1, not everyone wants that – even those who do have other goals as well.

Max de Pree describes the role of the leader as 'liberating people to do what is required of them in the most effective and humane way possible'.[6] If your change programme does not liberate your staff to do what is required of them, effectively and humanely, then reconsider it. The fact that people do have such different goals ensures that the means to liberate them differ. This allows you to design a change programme in which everyone gains.

Your staff may gain greater clarity about their role, more systematic and valuable feedback, the opportunity to develop a particular interest, the ability to influence service levels from an interdependent department, and have their views heard elsewhere in the organization. This is not bribery, this is a careful analysis of your staff and their interests (part of your '7 Ss' scrutiny) and an honest and creative attempt to liberate them. I say 'honest' because it is all too easy to meet the needs of people we like at the expense of those we do not; an honest attempt will preclude this.

You may like to consider that if, as a result of your change programme, anyone genuinely (as opposed to politically) feels they have been a loser, then you have failed: failed to construct a programme which takes account of their needs, failed to persuade them of the benefits, or failed to develop them to a point on the maturity continuum where they can recognize the benefits. At the same time, they must take responsibility for their own reactions and consider whether they have enabled you to meet their needs. A culture in which blame is routinely taken in this way, rather than given, would be novel (and enormously helpful) in health care.

It can never be said that a change is 'for the best', simply because there is no best, just as there is no right or wrong, no solution to a problem. Let me introduce a terminological nicety here. A puzzle has one right answer and if you search hard and wide and long enough you may find it. A problem has no answer. A problem is so multidimensional that it can be addressed in a number of different ways.[7] None of them will be right or wrong, none will be the 'best', but some will be more or less appropriate in the prevailing circumstances. In other words, some will be better, or worse, for now. At different times and in different circumstances, the same problem will be addressed in different ways. This leads to talk of pendulums and swings.

In any situation, we tend to spot problems and ignore all the features that are working well. We then implement a change programme designed to solve the problems and only then realize that in doing so we have created a number of new ones. Our successor attempts to remove these by introducing a system very similar to the one we were so keen to change, and so it goes on. The more we can remember that there is no right or wrong, that our solutions will be found wanting by others, that the situation we inherit was devised by people as committed and as able as ourselves, then the more easily we can avoid two temptations: first, to change everything immediately and, second, to blame and scapegoat our predecessor and assume the clock only started when we came into post.

As a result of the lack of skill and integrity in this area, in many of the changes that take place in health care today there are winners and losers. Unfortunately, whether you and your team will be a winner or loser does not often depend on intrinsic merit. It does not depend on how great your contribution could have been clinically or technically, nor even on your combination of clinical skills and personal maturity, although the latter will certainly help you and your team cope with the changes. In addition to sheer luck (which does play some part), what it does depend on is your ability to analyse the situation, determine your goals, identify the obstacles and assisters to those goals, and deploy your resources tactically as a result. Whether the organization (and its clients) is a winner or a loser depends on the merit of the people who do that. Thus if your view is important, if your service has a valuable contribution to make, it is essential that you develop the skills discussed in this chapter to analyse, to plan and to *really manage* change.

5 Really managing money

Does the following sound familiar?

A survey in 1993 revealed that approximately 70% of the responding organisations used questionable financial information as a basis for decision making.

If you ask a healthcare professional showing an interest in management education what aspects of their management they particularly want to improve, nearly all of them will mention financial skills. The inadequacy felt by many in this area is exacerbated by surveys which apparently demonstrate that senior healthcare professionals do not understand balance sheets, budget reports and other financial statements. But it is time that 'financial skills' and their perceived shortage in healthcare organizations were put into perspective. The quote that opens this chapter refers not to health care but to UK manufacturing companies.[1] It may well be the case that healthcare professionals cannot read financial statements with any comprehension, but no-one has satisfactorily demonstrated a link between this and the ability to manage money. Indeed, in many industries, any 'failure' in such circumstances would be acknowledged by the finance staff who had prepared the statements.

Managing money owes more to an acceptance of the guidance of Mr Micawber than to anything else. It requires recognition of the fact that you have only one pound to spend, that if toward the end of the financial year you are confident that you will spend only nineteen shillings and sixpence, then you will have the happiness of sixpence to spend as you wish; but that if you spend one pound and sixpence the result will be the disaster of loss of contracts, or outside interference in the way you allocate your resources. Once this belief is firmly embedded then the greatest financial skill required is the ability to turn over to the back of the envelope. This all-important belief is endangered every time any department or service is 'bailed out', and judging the difference between a genuine (and genuinely unforeseeable) need for extra funds and arrogant or undisciplined profligacy is one of the reasons chief executives, and their most senior staff, must spend so much time out and about in their organization, as described in Chapter 7.

Contrary to the wishful thinking of many, improving your financial skills will not in itself make any more money available to you. Nor will it allow you to achieve any more with the money you have – that is the result of the skills discussed in the previous chapters. It will, however, help you understand the impact on your financial position of a particular proposal, increase your ability to calculate how much your services are costing, and monitor how you are managing your money.

There are two sets of users of accounting information: people inside the organization and agencies outside it. Generally the internal users require it for decision-making and the external for regulatory purposes. The two sets of users and uses have given rise to two kinds of accounting – financial accounting (for external parties) and management accounting (for internal). A set of financial accounts is generally required once a year, in a statutory format, prepared in accordance with accepted accounting principles, referring to the past year and encompassing the organization as a whole. Their emphasis is on precision rather than speed. Normally they are written by accountants for accountants, or at any rate for people with some specialist expertise in deciphering them, analysing them, seeing behind them, and knowing what questions to ask of the organization's top management. If you are ever required to help put these together, or to read them, then you will have specialist advice and assistance available. A failure among healthcare professionals to make head or tail of a set of financial accounting statements is to be *expected*. It will be the norm, and rightly so.

Management accounts are produced for use within the organization. They are outside statutory regulation; they can be presented, commissioned and used entirely at the discretion of the organization and the people within it. In many respects, they are the converse of the financial accounts. They are produced not once a year but on an ongoing basis; they refer not to the past but to the present and future; they describe parts of the organization, rather than the whole; and they occasionally sacrifice precision for the sake of speed. We could perhaps characterize the difference between the two kinds of accounting by suggesting that financial accounting is the 'complicated easy', whereas management accounting is the 'simple hard'.

The aim of this chapter is to arm you with sufficient understanding of the principles of management accounting for you to be able to have a sensible discussion with your director of finance, finance department or management accountant about the kind of information you require from them if you are to manage your resources. Incidentally, you may be interested to know that accountants are taught that part of their role is to produce performance reports that list actual outcomes and planned outcomes and highlight the differences. Furthermore, these performance reports are intended to 'motivate desirable individual performances by communicating performance information in relation to the targets set' in the budget.[2] I am yet to encounter a healthcare professional who finds their monthly budget statement motivational, and this major difference in perspective may go some way to explaining why accountants, even those with talent and good-will, find healthcare organizations so challenging and exasperating.

If you enhance your financial skills in the ways outlined in this chapter, you will improve your ability to do three things:

1 Calculate your costs.
2 Look at the impact on your financial position of any clinical or managerial decisions.
3 Set up mechanisms for monitoring (not 'controlling', which is the accountant's choice of word) your financial performance.

All of these are far too important for you to leave to somebody who does not understand your service the way you do. You cannot leave this to the finance department – I am sorry, but it is *your* job. If your response to this is that you did not enter health care to become an accountant, then think clearly, because this is not what you are being asked to do. In any setting, anywhere, the use of any resource has to be justified, and health care is no exception. The resources you use or commit must be justified; either by you, or by somebody else who will then have the right to tell you what you can or cannot do. Nobody is asking you to concentrate solely on financial figures; those figures are but one way of capturing what you and your service is doing, but unless you give them your attention someone else will give them theirs.

Calculating costs

Calculating costs, even in industries where the products are much simpler than those in health care, is not as straightforward as it may seem. Dividing the total costs of production by the number of widgets[3] produced may sound simple, but the difficulty arises when we start to consider what to include in those 'total costs'.

Clearly, we must include all the costs of the materials used up in the manufacture of the widgets. Also, the costs of the labour hours spent on making them. But if the machines used in their production also produce other goods, then any costs of maintaining these machines cannot be borne entirely by the widgets. And yet, if the other goods were to go out of production, then the entire machine maintenance cost would have to be recouped from the widgets. The widget-making machine will be housed in factory premises which incur rates – should these be included in our 'total' costs? And what about the expense of the staff canteen? Already we can see that there are different kinds of costs.

The cost of any goods or service can be thought of as made up of three parts: direct costs, indirect costs and overheads. *Direct costs* are those which are used only for, and entirely by, the product we are trying to cost. In our widget example, these would be the materials and labour. *Indirect costs* cannot be linked solely to one product but with several. Machine maintenance would fall into this category, as would any holiday pay for the operator. *Overheads* are incurred on an organization-wide basis; in our example, the building rates and staff canteen are overheads.

If instead of trying to cost a widget we were attempting to calculate the average cost of all the products made by the widget-making machine, then clearly the machine maintenance switches from being an indirect cost to a direct cost. So whether a particular cost is direct or indirect depends on the *cost objective*; that is, exactly what it is we are trying to cost. It is therefore not possible to say that study leave, for example, is invariably a direct or an indirect cost, since it will depend on whether the individual taking it is engaged in providing more than one service and on what is the cost objective.

Indirect costs must be allocated to the cost objective, but normally the means of doing so are not contentious and require only the deployment of common sense. Machine maintenance costs, for example, could be split according to the ratio of the number of widgets produced to the number of other products produced on the same machine. Alternatively, the machine hours spent on each could be used. Another possibility would be the weight of the materials used in production. A knowledge of the machine and its propensity for malfunction would be needed in order to choose between them, but to someone with this knowledge the appropriate option would be self-evident.

When it comes to overhead costs, however, the allocation process is almost invariably a two-stage process, the alternatives are greater in number and the option selected can have an impact on the decision-making behaviour of departments and budget-holders. In the widget example, the building rates and the costs of running the staff canteen need to be allocated. A sensible rationale for apportioning the rates would be the floor area each department occupies. Using floor area as the basis for allocating canteen costs would be ridiculous; instead, the number of employees would make more sense. The canteen will also have received its portion of the rates bill and will be passing this on when its total costs are allocated. Suppose that when the rates, the salary of the chief executive and the renovation of the building's exterior are included in the canteen costs, they exceed the prices on offer elsewhere? Suppose departments could feed their staff more cheaply by giving them an allowance to buy meals at a local cafe? If the canteen closed, the rates, chief executive's salary and renovation expenses would still have to be paid, so should they be included in the 'total costs' of the canteen? Is the answer influenced by the fact that the chief executive spends no time at all worrying about the canteen service or management, or that the canteen is in an interior room with no exterior walls? Management accounting is not simply a question of knowing where to wield your calculator; it requires careful consideration of behaviours.

The different ways in which overhead costs are allocated may all have their basis in logic but lead to very different figures being produced. This is why there are tomes written purely on this subject, and why, in financial – but not management – accounting there are a number of rules about how it must be done.

When overhead costs have been allocated to goods- or service-producing departments, they can then be allocated to the goods or services themselves as a basis for pricing. This allocation is usually a volume-related one, based on the labour hours spent on one product as opposed to another. Since it is volume-related, any change in activity levels will lead to over- or under-recovery of overheads. This leads to the need to charge different prices based on the quantity ordered. Sometimes seen as a cynical inducement to buy more than you need, it is often merely a reflection of the fact that costs (and therefore prices) *do* vary with volume.

This leads us onto *cost behaviour*, one of the most important concepts when financially appraising different options.

Financially appraising options

Cost structures

We have already seen that costs vary according to the volume of production and according to the method chosen for the allocation of overheads. Since we will need to analyse the impact of any proposed change in type of activity or method of delivery on our financial position, we need to understand rather more about the behaviour of costs.

In the previous section, we saw how costs can be divided into direct costs, indirect costs and overheads. To investigate cost behaviour, we need to use another classification, this time fixed, variable, semi-fixed and semi-variable costs. You may be tempted to try and equate the two classifications (fixed with indirect and overheads, variable with direct). Remember that they have two different purposes, one to calculate costs at a given level of activity, the other to explore their behaviour at different activity levels.

Variable costs change in direct proportion to your activity level (see Figure 5.1). You double or treble your volume of activity and your variable costs double or treble accordingly. They include all the materials used in the production process. *Fixed costs* remain the same regardless of activity levels. The salary of the chief executive is a fixed cost. Variable costs therefore remain the same per unit as activity levels rise or fall. The total expenditure on variable costs of course rises or falls (varies). Fixed costs, on the other hand, rise per unit if the activity level falls, because the number of units which must bear them has fallen. Similarly, they fall, per unit, if the activity levels rise. The total amount though remains the same.

Staff salaries are not a variable cost, since a rise or fall in activity levels does not precipitate an immediate and consequent change in salaried hours. But if volume increased or decreased to the point where an extra post could be justified, or an existing one jeopardized, then the salary figure

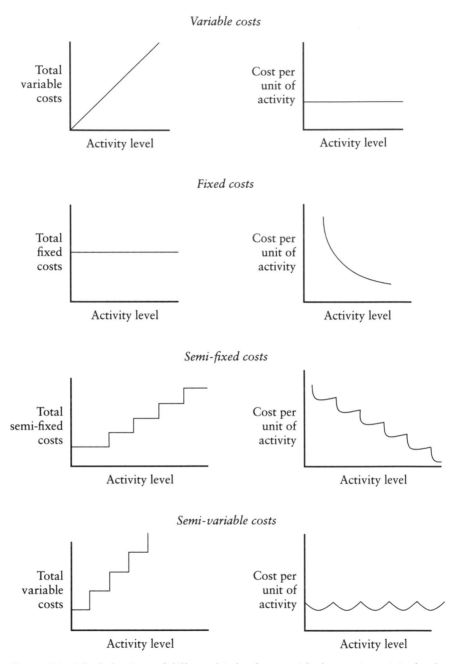

Figure 5.1   The behaviour of different kinds of costs with changes in activity level

would change. Such costs are called *semi-fixed costs*, or *step-fixed costs*, since they remain the same over a given range of activity levels and then increase or decrease in steps. Equipment maintenance costs, which are incurred with greater frequency as activity increases, are not fixed costs, but neither are they variable, since they do not increase or decrease with every unit of activity. These are *semi-variable* or *step-variable costs*.

Imagine the range of activity levels changing from zero to ten times the current level, and you will see that almost no cost is completely fixed. Ultimately all staff can be made redundant and premises sold; conversely, staff numbers could increase ten-fold and a new site be acquired. So when we consider the breakdown of costs into fixed and variable, we are doing so over a limited range, otherwise known as the *relevant range*.

Identifying which elements of the costs are fixed and which are variable enables us to differentiate between the *average cost* and *marginal cost*. The average cost is just what it says: the fixed plus variable costs divided by the number of units of activity. The marginal cost is that of providing one more unit. Unless you are right at the limit of a step cost, the marginal cost is the variable cost. Obviously, once you have recovered all your fixed costs, you are able to afford to offer your services at a price lower than the average cost, without losing money, as long as you recover at least your marginal costs.

Understanding how costs behave in relation to changes in activity levels enables us to answer such fundamental questions as:

- How many units do we need to sell at price y in order to break even?
- What must our price be if we are to break even on a given number of units?
- If we can only sell x units at price y, what must we reduce our fixed costs by (usually staff numbers) if we are to break even?
- How many more units would we need to sell to pay for an extra member of staff in the department?

As long as all the variables except the volume remain constant, the costs can be accurately divided into fixed and variable components and the question falls within the relevant range, then the *breakeven point* is where the cost of the units sold is equal to the income from those units:

$$(\text{number of units sold} \times \text{variable costs}) + \text{fixed costs} =$$
$$\text{number of units sold} \times \text{sale price}$$

Whatever price is charged, as long as it is in excess of the variable costs, it will make a contribution to the fixed costs. The amount of contribution is known as the *contribution margin*:

$$\text{contribution margin} = \text{sales income} - \text{variable costs}$$

Thus an alternative way of calculating the breakeven point is:

$$\text{number of units at breakeven point} = \frac{\text{fixed costs}}{\text{contribution per unit}}$$

These calculations are simple and the value of the answers relies on the validity of your forecasts about demand, prices, fixed and variable costs. *Sensitivity analysis* is the term coined for investigating the impact on the final financial picture if your assumptions and forecasts turn out to be incorrect. In essence, it asks the question 'what if?' about every element of costs and revenues. Tedious and time-consuming manually, it is usually undertaken on computer spreadsheet.

In addition to the questions posed above, you may need to consider such issues as:

• Should we 'make or buy' (i.e. undertake a service ourselves or buy it in)?
• Would a new piece of equipment help us to reduce our costs?
• What will happen to the costs of service x if we stop offering service y from the same department?
• If a commercial company would like to buy services from us, but at less than the average cost, should we supply them?

In order to answer these questions satisfactorily, there is another concept that must be understood. When it comes to these sorts of decisions, not all costs matter.

Relevant costs

Whereas when you are calculating costs all elements of the cost are *relevant*, when you are making decisions about different options some of them become *irrelevant*. This is because they have been incurred anyway: they are irretrievably committed, they are unavoidable. No matter what you do you cannot influence them. These costs are termed *sunk costs*. You can ignore them, no matter how big they are, because nothing will change them. Since your decision cannot change them, it must not be influenced by them. I stress this because emotionally this can be difficult. The fact that a million pounds has been spent on a piece of equipment would be difficult to ignore. If, however, using that equipment is going to cost you more money for a given outcome than a different alternative (once you have included all purchase and related costs in your calculations), then you must be able to say goodbye to the million pounds. The decision to purchase that machine may have been absolutely the right one at the time, or it may have been a misguided one; but whichever is the case, insisting on its use when there are cheaper alternatives which give clinical results that are just as good is indisputably wasteful.

When you are financially appraising different options, you need to consider only the costs which differ between them. If both options require the additional employment of a member of staff, or if they can both be accommodated within the existing establishment with neither permitting any staff reduction, then staffing costs are irrelevant to your decision: they do not need to be included in your calculations. You compare the position with and without that option and write a *with/without* case.

The staff costs mentioned are irrelevant costs, but they are not sunk costs. Thus all sunk costs are irrelevant, but not all irrelevant costs are sunk.

Irrelevant costs, despite being ignored in your calculations, are real in that they have been spent. There is a class of costs that are *relevant* even though they are only ever hypothetical, and these are called *opportunity costs*. Whenever you have any money to spend (or any other resources to allocate for that matter), there is always something else you could choose to spend it on. The benefits of this alternative are closed to you if you choose the option under consideration. An opportunity cost measures the opportunity that you must forego when your selection of one option means you cannot pursue another. If you can pursue both, then there is no sacrifice of opportunity, so opportunity costs are only incurred where there is a scarcity of resources (so there are a lot of opportunity costs in health care!).

Moving away from imaginary costs back to real ones, let us now look at ways of monitoring the costs actually incurred by individuals and departments.

Monitoring costs

The first stage in any monitoring exercise is to set targets against which performance can be measured. When managing money, the targets take the form of the annual budget. The budget-setting process largely determines the robustness of the budget produced and its likelihood of being delivered. It should include all of the following stages:

1 *Framework*. Top management describes relevant details of budget policy and provides guidelines to the individuals in each department, who will be responsible for preparing their budgets.
2 *Limiting factors*. Any factor which restricts performance can be described as a limiting factor. Usually, this is sales demand, but it could be a restricted number (due to national or local shortage) of staff with particular skills, or a capacity limit on a machine. The next stage in the budgeting process is to identify what these limiting factors are. Since these determine the activity levels, only when they have been highlighted can achievable activity levels be set.
3 *Activity level budget*. Activity levels determine expenditure, so these must be agreed before sensible discussions can take place.
4 *Bottom-up preparation of budgets*. When departments know what activity is required of them, they can use their detailed knowledge of their services and their cost structures to put together a schedule of expenditure.
5 *Negotiation*. Human nature being what it is, departments are likely to set budgets which they believe they will achieve without too much effort. Some negotiation needs to take place between these departments and an individual with experience of managing individuals in similar settings, who will know where any 'padding' can be found. This individual is usually the line manager of the departmental heads, and this closeness

to budget detail is another reason why such managers should have had significant operational experience and should be in close contact on a regular basis. The ability of the individuals concerned to negotiate fruitfully and not emotionally requires a relationship between them of the kind described in Chapter 7.

6 *Coordination.* Only when all the budgets are brought together can the total costs be projected, and they may be unaffordable as they stand. There may also be inconsistencies between departmental assumptions. Thus a coordination phase is required and this may necessitate a second or even third or fourth reworking of stages 4 and 5 before a feasible, affordable organization-wide set of budgets can be finalized.

7 *Acceptance.* When the budgets have been agreed by all parties, they are summarized into a 'master' budget.

8 *Monitoring and review.* In the master budget, all costs should be allocated to a responsibility centre as close as possible to the individual who commits these costs. Thereafter at monthly intervals reports can be generated which compare predicted expenditure with actual expenditure.

We now come to the third (and final) classification of costs in this chapter. Where costs can reasonably be expected to be regulated by the individual to whom they are allocated, then those costs are *controllable*. Clearly, overhead costs (e.g. the canteen), although they need to be apportioned for cost calculation purposes, must be awarded to their own managers when it comes to monitoring and review. Costs outside the control of anyone in the organization (e.g. many supplies) are known as *non-controllable* costs. They must also be monitored, but their uncontrollable nature acknowledged. In practice, this means holding a contingency fund centrally once the scale of the uncontrollable element is known.

Any disparity between actual and predicted expenditure or income is known as a 'variance'. Most variances are due to one or both of two factors: the price paid per unit of activity and the activity levels. A projected spend of £10,000 on material A will give rise to a favourable variance of £2000 when only £8000 is spent. However, if the activity level on which the £10,000 projection was based is 100 and only 70 cases have been treated, then the picture no longer looks so rosy. For this reason, budgets should not be *fixed* but be *flexible*. They should change the expenditure projections as any changes in activity levels occur. Frankly this is asking too much of most finance departments in the complex world of health care. Since you are the one who needs to know how well you are doing at keeping within your budget, you need to keep a record of expenditure committed and activity undertaken. You will probably not want to do the variance analysis yourself, so give your figures to the finance department so that they can do it for you.

Counting your own money is an important aspect of real management. You understand better than anyone else how your costs are incurred, the factors which influence them, and the *cost drivers* (those activities by which it makes most sense to monitor costs). You also know better than anyone else your workload. You could, of course, wait for the conventional monthly reports based on information you and your team have given to the finance department (in one form or another), presented in a form which you find unhelpful if not unintelligible, in which costs are analysed under headings which are not meaningful in the context of your services. You could, but it would take less time than deciphering and analysing these to do the counting yourself, detailing someone in your team or department (or everyone) to enter details of costs and activities onto a dedicated programme.

You could do neither, stuffing the budget statements in a drawer unread or barely skimmed. But then you would not be managing money, it would be managing you. You would be at its mercy, being forced to reduce activity because of overspends, or to do without support staff while there is no let-up in workload. This is so intolerable a position for the responsible healthcare professional that you really have no choice. Managing money is part of the professional role and requires the kind of effort described here.

I suggested at the beginning of this chapter that management accounting is simple and hard. Conceptually, like everything else in this book, it is undemanding. The discipline required to keep on top of it is, like everything else in this book, very great.

In this chapter, I have not touched on any of the principles of health economics which seem to offer assistance with many of the tough decisions which healthcare professionals have to make. As there are many excellent books on the subject, I will go into no details here, but would remind you that tough decisions are always going to be tough decisions, and no economic tools devised will stop them being tough to take. In certain circumstances, these tools will help clarify for you exactly what the decision to be taken is. They may even inform you what other people claim their decision would be in somewhat similar circumstances. But they do not and cannot remove from you the difficulty of the decision.

The toughest decisions healthcare professionals have to make centre on shortages of resources, so the only way to reduce the number of times those decisions have to be made is to ensure that every resource is used to its optimum. That is what *real management* is about.

6 Really managing yourself

- Are you surrounded by people who prevent you from achieving all you could?
- Are you often disappointed in the performance of your juniors?
- Are the managers in your organization ill-informed, remote, prone to imposing diktats without seeking your opinion?
- Do some of your patients have unrealistic expectations of the NHS?
- Are there more and more demands on your time?
- Do colleagues in other professions or disciplines seem not to understand the pressures you are under?
- Are other professionals trying to take over some of your role?
- Are politicians trying to wreck the NHS?
- Is a lot of the information you provide misused?
- Have you had change, change and more change imposed on you?
- Is it impossible for you to achieve any more without greater resources?

Then naturally you are unhappy, frustrated and dissatisfied. You are wondering whether you made the right career choice or are discouraging your children from following in your footsteps. You are not in control and since childhood most of us have been striving to be in control over our worlds rather than in thrall to others. This chapter is about putting you back in control.

Exercising control is difficult unless we have a clear idea of direction, of what it is we are trying to achieve or contribute. If we do not know what our aspirations are, we have no way of reaching them, and we can only *react* to events. We all know of people who become so 'driven' that they lose the ability to relax and enjoy life, so when we define our direction we must remember to include family, social and personal enjoyment. We must also remember to define our direction in terms of outcomes rather than processes, so that we can make the most of new opportunities that arise along the way.

Articulating the meaning we wish to give to our life is no trivial matter and it can be difficult to know where to start. Many of the people I have worked with have found the following method helpful. It is derived largely from Stephen Covey's book, *The Seven Habits of Highly Effective People*.[1]

Personal goals

When in 30 years time, say, your grandchildren describe you to their schoolfriends, what would you want them to say? How would you like colleagues to recall you once you have retired? If you were writing your own obituary, what would you like to include? Thinking about what we would like to have done with our lives begins to give us a sense of direction. Try writing down your responses to these questions. When you have done so, list all the different roles you play in your life. As a healthcare professional, you have many roles. You have the roles of assessor and provider of care to individual patients. You are also an educator, a supervisor, a researcher or evaluator, a colleague, a member of your professional body, a member of a healthcare organization. But you are not only a HCP, you are a member of a family, of a community or neighbourhood, you are a friend. In each of these roles, you will want to achieve or contribute something. Try writing a short description of the contribution you want to make for each one. This is not something that you can start and finish satisfactorily in one short session. If it is to make a difference, to really help put you back in control, you will need to contemplate these roles and contributions over a period of weeks or even months. When you feel that the roles and contributions which you have envisaged accurately depict what you want your life to be about, then write them down as a personal mission or direction statement.

Now that the end is clear you are ready to consider the means. Taking the roles in turn, formulate a set of long- and short-term objectives for each. From these objectives, draw up a list of actions that you need to engage in in the near future. Take your diary for the week ahead and see what opportunities you have in that time to complete these actions. If you have identified your roles adequately, then every appointment during the week will give you a chance to work towards at least one of your objectives. If it does not, you can cancel it! Schedule in all the actions you believe you can tackle in the week and highlight priorities among those left for future weeks. Remember to build in some time for planning next week's schedule.

Many people report that the positive results of such an exercise are apparent almost immediately. The small but significant tasks that otherwise tend to be left and to form part of an overall feeling of pressure (a 'phone call to arrange to meet, sending a document requested, retrieving said document from its file, drafting a memo about leave arrangements or a student visit) will now all be scheduled and tackled. When aware of just how many other commitments they have in a day, and the precise nature of those commitments, most people report a reduction in the time they spend in pleasant but unproductive activities – gossip, speculation, complaining about (but not to), etc. Being able to tick off these activities as they are completed gives a satisfaction that is lost when the pressures are perceived as an amorphous and irreducible mass.

In working with clinicians of various sorts over the last 20 years, I have observed that it is often the most highly intelligent, the most incisive and decisive who are the most disorganized. They feel under enormous pressure but fail to recognize that it is greatly increased by their profligate use of their greatest resource – their own time. So the more you think that this approach may be fine in theory but that you do not have the time to put it into practice, the more you are irritated at my naivety and lack of understanding of your service and the pressures you are under, the more strongly I recommend that you try it. If you are thinking about suggesting it to a disorganized junior member of your team, then do so – but also try it yourself.

If you find that this method does not relieve the pressure on your diary, this is probably because you have been insufficiently rigorous in restricting your goals to the activities that are *critical* to the successful achievement of your mission. It is easy to get bogged down in 'process' rather than 'outcome' tasks, to get trapped in a cycle of meetings when there are other, more time-effective ways of achieving the same aim.

If, after further reflection, you still cannot fit all your goals into your schedule, you must reconsider your mission. You are probably asking too much of yourself, setting yourself up to fail, making feelings of stress, anger and helplessness inevitable. Occasionally people find that they are not in the right position to achieve their mission. If they do not want to relinquish that, then they have to change job.

You now have a list of tasks and behaviours for every day of the week ahead, and each of these is important if you are to achieve your very personal life goals. Delaying a few until next week (if you choose to spend the time tackling another goal-oriented task instead) will be fine, but just how good are you at sticking to lists? This is going to require discipline and here it is useful to consider just what the elements of discipline are.

Discipline

Peck (introduced in Chapter 2) describes discipline as having four component behaviours: (1) the delaying of gratification, (2) acceptance of responsibility, (3) dedication to reality and (4) balancing.[2]

Delaying of gratification

'Delaying gratification is a process of scheduling the pain and pleasure of life in such a way as to enhance the pleasure by meeting and experiencing the pain first and getting it over with. It is the only decent way to live.'³ In practice, this means that if your scheduled tasks for the day include two you will dislike, eight you feel neutral about and three you will enjoy, then you tackle them in that order – delay gratification and start with those activities you like least. This does not mean that you rush through those displeasing activities. Indeed, because you are dealing with them when you are at your freshest, you will handle them better. The impact on your feelings for the rest of the day will be immense. There is a great release of pressure when you have given somebody the bad news, have written that report, have telephoned to make a complaint, or (worse still) have apologized. We all know we should live this way, but we very easily find reasons not to. Scheduling will help remind you to delay gratification, and delaying gratification will keep you on schedule.

Acceptance of responsibility

If you have a problem, then *you* have a problem. It is your problem and you must try and resolve it. It doesn't matter if the problem is caused by other people; you cannot leave it to them to solve because it is *you* who has the problem.

If managers are making your life difficult because they do not understand the impact of their requirements or decisions on you and your team, then you have a problem. Complaining to colleagues about the remoteness of management will not solve the problem. Waiting for management to come to you and ask you if you have a problem will not solve it. The only way to solve it is to get them to see how much better you and your team can perform if they change their policy. You could try telling them in no uncertain terms about how difficult they are making things for you, in front of your colleagues. You could try and secure a vote of no confidence. Or you could find out the reasons behind their decisions and work with them to find a solution to meet both sets of needs. Only the latter is 'accepting responsibility'.

Similarly, if you are disappointed in the performance of some of your staff, then you have a problem: the problem of having to be available to them more often than you would like, or of exposing your patients to greater risk. Blaming them does nothing to solve your problem. Making sure that they have clear instructions, guidelines, access to training and support, and proper feedback will all help. So will reviewing your recruitment procedures to see whether you can avoid creating problems for yourself in the future.

Whenever you are experiencing discomfort, *you* have a problem and it is up to *you* to solve it. Often when teaching on short courses I hear from HCPs a list of their woes. When I ask them what they can do to improve their situation, I am normally regaled with a lengthy list of all the things they cannot do. Only when I point out to them what they have just done and ask them again what they *can* do, do some of them start to accept responsibility and recognize their own role in the creation of the difficulty.

Dedication to reality

'The more clearly we see the reality of the world, the better equipped we are to deal with the world.'[4] The way we see the world changes with our life stages, the circumstances we are in, the information we gain. At no stage can we know everything about everything, so our view of the world is, of necessity, a model of it – a simplified version of it. The closer our model approximates reality, the more effective we can be in our inter-actions with the world. We all know individuals whose model is a very jaundiced one, others whose model is an over-rosy, optimistic one. We can see when the models of other people are faulty, but can we recognize the flaws in our own?

The most important determinant of our model is the modeller – that is, us. So dedication to reality requires 'continuous and never-ending stringent self-examination'.[5] In practice, this has two essential elements: an openness to challenge from others and a preparedness to challenge ourselves. If we are able to take criticism from our children, spouse, colleagues, staff, students, and are able to accept its validity, then we are enabled to increase our effectiveness, by making some changes to the ways we operate. If we reject it as ill-informed, prejudiced or non-valid, then we cut ourselves off from that opportunity.

We all make mistakes. If a meeting has gone badly, we can either blame the other party and protect our self-image or we can challenge ourselves: How could I have been more persuasive? What was I doing when the meeting cooled? If we recognize that we have made a mistake, we can work to avoid making it again. We need not blame ourselves, just learn from the experience. If we deny the mistake, then again we deny ourselves the chance of increasing our abilities, of becoming better at interacting with the world. Often we trap ourselves in what Chris Argyris describes as 'defensive routines', habitual reactions to situations which we perceive as threatening or painful, but which could be, if we behaved differently and were prepared to challenge the mental model we have of it, opportunities for us to learn. Argyris describes this process as leading to 'skilled incompetence'.[6] We become better and better at not learning because we become better and better at avoiding looking at reality.

Are the people around you, the ones who prevent you from achieving more, actively setting out to do so? In some cases, they may believe they are doing the opposite – that is, helping you. Others are simply not aware of how, in seeking to achieve their own goals, they impinge on yours. In a few cases, they may be feeling punitive towards you. Why? How could they be interpreting your actions as hostile? In situations involving people (i.e. at the higher levels of the hierarchy of natural descriptions discussed in Chapter 2), there is rarely a single cause resulting in a particular effect. Here linear thinking needs to give way to systems thinking, to an appre-ciation that we ourselves are part of an open system and influence other components of it.

If we are dedicated to reality, then we will want other people to have all the information they require if they are to perceive the world as it is. We must therefore find ways of challenging their perceptions, of telling them how their actions are being interpreted, of the difficulties their decisions are causing, of persuading them of the innocence (rather than malevolence) of ourselves and others. Not everyone can handle the whole truth (indeed not many of us), so we sometimes need to impart less than the whole truth, but as we saw in Chapter 2, Peck provides us with useful guidelines to follow when wondering just how much to give and how much to hold back. As HCPs, we are in possession of more truth about more people than are our counterparts in other walks of life, so these guidelines are all the more important and relevant for us.

Balancing

'. . . the capacity to flexibly strike and continually restrike a delicate balance between conflicting needs, goals, duties, responsibilities, directions etc.'.[7] There are many instances every day when we have to strike a balance. For example, we may have to choose between being completely honest or withholding some truth; between taking responsibility for something or encouraging others to do so: between delaying gratification or enjoying the present. Mostly we do this on autopilot, unaware of how often such a choice is required. The autopilot is often governed by our emotions, and this element of discipline requires us to become conscious of the occasions when a choice must be made and to subordinate our emotions to our judgement.

Many of our emotional responses were programmed into us as children but as adults we can choose how we feel.[8] We can choose whether to revert to an emotional response which has served us well in the past (e.g. helpless victim, aggressive competitor) or whether to override it. If we choose the latter, we respond to the present, not the past; we observe, analyse and reach conclusions about the behaviour needed, and then we select that behaviour.

Mastering feelings

Implementing the suggestions thus far will give you greater control of your direction and your time. However, you are still surrounded by people who, for whatever reason (and we have seen that this is often inadvertent), take a course of action which irritates, frustrates or impedes you. How can these be controlled? Stephen Covey quotes Eleanor Roosevelt: 'No-one can hurt you without your consent'.[9] He reminds us that between stimulus and response we have the freedom to choose; that is, between stimulus (other people's actions) and response (our own feelings) we have the freedom to choose how we will feel and hence behave. In other words, we cannot control the actions taken by other people, but we can choose not to let them irritate or anger us.

A number of psychologists suggest that all our negative or upsetting emotions (anger, jealousy, resentment, depression) represent some form of fear. That it is our own fear that leads us to respond negatively; that it is other people's fear that leads them to behave in a hostile fashion. This idea allows two helpful thought processes. First, that if you can identify the cause of your fear, the reason you become angry, resentful or frustrated, you can often tackle that cause and achieve longstanding release from those negative feelings. For example, if a colleague uses some of your ideas in a paper and fails to attribute them to you, you may well feel angry. What is the fear behind the anger? The fear may be that others will not credit you with those ideas, that they will not think as highly of you as they might. Is your reputation really as fragile as that? If it is and there is a promotion round coming up, then you must address it, but in many cases you will realize that it is not. Sometimes it can be helpful to think through the worst possible consequences. Often the very worst that can happen is something you can live with. In many cases, people find that when they have analysed their fear once, they can be relieved of the feeling of anger on many similar occasions.

Second, that you can choose to see everyone as either behaving generously or behaving fearfully and jealously. Approached in this way a colleague who behaves in a hostile or predatory fashion can be thought of as fearful, of needing your help to overcome that fear. If you can identify the source of their fear, then again you will find it easier to respond constructively, to lose your anger and replace it with concern or compassion. This does not turn you into a doormat. If your colleague's behaviour threatens your ability to achieve your personal goals, then you must attack. Compassion does not equate with tolerance. However, you attack their arguments or their behaviour, not them. You use logic and reason to defend yourself, not emotion.

Very often our fear is of how other people will respond to us. We want them to think well of us. If we can fully appreciate that how they think of us depends less on our own merits than on their feelings about themselves, then we are ready to take one of the biggest steps to becoming a *real* manager. This is the step when we stop worrying about how other people see us and instead devote that energy to considering what we think of them. Are they genuinely confident enough to respond generously to our ideas, to our initiatives, to our mistakes. Or will they be critical of our ideas, resistant to our initiatives and jealously triumphant about our mistakes? Forging a network of people who are both generous and disciplined, with whom you can enter into open, honest relationships based on confidence and trust, is the way that you will increase your influence and achieve your goals. Trying to impress the unimpressible is not. You will need to engage with these but must not allow your self-image to be determined by them.

Nevertheless we can, and should, *help* people respond favourably to us by exploiting the 'halo' effect. If we like certain things about a person –

the way she looks, the way she sounds – then the 'halo effect' predisposes us to like other aspects, her arguments for example. Paying attention to how we present ourselves – voice and posture, colour and style of clothing – can help us to influence others and achieve our goals. Professional advice in these areas is well worth taking.[10] However, although they are a valuable aid in getting a message across, they do not replace the need for a valid message! Without this change of outlook, without a determination to concentrate our attention on others rather than on ourselves, to become a 'go-giver' rather than a 'go-getter',[11] then no matter how classy our presentation skills, our effectiveness will be severely limited.

Taking this step requires an initial change in attitude and constant work on feelings, on the way we respond to others, and on the way we can frame arguments to persuade others. This takes time.

Preparation

Work on feelings, on generosity and discipline was for centuries the province of religion. With the decline of theism over the last 150 years, many of the routines associated with religions have all but disappeared. Yet there is much benefit to be gained from a period of reflection and preparation on a daily basis, a weekly review and an annual period of questioning and reaffirming of goals. This is a pattern you will recognize as occurring in many of the major world religions.

We have already considered an important function of the *weekly* review, the scheduling of your time to work towards your own goals. The *daily* session need not take long, 10 minutes perhaps, and most people seem to find it most valuable at either end of the day – on waking or before sleeping. The first part of the session is spent reflecting on the day just completed, remembering especially the feelings experienced. Whenever you have experienced a 'negative' emotion – anger, frustration, resentment – challenge yourself. Is there a lesson for you to draw from it? Identify the cause of those feelings. See if you can reach a feeling of calm about the situations that previously enervated you.

The second purpose of the session is preparation for the day ahead. Consider your agenda. How do you feel about the tasks to be undertaken? Are you accepting all your responsibilities and owning all your problems, or are you trying to offload them on to others? What is the problem you have? How could you resolve it? If you have a meeting with someone you find difficult, when you know you are likely to respond in anger, imagine yourself in the meeting. Imagine their behaviour, their arguments, feel yourself getting angry and practise losing that anger. Practise choosing concern or compassion as your response instead. Is there a meeting with colleagues where you will be tempted to join with them in a general condemnation of the *status quo*, of management, of other professions? You can practise choosing not to diminish yourself by joining in, practise encouraging them to accept their responsibilities by refuting notions of censure and blame. Perhaps there is a session when you have to give someone some bad news – a patient perhaps or a junior member of your team who needs to improve their performance. Your feelings will drive your behaviours, so it is essential to work on these. When you have imagined your feelings of discomfort, embarrassment or self-consciousness, imagine replacing those with feelings of concern for the other; imagine forgetting about yourself and concentrating entirely on the needs of the other. The more vividly you can imagine these new feelings, the more easily will you experience them when the time comes.

Sometimes it is difficult to challenge ourselves; either we are too gentle or too condemnatory. For that reason, some people choose to seek that challenge in other ways. Some find 'action learning sets' a valuable resource, others look for a mentor (either formally or informally), some book regular 'supervision' sessions with an individual outside the workplace, whereas others have a particularly open, honest and challenging relationship with their spouse or a friend. Unfortunately, the more senior one becomes, and the more important is this challenge, the more difficult it can be to find it informally or within one's organization. You are more likely to find an external arrangement most satisfactory. The time spent on such support must, of course, be limited. While important, its purpose is to help people to be more effective, not just to understand why they are not. A few individuals appear to derive so much support from their set or their mentor, that they do little to tackle the problems they experience. Making decisions about the source of such a challenge can form a valuable part of an *annual* review of progress towards goals. This is also an opportunity to consider any need for skills development.

In Chapter 3 we noted that the role of a *real* manager is to develop the maturity of an organization by increasing the confidence of its members. Engendering confidence in others requires us to have confidence in ourselves and in managing yourself you will nurture this self-confidence. Confidence results when the demands made of us are within our competence, and when our competences are steadily growing. We have a confidence problem whenever what our intellect tells us we can do, what our ambition tells us we ought to do, is not in harmony with what we believe we are able to do. Other people have a problem with our confidence when what they think we can achieve is less than we believe it to be. Whichever confidence problem we have (and most of us experience both from time to time), self-awareness is the route to its solution. A realistic assessment of our abilities is needed, and also of our feelings.

When assessing our skills, we must do so in all of the four skills areas defined in Chapter 4: clinical/technical, behavioural, managerial and evaluative. When we bring them to bear, we do so as a package of skills, each supporting the others, and it is how this package allows us to make progress towards our goals that we must consider. Comparing our own skill levels honestly with those of others allows us to identify areas of relative strength or weakness and thus opportunities to offer assistance or seek development.

If you find such a comparison disheartening, check that you are using an appropriate comparator and not a known paragon of virtue in this field. Check also that you are remembering your 'package' of skills. You will always find others whose prowess exceeds your own on one of the dimensions; however, it is the four together that enable you to contribute. Refer back also to your personal goals. If your aim is to make a difference to the lives of a particular group of patients, then you will need a skills package that differs from that required if you wish to take a high-profile national role. Always remember, too, that the most influential individuals are not necessarily the most charismatic, they are simply effective.

If this comparison leaves you with a fiery glow of satisfaction, then you also have some checking to do. Have you sought any more objective appraisal of your competences and qualities than your own analysis? Are you confusing the ability to acquire a competence with its acquisition? The intelligence to understand how to undertake certain roles is not in itself something deserving of self-congratulation.

Whenever we behave in a way that differs from the behaviour of the person we would like to be we damage our confidence. When we adopt behaviours of which we approve our confidence increases. So since we can choose our behaviours, our level of confidence is largely in our own hands.

Genuine (as opposed to misplaced) confidence is not empty self-belief, it will not arise from simply telling ourselves that we are okay. It is acquired gradually as we exercise discipline to choose our behaviours, to make and keep commitments to ourselves and to others. Every time we make a commitment we do not keep we diminish our self-esteem. We should therefore make commitments carefully and sparingly, in full knowledge of what the commitment will require of us. To ensure that you only make commitments that you can keep, and that they are worthy of your energy and effort, always think through carefully what your own contribution to a particular task could be. Make sure that you have something to offer. Other people may be more experienced in this field but unavailable. Your availability is important. Others may have a higher level of technical expertise but not be able to get on with colleagues. Your interpersonal skills are your asset. You may be more junior than others, but your knowledge of operational detail may be just what is needed. Only if you assess correctly what your contribution could be can you ensure that you make it. You won't then be tempted to limit your availability by going on holiday, or to beef up on technical detail when you are needed for your ability to build a team.

If we want to build our competences we must also operate, at least some of the time, right at the edge (or outside) of our comfort zone. It is only when we experiment or when we make mistakes that we learn. As Benjamin Franklin put it, 'that which hurts instructs'. Unfortunately, that which hurts, well, hurts! The trick here is to make sure that we do learn from every painful experience. That way we can reflect on our increased competence as we smile ruefully about the time when . . .

Being aware of our feelings is the other self-assessment we must make and on a continuing basis. How did/do I feel and why? Is that a good enough reason to commit my time? Is the feeling justified? If not, can I lose it? Knowing how we respond is the necessary first step to understanding why we do so and thence to changing that response so that our feelings about our abilities coincide with our rational assessment of them.

Circumstances beyond our control

You may be thinking that none of this will help when the pressures are societal, or at such a macro level that you can have no influence. Patients, for instance, have expectations that you cannot possibly meet, and politicians, driven by a political and ideological agenda, are trying to destroy the very system to which you chose to devote my career. Here again we can choose to respond generously or jealously to the individuals exerting these pressures. Don Berwick phrased it very neatly when he said about patients: 'behind every unreasonable demand there is a reasonable expectation'.[12]

Certainly there are people whose expectations are unrealistic, often because they do not appreciate the complexity of the system that is required to meet what, to them, appears a simple need. A few others, unfortunately, have an aggressive expectation of poor service and, by their demeanour, contribute to the fact that they receive it. Some are thoughtless about their use of services and some are over-anxious. Many are worried and not as accommodating as they might be when dealing with other services. But, on the whole, patients simply expect to be treated in the way that they are when in other service settings. What is more they exhibit great tolerance of poor service and sympathy for its providers, and complain far less often than they might. The generous response, when a patient expects something of your service that you cannot provide, is to let that expectation challenge your thinking. Could we provide this? Should we provide this? How could we organize things differently in order to do so? Would doing so be more in harmony with my goals than not doing so? As HCPs we have the ability to devise systems that meet most expectations, or at the very least to influence those expectations to a level we can meet. When we become self-absorbed, or precious, or a victim, we lose that ability.

Somehow we have come to expect stability. We have come to believe that if we pass through the life stages of dependency, development and education, then eventually we shall reach a point when we have learned all we need to know in order to meet a fairly predictable set of demands. This is a new belief that has accompanied the massive increase in life expectancy and the absence for 50 years, in the UK anyway, of a major destabilizing factor such as war. We have no right to such an expectation. Until relatively recently, as a visit to any graveyard reminds us, early death was commonplace. Family life and individual well-being was very far from predictable. Advances in knowledge have granted, to populations able to exploit them, longevity and predictability undreamed of by our ancestors. But with those advances have come others and the tremendous developments in technology have led to changes in systems and structures – and also in opportunities – that affect us all. Alvin Toffler wrote *Future Shock*, a book about the rate of change 20 years ago;[13] some of us are now experiencing 'present shock'. And yet we must learn to deal with change, because not only is it here to stay but its rate is accelerating. Generally in the UK there has been much less change in the healthcare system than there has been in other sectors where new technology has reduced workforces by 50 or even 70 per cent in some cases. We must expect more and more change, arriving faster and faster. Our ability to respond to change is a critical area to develop – in ourselves and, even more crucially, in our children.

Who knows, the chaos theorists may yet demonstrate to us that the foundations of current medical science are suspect; that, like Ptolemy's understanding of the heavens, it has proved usefully predictive but is fundamentally flawed. Future generations of healthcare professionals may view our interventions with amusement. The point is, we do not know and we cannot begin to imagine, but we must be able to respond.

Given the changes in technology and increases in longevity, politicians (of whatever flavour) do what you or I would do in their place. They aim to contain the explosion in funding that could take place, while requiring accountability for the way current monies are spent. We can quibble with their choice of methods, or the way they choose to sell it to the electorate, but not with the task. Our ability to respond is diminished when we personalize issues and attribute blame to individuals and parties instead of recognizing that our world is changing and that we cannot expect anything else.

There is an old Christian prayer, a version of which is used by Alcoholics Anonymous, which asks, 'Lord, grant me the courage to change the things I can change, the grace to accept those I cannot, and the wisdom to know the difference'. As running into a brick wall, either literally or metaphorically, is both painful and damaging, it is worth trying to recognize a brick wall when we see one. Covey suggests drawing two circles (Figure 6.1).[14] The first should include all the issues, events and people you care about (this is your circle of concern). The second encompasses all the issues, events and people you can influence in some way (your circle of influence). Most people have circles of concern and influence which have much in common, but find there are many things they are concerned about but which they cannot influence. Thus their circle of concern includes, but is greater than, their circle of influence.

Spending time and energy in our circle of concern, where we can achieve nothing, is counterproductive. It diminishes our ability to work within our circle of influence, where we can and will have an impact. Thus when we come across a situation which angers or saddens us, the effective response is to determine whether it lies within our circle of concern or our circle of influence. If it falls within the latter, we should take appropriate action; if

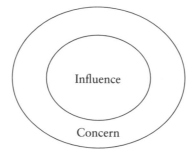

Figure 6.1   The circles of concern and influence

the former, we should not dwell there for long. We do not improve that state of affairs by indulging in unproductive anger. Sometimes there are actions we can take which may contribute to a solution, for example writing to an MP or forming a lobby group. These actions and the research they require are now part of our circle of influence, but the rest of the issue remains in the outer circle of concern. Again we must focus on what we can do rather than on what we cannot if we are to contribute without burning out.

   We shall always be surrounded by events we cannot influence, but we can control how we respond to them. To do so requires work. Most of us will not invest in the work required and will remain out of control. But that is our choice. We cannot (although we will try very hard to) blame anyone else.

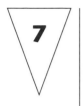

7 Really managing organizations

Imagine a machine, a complex machine with numerous parts, all of which have irregular movements, in the course of which they interact with a large number of other parts. Running into and out of the machine linking several of the parts to other machines are cords, some of which are more flexible than others.

To predict the output of such a machine, we could sit and watch it and count the different widgets it produces and perhaps measure their quality. If we wanted to change either the number or quality of some of the varieties of widgets produced, we would have two options. First, we could try and identify which parts of the machine are involved in the production of this type of widget, and then we could intervene to change the part or the movement, or both. Second, we could, instead, really get to know all the workings of the machine – all of its parts and all their movements. As a result, we would know how any changes to parts or movements or, for that matter, grade of fuel, will impact on outputs. We would also know just what lubricant is required and whether any part is about to seize up for lack of it.

The machine, of course, is the healthcare organization and the two options describe the difference between traditional and *real* management. *Real managers* (when in chief executive positions) take responsibility for the output of their machines by taking responsibility for three critical elements:

1 *The reliability of the parts*: by knowing the strengths and weaknesses of their staff and ensuring that people are in positions where they can play to their strengths.
2 *The precision of the movements*: by ensuring, through example and

expectation, that there are high-quality relationships in all parts of the organization.

3 *The grade of fuel*: by enabling everyone to have access to the information they need.

The difference between the two approaches is greater than may first appear. The first option, the traditional management role in health care, is an intellectual puzzle. The second requires a commitment, a conviction and a personal involvement that is altogether different. And where this can be found, the payoffs are also just as dramatically different. Neither commitment nor conviction can be gained and maintained without a high degree of personal involvement. Commitment accompanies an intimacy with the core of the organization – that is, clinical care. Conviction springs from a deep understanding of the people who comprise the organization and a real belief in their potential contribution (albeit accompanied by a realistic assessment of the personal factors preventing them from realizing that potential). Only when commitment and conviction have been gained can a chief executive build the systems and develop the relationships that will allow the organization to become greater than the sum of its parts. The staff in any healthcare organization include some of the most able and the most committed in society. That is why it is so regrettable that in most of these organizations there is negative synergy, the whole is very much *less* than the sum of these parts.

The parts

Commitment

Commitment accompanies intimacy – intimacy with the core of the organization, the guts of the machine. This is what allows the chief executive to have a real feeling for the shared beliefs, behaviours, feelings and sensibilities that are engendered in response to pressures, to opportunities, to frustrations and to successes. It is, after all, these responses which determine overall performance. Managers who do not regularly spend time on the frontline lose this feeling (or never gain it), and without it they lose both the credibility that accompanies a sound grasp of operational detail and the ability to predict trouble – to know almost intuitively when things are going wrong. Without these they cannot engage in one of their most important functions, that of selling problems, and they will be tempted to try and solve them. Instead of calling upon the skills and insights of the people who understand the complexities of the factors which contribute to the problem, an ineffective chief executive, advised by others equally removed from the frontline, imposes a course of action that solves part of the problem but creates many more in the process. Time-consuming though it undoubtedly is, *selling* problems to the people who are most affected by them will be far more successful than taking decisions without them.

So time on the frontline, and throughout the organization, is an important and protected part of a chief executive's schedule if he is a *real manager*. There is just no substitute for actually being there, and not just during weekday and daylight hours either. This is not a one-off shadowing exercise for the superficial education of the chief executive, nor is it a means of policing. The benefit of this investment of time is not realized by the chief executive, but by the organization and the people who comprise it. The chief executive's interests when spending time becoming fully familiar with her machine will include:

• Exactly what is required of these staff?
• Are they adequately skilled and resourced?
• Do the organizational systems support them?
• Do those systems work with or against human nature?
• Are staff learning from their mistakes?
• Are there systems for the organization and myself to learn from those mistakes?
• Are individuals in positions where they can play to their strengths?
• How can they be liberated to achieve what is required of them?

It can be a useful mental shift for chief executives to consider that they themselves do not generate any income for their organization, that it is the provider departments, the frontline, which do so. In this scenario, it is not managers who give resources to departments and services, but the other way around. Departments and services pay a 'management tax', to pay for certain common support services and for ensuring that interdependency is achieved, but the bulk of their income remains their own. With this mindset it is clear that chief executives, with no spare financial resources of their own, have no choice but to fully engage with their frontline, gaining their support for any initiatives, or any changes, persuading these departments to bankroll them.

A chief executive intimate with the business at the heart of their organization will take an interest in relevant research, discuss new developments and approaches, and be fully committed to optimal clinical outcomes. Moreover, she will be perceived as a resource by her clinicians, for her clarity of thought, her enthusiasm, her concern. If she is to be seen in this way, then she needs to be aware of the boundary between decisions that are clinical and those which are managerial. Confusion over where this boundary lies has allowed individuals and groups to either over- or under-step it. The former causes resentment, the latter an absence of accountability. It is important therefore that there is agreement on its position. One of the easiest ways of determining this is to apply a widely known systems science concept to health care. This is that every system has a structure, a process and an outcome and, contrary to popular healthcare opinion, it is a concept whose origins are lost in antiquity. Aristotle's definition of four types of cause, for example (formal, material, efficient and final), are very similar.

In the 1970s, Donabedian applied it to medical care in the United States as follows:[1]

> Structure: The relatively stable characteristics of the providers of care, of the tools and resources at their disposal, and of the physical and organizational settings in which they work
> Process: The set of activities that go on between clinicians and clients
> Outcome: Any change in current and future health status that can be attributed to antecedent health care

To make this relevant to the UK in the 1990s and beyond we need to (1) widen the application to health, rather than solely medical, care, (2) include the consumer perspective, and (3) include the organizational system of which HCPs in the UK (unlike doctors in the USA at that time) are a part. When we do so, we will see that the structure, process and outcome differs for managers, clinicians and clients.

> **For the manager**
>
> Structure: Money, people, equipment, materials, premises, activity requirements, etc.
> Process: Taking responsibility for the seven Ss described in Chapter 4 (strategy, staff, skills, systems, style, structure and shared values)
> Outcome: HCPs have skills, resources and motivation to diagnose and meet the needs of their clients

> **For the clinician**
>
> Structure: The relatively stable characteristics of the providers of care, of the tools and resources they have at their disposal, and of the physical and organizational settings in which they work
> Process: The set of activities that go on between clinicians and clients
> Outcome: The client is informed about, and supported in decisions about, treatment

> **For the client**
>
> Structure: The consultation with the HCP, information about clinical condition and treatment options
> Process: The programme of treatment
> Outcome: The change in current and future health status that can be attributed to antecedent health care

A number of interesting points arise from this. First, the 'outcome' for one stakeholder is the 'structure' for another. This means that none of these three stakeholders can, alone, ensure an optimum final outcome. All have an essential part to play and deserve the respect of the other stakeholders when they play that part well.

Second, a manager (even a real manager) has no role in the interaction between an autonomous, fully trained clinician and an individual patient – this is the realm of clinical judgement. And this is true even when the manager is a clinician, for example when a GP employs a physiotherapist or when a number of consultants form a directorate managed by a clinical director. Where patients can be grouped together, however (by diagnosis, particular clinical features, age, ethnicity, clinician), then there will be a managerial role, for there will be issues of system design; for example, means of enhancing the application of research evidence, of ensuring clinical competence, of enabling patients to have access to an interpreter, of re-enthusing a clinical carer who is no longer caring. The actual design of such systems is best carried out by the people most closely involved or affected, but the responsibility for ensuring they are in place rests with the manager.

Third, just as there is a need to observe the boundary between clinical and managerial decisions, that between clinician and client responsibilities must be borne in mind. If patients are not given all the information they need on which to base a decision, if that information is meaningless to them or if they are not accorded the respect and the time which allows them to take decisions, then there has been trespass over that boundary. Another role of the chief executive when spending time with clinicians is to challenge systems (and individuals) which lead to that trespass.

Many of the healthcare professions continue to equate the outcome as perceived by the clinician with that of the client, so this boundary is also worthy of further consideration. As many clinicians, philosophers and policy-makers have observed, health is very much more than the absence of disease. Health status can be thought of as the outcome of the interaction of two highly complex systems – the individual human and their environment. Both of these systems have a large number of component elements and influencing one or more of these elements in either system may alter the health status. In complex, dynamic, non-linear systems, the nature of the outcome of an intervention cannot always be predicted, nor indeed can any system malfunction always be correctly pinned down to the behaviour of one particular element. The nature of clinical decision-making has to reflect the lack of certainty inherent here, a point not always appreciated by the public, the media or lay managers. And if managers are to achieve an intimacy with the clinical task, then they need to have an understanding of this uncertainty.

The complexity of both of these systems (the individual and their environment) requires the involvement of a number of different specialists if the health status is to be maximized. Unfortunately, specialists, as we saw in Chapter 2, are prone to take responsibility only for their specialist task and not for the overall outcome. In other words, members of healthcare professions can become desensitized to the *health* needs of clients in their efforts to rid them of disease. One of the roles of the real manager of an interdependent organization is to keep the attention of their specialists focused on that overall outcome, health. Seedhouse suggests that the role of the clinician is to create, maintain and respect the autonomy of their patients.[2] Real managers enable them to do so. They do this by encouraging reflective practice and freshening up reactions that have become jaded; never allowing 'we always do it this way' or 'this isn't as bad as some cases' to justify an approach to care they would not wish to receive themselves.

There is much talk nowadays about managing for or by outcomes, so let us think clearly about this. Structure is a given. In some cases, representations can be made to influence it, but then the ability to make those representations can be considered part of the structure. Outcomes are the results of the processes to which the structure is subjected. Process is therefore where we spend our time. Where the link between process and outcome is known, then our performance can be judged by monitoring either process *or* outcome and 'managing for outcomes' becomes a possibility. However, in the vast majority of cases (both clinical and managerial), this link has not been demonstrated, and in these cases managers and clinicians have two relevant roles: first, to manage the process and, second, where possible, to establish the link between process and outcome. There is now much more support in this latter role than hitherto in the clinical arena. Initiatives in 'evidence-based health care' abound. Much less interest and resource is invested in evidence-based management practice.

Management by structure, simply gathering the elements of the healthcare organization together, is unfortunately still common. Wherever the three rules of Chapter 1 are not observed, and that means at every level in the organization, then it is inevitable.

Conviction

Conviction springs from a deep understanding of the people who comprise the organization and a real belief in their potential contribution. This is not the same as wishful thinking on the part of an ineffectual 'mister nice guy'. It requires an ability, and a preparedness, to make judgements about performance.

By becoming familiar with the machine that is her organization, the real manager will be able to make judgements about the reliability of its parts. If, knowing that certain parts are unreliable, she continues to rely on them, then the responsibility for any failure lies with her. There is no avoiding the need to develop an ability to make judgements about the reliability of individuals in performing what is asked of them. This can only happen with time, with exposure to the kinds of people she will be managing, and by making mistakes. This latter is particularly important, although always disappointing or painful.

As we saw in Chapter 4, it can be helpful to think of the skills of staff falling into four categories, all of which are necessary in any healthcare worker: (1) clinical or technical, (2) behavioural, (3) managerial and (4) research and reflection. The demarcation between them is fuzzy because the application of clinical and research skills requires behavioural and managerial skills, and the personal maturity that underpins behavioural and managerial skills often develops from a competence (and hence confidence) in clinical, technical or research arenas. However, to distinguish between areas in which further development is needed and those where performance is reliably unproblematic, the classification is useful. Certainly within the organization there must be systems for appraising all four kinds of skills.

All four? Does a lay manager really have the right to make judgements about *clinical* skills? For a number of reasons they do. Really managing an organization means taking responsibility for its outputs. In healthcare organizations, this means managing clinical risk. To manage risk requires a knowledge of the size and nature of the risk. This cannot be acquired without an appreciation of the clinical skills of staff. Really managing an organization also involves ensuring its viability, which requires the ability to compete for contracts. The nature of the competition is determined by whether the service offered is a commodity one (and must therefore compete on price) or one that is differentiated from competitors by virtue of superior outcomes or the ability to tackle more complex cases. Knowing which competitive strategy to adopt and hence ensure the financial health of the organization also requires a knowledge of clinical skill levels.

Research and reflection skills allow the links between process and outcome to be established and must be encouraged. To develop a culture of reflective practice, the chief executive must personally take an active interest in research and understand different research methods and their appropriateness in different situations. He must also believe (and demonstrate this belief) that mistakes made are opportunities for people to learn and progress, and that complaints are valuable sources of the feedback which we all need in order to improve our performance. Research and reflection skills must be applied to every aspect of performance, giving rise to a culture of ongoing review, rather than be confined to particular clinical areas.

Where behavioural and managerial skill levels are high, the individuals concerned are likely to be the real managers of the organization, its leaders, its opinion-formers. Most often, these real managers will not be termed or think of themselves as managers, but as clinicians. Identifying these *real managers* is the key to *really managing* an organization. Unless organization charts accord with these realities they will be ignored, no matter how fancy the titles given.

The easiest way of assessing leadership abilities is to examine the people who are following. de Pree puts it thus: 'Signs of outstanding leadership appear primarily among the followers. Are the followers reaching their potential? are they learning? serving? Do they achieve the required results? Do they change with grace? manage conflict?'.[3] *Real* managers are perceived by their teams and departments as a resource, a means of helping them to contribute, not as a policeman constantly looking over their shoulders to see that they are obeying the letter of the law. Real managers, in the words of E. Deming, a quality guru, 'drive out fear', so they engender confidence and faith in others.[4]

Fear is the big enemy of *real* management. Fear is the root cause of immaturity in individuals and in organizations. Recognizing, gracefully acknowledging and learning from mistakes; respecting, crediting and assisting colleagues; supporting motivating and developing staff; these are all behaviours only consistently contributed by the individual (or organization) who is not afraid, who is confident in him or herself and in his or her potential. In looking for real managers we should therefore look for signs of generosity, of open, honest relationships, of individuals and teams prepared to risk making themselves vulnerable by relying on others. Alongside this there will be evidence of discipline – no scapegoating, no self-righteousness, no culture of gossip and blame.

Real managers, aware of the sometimes thin line between delegation and 'copping out', will help members of their teams with aspects of their role that they themselves find unpleasant. Most people, for example, do not enjoy dealing with poor performance, nor the giving of bad news, nor having to choose between two or more equally bad alternatives. The real manager will be a genuine resource here. She will physically accompany members of her staff, if appropriate, to meetings where there may be flack flying, and she will never send other people in to fight battles she would not want to fight herself. It is worth remembering that good managers are not necessarily those who naturally and easily handle these situations well. Paraphrasing only slightly, 'Those who can, do. It takes those who can't to teach'. Good managers are confident in their strengths and aware of (and comfortable with) the areas they find more difficult. They do not feel the need to hide these, nor fear exposure of them. They use their insight into their own feelings and reactions to assist others through situations where they will feel the same.

Another pointer to the identification of real managers is that we will find them listening. Listening rather than talking. In particular, they listen to information moving up an organization. Imagine an organization in which at every level of the hierarchy each individual has ten people accountable to them. Even if we assume that information moving up the organization has the same value as that moving down (and for many reasons we could suggest it was worth more), then every manager would need to listen to information coming from below ten times as often as to that coming from above. The reverse is a common complaint. As they listen they will also challenge and by doing so they will encourage their staff to accept their proper responsibilities, to interact effectively with others, to avoid group-think, to act rather than complain.

In *The Fifth Discipline*, Senge suggests that 'the hallmark of a great organization is how quickly bad news travels upwards'.[5] We can see why this is by considering the last two paragraphs. For news to travel quickly upwards, the organization must have managers who listen to information coming from the frontline. For *bad* news to travel, then these managers must feel sufficiently confident of their abilities and, even more important, open about their weaknesses, not to fear exposure.

The real manager also internalizes another of Deming's maxims, that it is systems that fail, not people. Don Berwick, an American physician responsible for championing Deming's ideas in his own organization, and now more widely, highlights the fact that across a large number of industries, scrutiny of the causes of product or service defects reveals that in 8 per cent of cases the blame can be attributed to the underperformance of an individual, who should have known better. In the other 92 per cent, the people involved behaved the way that anyone else would have done in a similar situation.[6] In other words, it is the situation, or system, that has led to the defect. Real managers, then, faced with a complaint, or an untoward incident, spend eleven times as much energy pursuing system faults as they do investigating the performance of their staff. The systems, naturally, include those of recruitment, development and appraisal, and there are times when the 'fit' between the task and the individual, or between the organization and the individual, is not right. In these cases, it is in the best interests of the organization and its customers (and, in the long term, the individual concerned, although this may not be apparent in the short term) for the mismatch to be resolved. This may mean different responsibilities within the organization or it may mean departure. In any instance, when an individual has been 'let go', a review of the organization's systems is needed. If, instead, all the blame is placed with the departing individual (as happens all too frequently), then the system failure that led to this untoward event cannot be remedied and it is likely to be repeated.

Systems must work with and not against human nature. In other words, it must be easier to comply with the required system than not to do so. If systems are not designed to take human nature into account, then when something goes wrong it is the system (and its architect) which must shoulder the blame. One important example of this is that systems must be designed with the implications of the hierarchy of clinical descriptions kept firmly in mind. As we saw in Chapter 2, different professions and disciplines will operate at different levels of the hierarchy. We also saw that it is very difficult (if not impossible) to focus on more than one level at a time. Clearly, therefore, someone doing valiant battle at electrolyte level (a senior house officer in accident and emergency, for example) is not simultaneously considering the needs of the patient for a 'good death'. If a complaint from relatives is forthcoming, instead of blaming the individuals concerned, the real manager will redesign his systems so that there is no reliance on his staff undertaking the impossible (or even the very difficult). Ensuring that every level in the hierarchy receives the attention it requires is one of the greatest challenges for healthcare organizations and their real managers.

The recruitment system is one which often fails, sometimes because in concern about the process, its purpose is forgotten. An appointment is an important decision for both parties, the appointer and the appointed. A bad decision is costly for both. People come in all shapes and sizes and so do their abilities, interests and attitudes. The hole that you have in your organization is unlikely to be exactly the same size and shape as any of the individuals applying to fill it. For positions that are critical to the success of the organization (and that includes *all* senior clinical ones), exploring ways in which your hole can be modified to mutual benefit is essential. Thus a service, department or organization will have a different feel depending on the candidate selected to join its leadership. The implications of this must be considered carefully by those individuals who will be affected. Job descriptions and person specifications are valuable starting points for discussion. Assessment centres can be helpful, too, but tend to be based on the principle that your hole is immutable and you want the closest fit. They and the short panel interview forget the needs of the candidates to assess the organization, the post and the 'fit' with their own profile. Again there is no getting away from the need to take time and exercise judgement. Although it may be useful to have decision support from the personality and other tests of an assessment centre, that is all they are – decision support – and *not* the decision.

A one-hour interview allows you to hear a candidate's response to the questions you ask. It does not allow you the time you need to decide whether you believe that they can deliver what they say. Many people can 'talk a good business' but not deliver it. Others undersell their abilities. Track record is important here, and the steady accumulation of experience and responsibilities is more likely to engender the confidence and insight required than are meteoric rises. de Pree warns that it is possible to mistake momentum for leadership, and nowhere is this more relevant than when making senior appointments.[7] Lack of significant experience at operational levels in the organization is difficult to compensate for later. A candidate with such experience can be exposed to the broader issues of top-level management much more successfully than can someone who understands only these broad issues be made familiar with operational complexities. One sign of people who merely 'talk a good business' are CVs which consistently list all achievements as individual, where the writer claims all the credit. In all senior positions the ability to work through and with other people will be paramount. The CV which talks of enabling the achievements of others, and that lists failures (and the lessons learned) as well as successes, is more likely to represent the successful *real* manager.

Personal involvement

Managing a healthcare organization, then, requires intimacy with its core business, a deep understanding of its members, and a genuine belief in their potential to contribute. When individual members are not realizing that potential, then the real managers (e.g. the chief executive), must ensure that they have opportunities to develop the ability to do so.

Individuals or groups stuck in dependency mode (as described in Chapter 3) will not realize their potential until they can be moved along the maturity continuum. They are dangerous at senior levels in an organization. Personal maturity must be one of the chief executive's criteria when she makes senior appointments. In many cases, she will not find the clinical/technical skills she needs in an individual with this maturity and she will have to develop it. This is one of her roles, perhaps the most important, and it should not frighten her. Some people, however, are so deeply into dependency mode that the time spent moving them forward will deprive others of her assistance. She must therefore select individuals who appear able to respond to her input. Belief in the latent capabilities of her staff is not enough on its own; the real manager also makes an assessment of the input required of her and others if these are to be released.

People are sometimes trapped in dependency mode because they are trapped in a dependency system. As Peters says, 'people want to be in control of their worlds'.[8] If your system does not allow them to be so, then you can expect resentful, immature behaviour. Where you observe this, investigate further. Would a dedicated lift or theatre change the mindset of a surgical team? If so, failing to provide it will be more expensive than doing so. A dedicated porter for the laboratories? Equipment budgets for each district nursing team? Real managers build systems of interdependency rather than dependency.

Moving people along the maturity continuum is easier said than done and requires the overcoming of the defensive routines (see Chapter 6) people adopt to protect themselves from the pain of acknowledging that they have learning needs. This is not an area that can be tackled by theorizing, it requires example and the modelling of the desired behaviour. It demands the disclosure of feelings and acknowledgement of insecurities to people who may believe this signifies weakness. The courage that this will require can only be found where there is intense personal involvement and a passionate desire for the organization and its members to succeed.

The movements

It is not enough for a chief executive to identify the real managers in his organization, he must now develop robust relationships with them. Relationships in which each can challenge the thinking, the behaviour and the self-image of the other, and be open to such challenges in return. These relationships will not always be comfortable, often the reverse, and developing and maintaining such relationships requires time, effort, courage and integrity. Above all, the latter, because he must *model* the behaviours he wishes to see in others.

A robust relationship contains no sycophancy, nor does it require that the parties like each other. They must trust and respect one another but if a manager is always liked by his staff, the chances are he is neither respected nor trusted. Developing these robust relationships is not an optional extra for the chief executive. Not something to be done when time permits. These relationships and those established by his team, with each other, and with their teams, throughout the organisation, are the means by which he manages, *really manages*. These relationships are his way of ensuring the organization is in control, achieving its potential, its vision.

What vision? Or rather, whose vision? Management orthodoxy has it that it is the chief executive who defines the vision of an organization. Indeed, many of the mission statements produced by healthcare Trusts over recent years are clearly the work of the top management team. Certainly a really managed service will be one *with* a vision, where people know the direction in which they are heading and are enthusiastic about travelling there. But the vision will not have come from the chief executive. The role of the chief executive (or any real manager) is not to create a vision but to find it – find it held by the people they are managing. According to Gary Hamel, a leading business strategist, companies the world over are now saying 'the last thing we want is a vision', that all too often 'a company vision statement is indistinguishable from the delusions of the chief executive'.[9] While delusions must be avoided, so too must allowing externally imposed targets to masquerade as the organizational purpose. The vision, the purpose, is in the commitment and enthusiasm of staff. Meeting waiting list targets or financial limits are merely 'table stakes', things you have to do to be in the game, but not the game itself and certainly not the prize.

Thus real managers as chief executives will be 'middle-up-down' managers in the terminology of Ikugiro Nonaka.[10] The middle-up-down management hierarchy is one in which the people at the top tend to lay down values (through their behaviour) and policies (arising from the constraints of the environment in which the organization operates). They then synthesize the innovative actions which flow up from those beneath. These managers spend most of their time listening, responding, nurturing and formulating policy from ideas and practices that have emerged from below.

As Senge points out, unless a shared vision is made up of personal visions, we can expect only compliance from our staff, not commitment.[11] Sometimes HCPs lose their vision and look back with frustration or embarrassment at the naive ideals that drew them in to health care. They need to be put back in touch with their vision, with those ideals. Since helplessness or powerlessness is one of the reasons they have lost sight of those ideals, they will need tangible encouragement – evidence that if they make a reasonable case they will receive a helpful response. This can only be achieved if managers are prepared to invest both time and emotional energy. It will certainly require of them that they master their feelings as discussed in Chapter 6 and do not back-off when they meet scornful resistance.

Pushing decisions right down to the people most affected by them is the way to ensure they are both informed and owned. Pushing decisions down is one of the most effective ways of creating systems of interdependency rather than dependency. But we need to be careful. Pushing decisions down is not the same as seeking specialist advice, although to a chief executive they may both appear to be delegation. Delegating decisions to specialist advisers ('staff' departments such as personnel, finance, planning and information technology, as opposed to 'line' or operational departments) is the very opposite of pushing decisions down, it is keeping them right at the top.

When seeking specialist advice, a chief executive should do so in two stages. In the first, she needs help in defining the dimensions of the problem. When restructuring (sigh!) her organization, for example, she should seek information from the personnel department on, perhaps, relevant employment law, local agreements with unions, national or locally agreed terms and conditions of employment, other local policies (e.g. equal opportunities). When those dimensions of the problem are clear, she must add in her other concerns – maintaining the commitment of her staff, increasing organizational effectiveness by identifying and recognizing the real managers – and also her personal values (do as you would be done by, perhaps). When she has defined her problem more fully in this way, she can now seek her second stage advice: What are the options? What are the risks? Specialist advisers will be tempted to try and sell their solutions to the problems as they see them. The chief executive must remember that she has other information, other concerns, not shared by the specialist, so she will see the problem differently. It is her job to do so. She must have the courage to reject advice (gracefully) in the wider interests of the organization and its clients. It is not difficult for people in departments away from the frontline to lose sight of the organization's purpose and lose the 'balance' described in Chapter 3. Asking management support departments to make a 'clinical case' for any recommendations they make, in the same way that clinical departments must make a 'business case', can help to restore this balance.

So the real manager manages the movements of her machine by putting people back in touch with their vision, with the reasons they came into health care, and removing the obstacles preventing them achieving it – poorly designed systems and antagonistic relationships. She develops and fosters robust, high-quality, challenging relationships throughout the organization. That's all. Simple. Simple but very hard.

The fuel

Every aspect of the clinical process involves the use and/or transfer of information. Information handling is also the very essence of management. As soon as we no longer perform a task ourselves but rely on someone else to do so, the two-way transfer of information (or 'communication') becomes essential. Information is therefore the fuel of the healthcare machine.

Ensuring that the correct grade is provided at the right intervals is another of the fundamental roles of the chief executive.

Information is needed for both operational and strategic purposes. It supports and arises out of the same events – patients being treated by staff – yet historically information collected for operational purposes has been kept completely separate from that used for strategy formulation. Strategic decisions do not require information at the same level of detail as do frontline clinical decision-makers; however, they rely on that detail being represented faithfully in the aggregate form that is made available to top levels in the organization. Where the link between strategic and operational information is unsound, the organization is quickly in trouble. In large part, the link between operational and strategic information is assured by the robust relationships described in the previous section. It is indeed the destruction of this link that guarantees the underperformance of the organization with low-quality relationships.

Ensuring that all the members of a large, complex organization receive the information they need, without having to waste time wading through lots of it that they do not, calls for an overview of just what information is needed, generated and transferred. It needs, in other words, an information and communication strategy. When formulating such a strategy, we must beware of confusion with two similar sounding concepts: the information strategy and the communication strategy.

Information strategies do not have a lengthy history, partly because large organizations with complex information and communication needs were not common until after the Second World War and partly because they have accompanied the development of the computer. The arrival of computers allowed data to be processed and moved around the organization, at a cost. It was important therefore to model the organization's flows of information so that the computer systems could be designed to replicate those flows. As computers were expensive and they were not all compatible with one another, a decision taken on one date to purchase a particular system would dictate future buying options and costs. A computing (or IT) strategy that considered future needs as well as present was thus sensible. Eventually, the technology was capable of doing more than reproducing existing data flows and clients and IT companies worked together to develop strategies for meeting the clients' information needs. These were called 'information strategies'. In other words, information strategies are nearly always developed or considered only when investment in IT is planned.

Communication strategies are much more recent and are often prefixed 'corporate' communication strategies. Their *raison d'être* is the presentation of the 'corporate' (top management they mean) view of the world to staff, clients and media.

An information and communication strategy is neither of these. It is just as interested in creating common coffee areas, setting up formal and informal meetings, or in revamping forms, as it is in computers, faxes and other information technology. It is just as concerned with management boards receiving news from the frontline as the other way around.

The first step in crafting such a strategy is to define the information that people require. This is far from easy and there have been several attempts at applying methodologies developed in commercial and industrial settings. Typically, these methodologies are 'top-down' or 'peeling the onion' approaches. Briefly, they ask managers from the most senior level down to define their objectives, factors critical to the successful achievement of those objectives and the information they receive and require. A parallel exercise identifies points at which data are collected and, after a series of complicated matrices, an 'information strategy' emerges.

There are a number of reasons why these techniques do not succeed in healthcare organizations. The most intractable is that objectives are as difficult to define as outcomes. When outcomes can be expressed in terms of numbers of widgets and financial figures, then objectives can be set tightly enough to be utilized in this way. Where precise definitions of outcomes are as elusive as they are in health care, then objectives are similarly wobbly. There will be some absolutes, the 'table stakes' mentioned earlier, but tight measurable objectives that together add up to the mission of the organization just cannot be written.

There is also the fact that top managers in health care cannot have experience of working in all the services they manage. This makes it very difficult for them to specify the information they need in order to manage them effectively. An added inhibitor to the successful application of these techniques is that the hierarchy utilized for the top-down interviewing programme is usually the official organization chart. As we have seen, most of these bear no resemblance to the realities of power (and sometimes forget clinicians almost altogether!).

If a top-down approach does not work, how does a bottom-up method succeed? Not well, because many frontline staff understand so incompletely the roles of others in the organization, particularly of those in more senior positions, that they are not able to imagine nor articulate the information flows involving those roles that would benefit them, their patients and the organization. What is needed in healthcare organizations is not a top-down or a bottom-up approach, but one that is service-led.

A service-led approach to information and communication strategies

Before we can define what information is needed, we have to identify *who* may need it. As a first step, representatives of a service identify all the people or agencies who are involved in any way with that service. Usually these 'stakeholders' fall into one or more of seven groupings: (1) client/carer, (2) service team (clinical and support), (3) referrers, (4) referees (a slightly confusing use of this word to mean people or agencies to whom the service team refers), (5) managers (i.e. anyone who can make resource

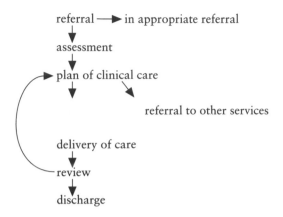

referral ⟶ in appropriate referral

assessment

plan of clinical care

referral to other services

delivery of care

review

discharge

Figure 7.1   Patient's pathway through the clinical process

allocation decisions which affect the team; it is helpful to include purchasers here), (6) professional advisers and (7) suppliers.

Next, we need to identify *when* information is required. Every service
can be thought of as a series of stages through which the client progresses.
The service representatives list the stages for their service and most services
find that they fall into the pattern shown in Figure 7.1. In addition, they
are asked to identify management processes and the stages of planning and
contracting are typically added.

The stakeholders can now be linked to the stages, thus clearly identifying everyone who is involved at each stage. Some are involved in several
stages, some (for example client and service team) in all of them, some in
only one. If anyone is involved in none of the stages, then he or she is not
a stakeholder. Clear thinking is necessary here. Typically the first attempt
by a community-based service nominates the GP at every single stage,
while their acute services colleagues deny the GP a role in any. The planning and contracting stages are normally considered the limits of legitim-
acy for managers, until there is a realization of the need to ensure capacity
at all the others.

It is now possible to look in detail at the information required by stakeholders if each stage is to be completed effectively and efficiently. If, in
addition, service representatives specify a number of standards or objectives for each stage, against which performance can be monitored, then the
information required for comprehensive service audits can also be identified. Although the process up to this point is best undertaken with a small
group of service representatives, the wider service membership can, and
should, now be consulted for their views.

It is once this process has been completed within a number of different
services in an organization that it becomes most useful. First, the requirements can be aggregated to form a set which, while it does not cover all
the requirements for every service, covers most of them; and is a set which

can form the basis of an appraisal of the various means by which the information can be provided. Second, portfolios of information requirements can be put together for groups and individuals who have a stake in more than one service. It is thus possible to generate a list of the information that is required by, for example, the chief executive or GPs, if the organization is to be able to provide its services well. Similarly, a list of information required from the chief executive or GPs can be pulled together. This is exciting because you are now in a position to tell people what information they need, rather than having to rely on what they think they want.

Any effective information and communication strategy needs to be service-led and it also requires a large amount of work at a detailed level. The temptation to offload this onto information (or even computing) specialists is very strong. It must be resisted. Managing information flows is the very essence of management. Information and responsibility walk hand in hand. There is one way and one way only of avoiding the need for the personal involvement of senior managers in such detailed work and that is for them to develop, maintain and rely on the robust relationships described in the previous section. Any organization which has neither robust relationships throughout, nor a detailed service-led information and communication strategy owned by the chief executive, is simply not being managed.

The lubricant

Our machine now has reliable parts (i.e. people in positions where they can play to their strengths and where they are being managed in accordance with the three rules of Chapter 1). It has precise movements: high-quality, robust relationships throughout the organization, and systems which work with rather than against human nature. The fuel is rich but not over-rich, with everyone receiving all the information they need (but not more). To run smoothly it still requires a lubricant, and the lubricant in healthcare organizations is a culture of generosity and of discipline.

The backbiting, backstabbing, criticism and blame that describe the culture of so many healthcare organizations are symptoms of exactly the opposite. How does this hostile culture develop? A culture reflects the shared beliefs of the individuals who make up an organization. So an organization-wide culture of generosity and discipline relies on its individuals to exhibit both. Similarly, a culture of defensiveness and gossip results from individuals who feel sufficiently insecure to find relief in disparaging others. This insecurity would be surprising given the intellectual abilities of those individuals, if it were not for what we know about the educational, formative and socialization processes required for entry into the healthcare professions. In medicine, 'education by humiliation' has still not been eliminated, and the still common 'see one, do one, teach one' approach in the training years does nothing to instil the sense of security needed if individuals are to relate productively with others. The other professions, in the course of educating and registering their members, engender a deep-seated perception of a hierarchy among the healthcare 'tribes'. Medicine holds unchallenged the first tier, with most of the others jockeying for a place on the second, often by disparaging the competition (i.e. other professions). Clearly, this does nothing to enhance the confidence and self-respect of individuals or the fruitful working relationships that spring from it.

Manifesting an interest in the education taking place in their machine will enable real managers to provide role models who are themselves deeply secure, and also to abandon practices which inhibit the development of the confidence and maturity of junior staff. The greatest contribution the chief executive can make to the development of this culture, however, is to ensure that they model the behaviour they want to see in others; that they expect of others that they behave in this way and that they gently challenge behaviours which spring from defensiveness. With their key staff they will explore any feelings of fear and help keep these in perspective. In particular, chief executives need to believe (and demonstrate) that strong management does not include the instant fisticuffs response; that strong management means developing healthy collaborative relationships with purchasers, other Trusts, indeed all other stakeholders; that an adversarial approach is not evidence of strength but of weakness. When their staff protest that purchasers, GP fundholders or other Trusts are behaving unreasonably, they will remind them of the typical parental response that 'it takes two to have a quarrel'. By rising above such behaviour themselves, they encourage the behaviours they want to see in their staff and their colleagues.

A common supportive culture does not in any way require conformity. Chief executives must remember that in their 'machine' they have some of the most specialized 'parts' produced by society. It can take more than 20 years to develop the skills that society requires of some of its clinicians. The rewards for this level of skill and degree of specialization are often not financial. Even consultants with substantial private practices may have made more money had they pursued a different career path. These individuals are more likely to be motivated by autonomy and the opportunity to continue being innovative and creative. If as a society we are to encourage the development of skills we need, we must cater for the idiosyncratic behaviours of such individuals. Behaviour breeds behaviour and if they are treated with generosity they are likely to respond similarly. Confining, curtailing or limiting will result in explosive resentment. Of course, there are organizational requirements of these individuals, for example budgets, contracts and the training needs of others. They cannot therefore be given complete autonomy, but so often the response to any difficulties here is for a solution to be imposed. As we have seen in several other sections, the role of the manager is to *sell* problems not to solve them.

Hamel draws a distinction between numerator managers and denominator managers.[12] The numerator and denominator in question are those in the following equation:

$$\text{return on investment} = \frac{\text{net return}}{\text{investment (or headcount)}}$$

A denominator manager is one who increases productivity by reducing manpower, impoverishing skill mix and downsizing. A numerator manager similarly increases productivity but by increasing the volume and/or value of goods and services produced. Numerator managers see highly qualified staff as assets that can provide more services of greater quality. Certainly these staff will need to be convinced of their ability to do so, but that is what numerator management is about, encouraging staff to blossom. Denominator managers see such staff as expensive, as the focus of skill mix reviews, whose departure will reduce unit costs. The difference between numerator and denominator managers appears to be cultural. The Japanese have managed numerators for decades, in the UK and USA we have managed denominators. Incidentally, Hamel points out that stock market investors are suspicious of denominator managers, that they require greater short-term returns (dividends) from them than they do of the numerator managers. He points out that UK and US stocks have the highest dividend yields in the financial world. If the stock market prefers numerator to denominator managers, should not the investors in the NHS – the taxpayers?

The cords

The machine I described had cords of varying flexibility running from various parts to other machines or fixtures. These machines form a wider system within which our machine must function. The cords are the regulatory, contractual and legislative framework of the organization. As the chief executive spends time with her frontline staff and real managers, she will be able to remind operational staff of the requirements of the wider system, thus providing explanations for actions which may otherwise appear incomprehensible. The nature of this system and the degree of flexibility of the cords needs to be understood throughout the organization. In the pre-management days of administrators, this understanding was widely available and there are a number of arguments in favour of reintroducing the administrative role.

Health services administration had a long, proud history as a profession (at least as long as several of the healthcare professions) until, in the UK, it imploded in the mid-1980s in the wake of the introduction of general management positions at unit and district level. Although Roy Griffiths in introducing those general management positions never suggested the demise of administration, the professional body (the IHSA) announced that it had metamorphosed into a profession of general management, encouraged the membership of individual general managers with no administrative knowledge base and ceased to teach or develop that knowledge base. The results are to be seen in cases where financial standing orders were ignored, good internal control (separation of duties, etc.) was not maintained, 'innovative' solutions to intractable problems have caused massive problems of their own, and where systems that worked have been allowed to fall (unnoticed in some cases, except to clients) into disuse as the people running them left and their significance was unrecognized in the higher echelons.

Complex organizations need both administrators *and* managers. They must both be developed and valued for their very different skills.

Really managing an organization is an intellectual challenge; however, it is also much more. It calls for commitment, conviction, personal involvement and integrity. Above all, it requires an ability and a willingness to actively engage with HCPs on their own ground. Whether these qualities are to be found in a chief executive can be judged by examining not reports, not papers, not even contracts or return on capital figures (although these are important), but the attitudes, behaviours and day-to-day decisions of frontline staff.

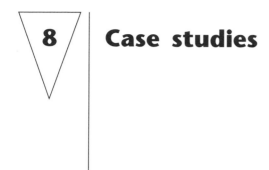

8 Case studies

These case studies were originally written as much to introduce the concerns of HCPs in a number of different settings as to illustrate management concepts; I hope that they do both. They are fictional sequences of events constructed from incidents which are wholly real. The characters in them are also fictional. They are composites built from people I have worked with, observed, met, conversed with or read. No-one should recognize themselves, nor their organization. Even where I have used a sustained series of events from one organization to provide a framework for the storyline, all the detail will have been drawn from elsewhere, and it will be peopled by individuals and groups who are foreign to it. All the discussion refers to these fictional characters and organizations.

If, as you read, you observe a detail that does not ring true, you could be right: I may have oversimplified in order to move the story along. I have written them in 'airport fiction' style, a style which I have noticed in my teaching experience, even those who profess to hate will actually read.

Hillside Hospital

Ruth Anderson, chief executive of Hillside Hospital Trust, parked her car on her return to the hospital and briefly thought back to the meeting she had just left. The Hillside and Donwich Health Commission had asked for a meeting to discuss the contract specification for palliative care. The contracts manager had invited the Trust's consultant in palliative care, Dr John Norland, to accompany him, and Ruth had decided to join them.

The Commission had expressed their concern about issues of equality in palliative care. They had observed that the local hospices tended to cater for white, middle-class patients with cancer and wanted to ensure that other cultural and diagnostic groups had access to support towards 'a good death'. Their research had suggested a level of unhappiness with the services available to patients who were known by their carers to be in the last stages of their life. This rarely gave rise to formal complaints, yet concern extended to both acute and community services, and the Commission was keen to promote the application of the philosophical principles of hospice care on a much wider basis.

There were four statistics that had prompted them to question current practices. The first was that recent local figures confirmed that nearly 70 per cent of deaths occurred in hospital. They contrasted this with the second, that several surveys had reported that 60 per cent of the people asked were strongly of the opinion that they wanted to die at home. The third was that a recent analysis had suggested that half of the per capita spent on the NHS was incurred in the last few months of an individual's life. The fourth was that of all deaths, only a third were due to cancer, yet this was where palliative care was concentrated.

John Norland had reassured them that patients on his palliative care ward did not fall into the white, middle-class category, indeed that his ward, on the fourth floor of a hospital originally built as a Victorian work-house, provided care for a wide range of people of which a current patient, homeless and in the final stages of liver disease, was not unrepresentative. He hadn't mentioned the concern he had expressed to Ruth on the journey, that his service was not attracting *enough* of the articulate white, middle class, that there was a danger of being seen as a 'sink' service, and thus he would be less and less able to influence practice on the other Hillside wards. However, the Commission had clearly been impressed with John, so she anticipated no problems with the placing of the contract.

Among the incoming post awaiting her when she reached her office was a letter which, with the morning's discussion fresh in her mind, Ruth read with especial interest.

The Chief Executive,
Hillside Hospital.

Dear Sir/Madam,

I have never previously complained about any aspect of care in your hos-pital, or indeed the NHS. However I do wish to register my concern at the way my aunt was treated in your hospital recently.

My aunt, Mrs Hilda Brady, was 89-years-old and was in your hospital (on Ward A) because she had had a bad fall at home and had broken her arm. While in hospital she suffered a stroke and her condition got worse and worse.

After two weeks it was clear to all her family that she was dying. My brother, her nephew, asked for her to be transferred to a hospice and it was agreed that the hospital and hospice staff would assess her so that she could move. Before that could be done she died.

My complaint is about the way she was treated in the last few days before she died. She was forced to get out of bed for most of every day in case she caught pneumonia. On the day before she died I was with her when she begged to go back to bed. She was told that she could 'soon', but it was over 90 minutes later when she was put back to bed.

When I protested to the nurse about the delay she said, and I quote, 'Everyone has to wait their turn'. I appreciate that she was trying to be fair and not to be cruel but the result of her actions *was* cruel to my aunt.

While my aunt was in hospital I tried to make sure I was there at lunch-time with her, because if I did not help her she did not eat anything. The meals seemed quite unsuitable, solid bits of meat and lots of vegetables. In the last few days my aunt only ate a bit of the custard.

When I asked a nurse if she could order some milky foods, she said that they had ordered a light diet but that 'the catering staff have a funny idea of a light diet here'.

All in all it seemed to our family that the whole of the ward was geared to those who are going to get well and come out of hospital. They never treated my aunt as someone who was dying.

I have written this letter because I would not want anyone else to suffer as my aunt did.

Yours sincerely,

Elizabeth Smith

When David Young came to see her a short time later, she showed him the letter and asked what he knew about Ward A and the staff involved. David, the operations director, had worked in the NHS since he left university. He had first met Ruth Anderson when he was on the administrative training scheme and he had been a trainee in her department. Since then, he had worked for her on several occasions, even following in her footsteps twice.

Ward A he knew little about, or rather he knew a lot about it – how the plumbing needed to be upgraded, the walls repainted, the bedside furniture replaced – but, in that, it was very similar to half a dozen other wards. He knew little that was peculiar to Ward A.

Of the staff on Ward A he knew similarly little detail, with one exception, the professions allied to medicine (PAMs). He had been managing physiotherapy, along with speech and language therapy, occupational therapy, radiography, dietetics and pharmacy, for some 6 months now. When the Trust had restructured into clinical directorates, no-one had known what to do with the PAMs. The professions themselves had been implacably opposed to being split into the clinical directorates, protesting that this would mean a loss in specialist skills and insufficient training opportunities. What they also objected to, and in David's view this was their real concern, was being managed by doctors. All the clinical directors were medically qualified.

When he had asked Ruth if he could manage them, knowing that some clinical management would strengthen his CV, they had been delighted. A clinical support directorate had been formed, headed by the ex-district occupational therapist. Their gratitude had not survived the next round of budget cuts, however, and he was now locked in conflict with them as he tried to implement the recommendations of an external management consultant on skill mix.

He thought back to the last meeting he had attended of the physiotherapy management team. There had been quite a lot of concern expressed about the way that certain consultants insisted on a very vigorous treatment regime even when the family, the patient and the physiotherapist concerned felt it was inappropriate. He mentioned this to Ruth. She asked what those at the meeting had decided to do about it. He reflected and replied that it was not action they had been after, but an opportunity to whinge.

Ruth re-read the letter and decided the proper course of action was to refer it to Anne Jones, director of nursing and quality. This she did, appending a short note asking to be kept personally informed of the outcome. After further thought, she also dropped a line to Jane Chisholm, medical director, asking her to investigate the apparent stand-off between medical and physiotherapy staff.

'Yes, the purchasers were being much more constructive these days', she reflected. Perhaps she could suggest to them a few areas where she would find it helpful if they were to require further service improvements. It was always easier to persuade her clinicians to change systems and practices if there was a threat of losing the contract.

In his office on Nightingale Ward, John Norland reflected on the figures he was incorporating into a paper. They showed that whereas he was achieving good pain control in 95 per cent of patients, on other Hillside wards the figure was under 50 per cent.

His length of stay figures (average 2 weeks) and discharge rates (60–70 per cent) had surprised his colleagues in the medical directorate. They had imagined that lengthy peaceful decline characterized his patients, whereas the reality was that he provided respite care, dealt with acute problems and even offered rehabilitation.

He had been trying for some time to interest his colleagues in palliative care. He firmly believed that the principles could be applied anywhere, not just in designated wards or hospices. 'It's the care, not the where' was the slogan he tried to keep in mind. They had not shown much interest to date, usually saying 'it's alright for you, you have the staffing levels and the technology', in spite of the fact that the staffing levels were similar and the technology available to all. Privately he thought that perhaps they were still not prepared to accept the concept of a good death – seeing death as a failure and wanting to postpone it for as long as possible.

On Nightingale Ward, Lesley Wilson, a senior I physiotherapist, was just arriving to see for the fifth time that day, Mrs Bird, an 80-year-old who had recently had a stroke and required physio input every hour. The staff nurse, Peggy Baker, greeted Lesley cheerfully and offered her a chocolate. Lesley asked how Mrs Bird seemed to be doing: 'Oh don't talk to me about Nellie Bird' said Peggy, 'I've had her son on to me all morning. He wants his mother transferred to a hospice. Says she hates it here.'

'Does he? I have been wondering about the physio regime' said Lesley. 'It seems *so* vigorous for someone so frail.' Peggy shrugged, 'Well that's Dr Kendal for you, he's always been the same. It's his ward round in half an hour.' Lesley sighed, 'Even when it is obvious that a patient is going to die, he insists on these regular passive movements and nasopharyngeal suction. Having a catheter repeatedly stuck up your nose is unpleasant for anyone but must be awful for someone who's so frail and elderly.'

'Why do it then?' said Peggy. 'I thought you were practitioners in your own right and could use your own clinical judgement? I'm sure you've told

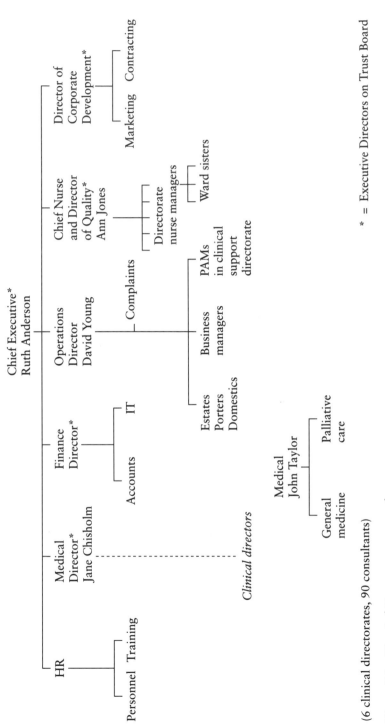

(6 clinical directorates, 90 consultants)

Figure 8.1 Hospital Trust management chart

me that before.' 'Well, we are, but in cases like this we must carry out the consultant's wishes, I do want to discuss it with him during the ward round, though.'

Both of them looked up as Katie Tyler, the complaints officer, walked in and asked to speak to sister. 'Oh no, just what we need, another complaint investigation' muttered Peggy. When Katie explained that she wanted to find out about a recent patient, Mrs Brady, Peggy knew nothing of her, pointing out that she had only recently moved to the ward. She offered to see if her notes were still to hand.

As she walked over to where Mrs Bird was lying, Lesley observed two young doctors poring over a set of notes, with a slightly anxious air. As she watched, a middle-aged man, sitting next to her patient, went over to them. She heard him ask about hospices or nursing homes and how to get his mother admitted to one. Both of them looked rather non-plussed and one said that social services might be able to help; perhaps Mr Bird should visit the hospital social work department. Given directions, Mr Bird disappeared in that direction. Lesley, despite knowing that this was not the best way to get Mrs Bird referred as he wished, did not stop him from going. She knew he would be distressed when she applied the suction and was relieved he would not be present.

A few minutes later, the source of the junior doctors' anxiety was apparent as Adrian Kendal, consultant in general medicine, entered the ward followed by a retinue of assorted white coats. Peggy Baker emerged, thrust the notes into Katie's hands and quickly joined the group, already at a bedside. Katie realized that she would gain no further information until the ward round had finished and decided she could usefully read the notes she had been given. She noticed they were only the nursing records, and she walked down to the day room at the end of the ward.

In the day room, a group of patients were exchanging views about the nursing staff. One complained that when she arrived on the ward she was scolded for wearing an expensive watch and bringing too much money with her: 'How was I to know what to bring' she demanded. 'I've never been to hospital before, not as a patient anyway. It's all very well giving me a booklet about it when I get here, but why didn't they tell me before I came?'

'Anyway', another responded, 'they had no right to tell you off like that, we're not children in a school'. 'And what about the way they treat Mr Lawrence?' said another. 'He'll starve to death soon. Every mealtime they plonk his food in front of him and then leave him to it. I haven't seen him eat anything. His relatives have complained about it but nothing seems to change.'

'Has your call button been fixed yet?' asked another, 'mine hasn't'. 'No, but it doesn't matter so much now I can get up' was the response. 'I just hated not being able to call for help when I could only lie there. And I know Miss Jones, in the bed next to me, was really upset last night, when she wet the bed because she couldn't get anyone to bring her a bed pan.

They told her she should have called out but she didn't want to, not about that and not in the middle of the night.'

'That poor Mrs Bird' said another, 'all that physio palaver every hour, all that noise behind the curtain. You can tell the old lady hates it. Be kinder to let her die in peace.'

The group turned their attention to an elderly man sitting by himself in the corner. Unlike the others he was dressed in day clothes, including an overcoat. 'Bert's waiting for an ambulance to go to a nursing home, he's been ready since just after breakfast' said one. 'I hope he doesn't have to wait as long as Elsie last week, they didn't collect her 'til tea time' responded another.

Katie recognized the problem, it was one that yielded a number of complaints. As the ambulance service was managed separately, the Trust had no direct control, and was not experiencing much cooperation in agreeing service standards. She did wonder whether Bert really needed to be kept quite so ready to leave however. Was the overcoat really necessary? She wondered briefly whether to raise this with the ward staff and decided against it. She would be seen as a 'snoop' she had no doubt.

The ward round was coming to an end. The last patient had no physio input, so Lesley left the group and made her way to the nursing office, furious at the way her view had, yet again, been overruled by Adrian Kendle. She had even been unable to persuade the group to await the return of Mrs Bird's son so that all involved could take part in the discussion. What made it worse was that she felt so helpless. She had complained so often to her head of service and absolutely nothing changed. As she watched from the office, one of the junior doctors peeled off from the group at the side of the last bed in the ward and came over. She had been on the receiving end of a particularly sharp response from Kendle, and Lesley wasn't surprised to see her looking distressed and angry. Peggy joined them and mentioned the complaints officer's visit. The response was defensive: 'When did you say she died? Three weeks ago? Well that's one thing, at least, that can't be my fault. I hadn't started here then. I'm sorry if I seem rude but I've been on call for over 24 hours now and in spite of doing my best I always seem to be being wrong-footed.'

Jane Chisholm, the medical director, thanked Adrian Kendle for sparing her some time, and reminded him what she wanted to discuss, relationships between medical and physio staff. Adrian responded that he was not aware of any problems and asked if there had been any complaints. 'Oh not formally' Jane replied, 'apparently David Young mentioned something to Ruth, in passing, and she's asked me to look into it'.

'Oh, thinks he can make clinical decisions now does he?' said Adrian. 'If the physios are unhappy why don't they come to see me. I know some of them aren't always too happy with my decisions, but they sometimes give up too easily. Just because a patient is elderly doesn't mean she should receive a lesser standard of care. A short period of discomfort may give them an extra ten years.'

'Yes, I thought it was probably another example of "doctor bashing" – it's going on everywhere these days' Jane sympathized. 'While you're here: Have you read John Norland's paper yet? Apparently he's achieving much better pain control on Nightingale Ward than we are elsewhere. Shall I ask him to come and discuss his approach at an audit meeting soon?'

She could hardly have achieved a more explosive response if she had lit a fuse. 'Nightingale Ward! If I had their staffing and their funding on my wards I'd offer a Rolls Royce treatment too.'

Question

How would you advise Ruth Anderson on her priorities if Hillside is to address the concerns of their purchasers, Hillside and Donwich Health Commission, over care for the dying?

Discussion

The purchasers' concerns can be summarized as follows: 'People are not dying *where* they want to, nor *how* they want to; although good practice is available, it isn't to the majority of patients'. People dying in the wrong way in the wrong place. Although simple to express, if we consider that this arises because of a large number of incremental decisions made about patients by different HCPs, then we can see that this is a multidimensional problem that will require changes on many fronts if it is to be resolved. It is a real test of the priorities and the effectiveness of the chief executive and senior clinical staff: frontline attitudes, behaviours and practices always are.

If individuals undergoing one of the most important of life events are to do so well, then Ruth Anderson must ensure that:

1 There is a culture of *real* management throughout the organization, so that frontline staff are led (motivated, supported and directed) by people for whom they have respect and with whom they have a relationship robust enough to withstand challenges to any unacceptable behaviours.
2 The interdependent specialists who comprise Hillside Hospital take individual responsibility for the total services provided to the patient. While operating primarily within their own professional boundaries, they keep the total 'service package' in mind and intervene across boundaries if they perceive there to be a problem.
3 Her organization as a healthcare system does not confuse the health of an individual with the absence of illness. It needs to retain and develop its expertise in secondary or tertiary medical care while also considering and meeting the psychological, social and personal growth needs of the individual patient.

In the case study, there is much evidence that Hillside is failing in all three respects.

1 *Lack of* real *management culture*

The management chart does not reflect reality (see Figure 8.1). Certainly David Young, Jane Chisholm and John Taylor are not among the organization's leaders – no-one is following. The David Young character is not uncommon in healthcare organizations. Such people will have proved themselves able in an administrative or non-clinical managerial role (business or facilities management). To make the increasingly large jump from this level to board and or chief executive posts, they require some experience of managing clinicians.

Should David Young have been 'given' the PAMs in order to strengthen his CV in this way? There is often understandable resentment when this happens from the HCPs concerned. And yet real managers can come from all backgrounds, and the health of the organization and its clients depends on the development of good, real managers, so it may be necessary. There are advantages and disadvantages in all management structures, and as long as the disadvantages of this one are recognized, then means of overcoming or minimizing them can be introduced.

But *is* David Young a *real* manager? Real managers as we have seen exhibit generosity and discipline. Does David Young?

1 He trivializes valid professional concerns expressed by the PAMs as 'not wishing to be managed by doctors'. At the very least he should ask 'why?'.
2 He does not require the physios to operate right up to the boundary between managerial and clinical decisions. He also stays far too far on his own side of the boundary, so that there is a void between them, into which Mrs Bird and others fall. As a manager he does not have any role in the treatment of Mrs Bird as an individual; that is a matter for the clinical judgement of clinicians. However, managers do have a role in the treatment of groups of patients. Groups such as the frail elderly prescribed nasopharyngeal suction, or patients over whom there is a dispute between clinicians about the most appropriate care. In either case, the managerial role would be to sell the problem to all the professionals involved, to persuade them to identify the causes of the problem, to constructively challenge their thinking, to resell to them the problem, to cajole them into working together to design a solution, to require them to review and evaluate their solution. David Young has not yet admitted that there is a problem.

There must be some doubt about the integrity of Jane Chisholm, the medical director. She appears to be more of a shop steward than a leader. Incumbents not infrequently appear uncomfortable in this role, feeling 'neither fish nor fowl'. As a result, they can be perceived to be 'running with the hare and with the hounds', as they seek to find points of agreement with whichever camp, management or medical, they are at that moment interacting. This limits their influence considerably. They would be far more effective highlighting issues of disagreement and providing explanations about the other party's reasoning. This discomfort should not surprise us if we consider that the medical career path never requires individuals to experience the feelings associated with a first managerial role. In other healthcare professions, and most other walks of life, people are promoted to an explicit management role while still in their twenties. The realization that they are no longer 'one of the boys', that they cannot be constantly popular *and* effective, that they must often choose between being liked and being respected, is often a painful one, but it is learned early. There are few parallels in the medical professions and it is asking a lot of individuals to experience this 20 years further on. Medical and clinical directors therefore need a lot of support, particularly regular constructive feedback and the opportunity of a credible mentor outside the profession.

John Taylor, as clinical director, is completely ignored, which indicates that he is one of those individuals whose appointment is unopposed, not as a result of his leadership skills, but because of their absence.

Further evidence of lack of a *real* management culture comes in the organizational separation of the contracting function from all clinical services and staff. Since the contract is a model of the work to be undertaken by clinicians over the contract period, all concerned must be involved if the model is to be robust. A Trust's best salespeople will be its best clinicians, so they must be actively involved. One way of achieving this is for the contracts department to become a support service to clinical departments who then negotiate their own contracts. This would require great confidence on the part of top management, as it sanctions the purchasers having direct access to Trust clinicians. This confidence is not enhanced if purchasers abuse this access. One director of public health, describing just this sort of joint working with Trust clinicians, has been known to express the view that this enables him to 'have the Trust chief executive over a barrel – the best place for a Trust chief executive'.

The attitude of staff to complaints is further evidence of a lack of real management. There is no suggestion in the case study that these are seen as opportunities for improvements in services to patients, only as problems for staff. This over-emphasis on the self at the expense of others reflects a shortage of both generosity and discipline and characterizes organizations lacking *real* managers.

Finally, Ruth Anderson herself is considering hiding behind a bogeyman (the Health Commission) rather than taking her proper responsibilities as a real manager. It is *her* role to convince her staff that their care for dying patients is not appropriate, *her* role to persuade them to develop ways of improving it. She will do so through the robust relationships she has with her senior clinicians. Pretending that it is the Health Commission who are the baddies, that she has protested to them but in vain, sends messages both that she is ineffectual in her negotiations and that what is being required is unreasonable. Neither message will increase the likelihood of a genuine change of practice.

2 The parts take responsibility for the whole

Let us now look at whether the characters in the case study take responsibility for the service as experienced by the patient.

David Young fails to realize that information and responsibility go hand in hand; he receives information about differences of professional opinion on care regimes and abdicates the responsibility conferred on him by failing to investigate any further.

John Norland, while ensuring that his own patients are relieved of pain, is aware that half of the patients in the care of his colleagues are suffering. The publication of papers on the subject is necessary both for his personal credibility and for the advancement of his specialization; however, he does not take opportunities to challenge the practice and the thinking of his peers, only privately concluding that they see death as a failure. More generosity on his part towards his colleagues would lead him to realize why this is the case and enable him to help design systems that permitted excellent medical or surgical interventions but within a framework of care with the patient's autonomy as its focus.

Lesley Wilson allows Mr Bird to waste his time finding the social workers because it will make her life easier. She also takes no responsibility for making her remonstrations to Adrian Kendle effective. To exercise real responsibility, she would need to find out his reasons, his concerns, check her own reasoning, address her arguments to his concerns and in a way that takes into account his motivation profile, preferred relationship style and conflict mode. Taking responsibility always requires a challenge to your own thinking and thorough preparation. If Lesley Wilson cares for her patients, she needs, in this situation, to engage in an act that will involve both work and courage (see Chapter 1). Unless she does, her care will remain idle ineffectual sentiment.

The ward nursing staff are also failing to take responsibility. When patients cannot eat the meals provided, they blame 'catering'. When patients, not knowing that it is better not to, bring money and valuables with them, they blame the patients. And when faulty call buttons cause distress, they blame both engineers and patients. Of course, the fact that nurses are more numerous than other professions involved and that their involvement with the patient is greater (nurses will be providing care 24 hours a day) mean that the opportunities for failure are more numerous. It is all the more important therefore that nurses, more than any other group, take responsibility for the total service that patients receive.

If the nursing staff on Ward A had been taking responsibility for the service experienced by their patients, how would they have behaved differently? Food that is inedible is not food. Nurses on Ward A are starving their patients. Their responsibility is to ensure that patients are offered an appropriate diet. Since this requires effective working relationships with the catering service, it is their responsibility to ensure that such a relationship exists. Incidentally, the ownership of the catering service (whether it is run by the Trust or by a commercial company) is irrelevant here. Taking responsibility also means making their experiences heard at top levels, if they themselves cannot achieve a change in service standard. This requires an understanding of decision-making processes. It is therefore a nursing responsibility to know how the organization is managed. Yet, to far too many nurses, outside the ward the organization is a non-specific 'they'.

Similar arguments apply to their relationships with both the engineering and patient information functions. In both cases, when other functions are failing, the nurses need to devise short-term solutions. These will probably require greater input from them (a system of checking every patient every half-hour to relieve the anxiety caused by the lack of a call button, for example) and they may take the decision that such short-term measures jeopardize the chance of a longer-term solution. In that case, they must make sure that the discomfort experienced by patients is made known. They must use it to ensure that the longer-term solution is realized. This must be a conscious decision, a weighing up of two unacceptable alternatives in the awareness of the negative consequences of each. This is very different from simply sending off a form, making a vituperative 'phone call, or complaining to each other about it.

Katie Tyler chooses not to question Bert's unnecessary overcoat with the ward staff, believing that it is more important that she is not thought a 'snoop' than that patients receive good care.

The junior doctors, not knowing the answer to Mr Bird's question, do not take the responsibility of finding out, or of telling him they do not know, but take a guess and send him off somewhere inappropriate. This ungenerous act is occasioned by their own apprehension – as ungenerous acts usually are.

Last but not least, Adrian Kendle has valid reasons for his clinical views, and his commitment to his patients is not in doubt. However, he allows no challenge to his perception of reality, either from the physios or from John Norland's paper on palliative care. The lack of this element of discipline makes him difficult to work with or for. In a system of interdependent specialists (indeed in any organization, as opposed to a one-man-band), it is everybody's responsibility to engage in productive working relationships. Kendle is probably one of the organization's leaders, one of the opinion-formers. His behaviour exerts a powerful influence on his junior staff, who are of critical importance to the service delivered. So, while Ruth Anderson may prefer to spend time with the more amenable Chisholm, she should choose to spend it developing the kind of robust relationship with Kendle that will enable her to challenge his mental models.

3 *Focusing on health rather than illness*

In part, this wide failure to accept responsibilities is due to a desensitizing of professionals to the needs of patients. Part of the role of a *real* manager is to keep reactions fresh.

The letter of complaint, research by the purchasers, concerns of the physios as a group, and disparity in practice between the palliative care ward and others, all indicate that parts of the Trust see their purpose as the treatment of a medical condition. If they saw it as 'the removal of obstacles to the achievement of patients' potentials' (Chapter 1), then they would have to give consideration to what those potentials were.

In some, perhaps many, cases where the outcomes are especially unclear, a decision must be made: whether to continue with treatment aimed at the lower levels in the hierarchy of clinical descriptions (pp. 21–2), which *may* prolong life and enable the patient to regain potentials at the higher levels, but may not, and will certainly prevent the patient from achieving their potential for a death that is a fitting end to their life.

Here the decision needs to be made by someone who has as their focus the potentials of the patient (levels 0, +1 and +2), while understanding levels −1 to −9 sufficiently to be able to assess probabilities of outcome. The clinician responsible for levels −5 to −9 is not, for the reasons discussed in Chapter 7, the best person to take this decision. In the case study, Adrian Kendle appears to do just that. What is more, the person with the greatest interest in Mrs Bird at levels 0, +1, +2 (her son) is dismissed by Peggy Baker as a problem and not allowed to contribute to the formal discussion of his mother's treatment because the ward round cannot wait for him to return.

This is such a thorny issue that solutions in different places will differ. The development of palliative care as a specialty is one response to the problem; GP beds in hospitals is another; perhaps the primary care led NHS is another. Chief executives will not know the solutions but they must persuade their staff to work together and with other agencies to try and develop one.

Hillside Trust has a centre of excellence, Nightingale Ward, and yet its philosophy, principles and practices of care are not shared more widely. Why not? There is a respectable volume of management literature analysing the reasons why dissemination of good practice does or does not occur. One of the issues identified is that of 'star-envy', a belief, among peers of the leaders of lauded projects, that 'it is alright for them because they've got extra resources, better people, better premises etc.'. What is more, this star-envy increases with the plaudits received. Successful dissemination has accompanied the rotation of staff through the project, particularly when project graduates are put in charge of similar initiatives elsewhere.

Ruth Anderson could consider drawing on this literature but must beware of simplistic solutions. She will need to analyse very carefully all the systems and individuals involved and design interventions tailor-made for her situation. She will need to consider what evidence Adrian Kendle and his colleagues will find credible, that will convince them there is a need for change, that Nightingale Ward can be a resource rather than a threat to them. She can only do this if she knows her staff, if senior opinion-formers respect her integrity and her understanding of their concerns – if, in short, she is a *real* manager.

Children's services

Seven per cent! A 7 per cent cut in the budget. Alison Brown knew there was still some slack in the children's services that she managed, but 7 per cent now and then another 5 per cent which the purchasers had agreed to discuss further . . .

The early retirement of her two senior clinical medical officers would make a substantial contribution; Alison knew they would be happy to take it. She was still calculating the gross savings the retirements would liberate as she walked into the meeting room. She was the last to arrive and Elizabeth Latham, consultant community paediatrician, welcomed her and introduced her to the few present who she did not know. The child mental health liaison meeting was a weekly event lasting about an hour and a half and the membership usually included consultant community paediatrician, consultant psychiatrist, psychologist, social worker, special needs counsellor, a health visitor, a clinical medical officer and an occupational therapist. Alison was not a member but had been invited along to see how they operated. She suspected that the team members wanted to remind her of the very difficult cases they dealt with. To her surprise, the entire meeting was devoted to one case, introduced by the social worker. It became apparent quite quickly that neither the social worker nor anyone else present had any evidence of the abuse that she feared was taking place, and the meeting concentrated on the social worker's feelings of anxiety and how she could deal with them.

When the meeting finished (with no recommendations with regard to the child in question but several for the social worker), five of those present remained seated. Elizabeth bade Alison goodbye, apologizing for having no time for further discussion as the special needs counsellor was now leading a two-hour workshop on family therapy. Alison reminded her of their meeting the next day and of its purpose – to discuss budgetary savings – and left.

So this was the regular family therapy workshop she had heard about last week when she discussed the role of the special needs counsellor with the current post-holder, Lydia Wright. The special needs counsellor was a half-time post, created to meet the needs of children with special needs and, just as important, their families. The special needs usually required input from such a large number of agencies that parents often found it very difficult to negotiate their way between them. One of the roles of the counsellor was to help them do so.

JOB DESCRIPTION

Special needs counsellor

Job purpose

To support and counsel children with special needs and their families and to liaise on their behalf with other agencies.

Key tasks

1 To offer support and advice to children with special needs, and to their families/carers, who are referred to the child health service.
2 To give information about range of services available across agency boundaries.
3 To act as an advocate for childrens' needs.
4 To contribute to the drawing up of care plans for children with special needs and their families.
5 To liaise with staff from other professions within the Trust and in other agencies to coordinate services for individual children.

Hours of work: 17½ hours

Responsible to: Community paediatrician

The post had never been properly funded, the salary was currently met from a CMO vacancy. It had been created 12 months previously by Alison's predecessor. Recently, when the purchasers requested more counselling sessions for special needs children, Alison had reviewed Lydia's workload. She recalled the letter she had sent her as a result:

Dear Lydia,

Thank you for coming to see me yesterday to discuss your work. I summarize below the salient points of our discussion.

You told me that you work in excess of your contracted hours, normally approximately twenty hours per week. Of that twenty hours, roughly five are spent with children with special needs and/or their families. You receive one new referral a week and your current caseload is twelve children.

Your timetable is not a regular one as you respond to requests, from other Trust staff, for your attendance at meetings.

These meetings include:

Child mental health liaison meeting	once a week, 1½ hours
Child development team	once a fortnight, 3 hours
Workshop on family therapy (organized and run by you)	weekly, 2 hours
Heads of service meeting	monthly, 1½ hours

You also meet with physiotherapists, health visitors and speech and language therapists, at their request, to discuss individual cases.

When we compared your schedule with your job description, we both agreed that there was little similarity. We agreed that I would discuss with your line manager, Elizabeth Latham, the means by which we can bring the two into line.

Yours sincerely,

Alison Brown

Alison sighed. Another item for discussion with Elizabeth, Lydia's line manager, the next day.

'I know you won't find it easy to make these savings' said Alison, 'none of us will, but I'm afraid there is absolutely no choice'.

'Savings!' said Elizabeth, 'now that's positively Orwellian. Savings are what you choose to put in the bank now, to spend later. This isn't saving, its robbery, and robbing some of the most defenceless people in the country at that.'

'The money will still be spent on health care' said Alison, 'it's more reallocation than robbery, but we can agree to call them cuts if you like'.

'Even if it is spent on health care and not just on more managers and accountants, it really must *not* come from the special needs budget' said Elizabeth. 'Have you any idea of the scale of the problem we're trying to deal with? One in every six children needs us at some time or another, for problems with hearing, or speech, really severe asthma and so on. Two in every hundred have severe needs and will need support for long periods or throughout their lives. Then there's a further group who need emotional support. Of course it doesn't help when GPs won't refer appropriately. Even when they notice some developmental delay they don't seem to know where to refer to. I was talking to one the other day who had never heard of our enuresis clinic and was having no success with her own treatment. And they really have no idea when to use the speech therapists. Mind you I've almost given up referring cases to them. They take months to see the child, then insist on redoing the assessment I've already done, and then say they haven't got the staff to offer any therapy. Perhaps we should change their title from speech therapists to speech assessors!'

Alison smiled and was about to speak when Elizabeth continued, as vehemently as before.

'What you don't understand is that the parents of these children are in a state of permanent bereavement. They need a lot of support and the children often cannot fulfil their potential simply because of lack of aids and equipment. The technology is available – it's just the *money* that can't be found. I've got a case at the moment of an intelligent lad of eleven, who needs an artificial voice box (like Stephen Hawking's) to be able to communicate. With it he could cope with school and do really quite well; without it there's a bright mind completely trapped. Education say they won't pay for it, because (a) he can use it outside school and (b) other children can't use it. Social services say they don't have a budget for under-eighteens, and when I asked you last week you said we didn't have the money for it either. Perhaps one of the speech therapists could usefully take a collecting box to Charing Cross Station, or one of the managers come to that! It's all got so much worse since the purchaser:provider split.'

Alison asked if she was thinking of the Green Glades case and Elizabeth nodded.

A multidisciplinary, multi-agency team had agreed, at a case conference about a particular child, that the child and her mother should both be sent to the Green Glades Centre for a year, with other family members attending weekly sessions there. Green Glades was a psychotherapeutic community that the local professionals had referred to previously. The health authority (HA), however, had baulked at the £X00,000 price tag for the year's treatment, and discussions were still under way.

'I know you deal with some very difficult cases' said Alison, 'and we can certainly make a case to the HA to exempt you from the further 5 per cent they want later in the year. Let's look at your activity figures. Is your activity increasing and, if so, by how much?'

'No I won't play at your game' Elizabeth responded, 'I came into medicine to help patients not collect numbers'.

'But I can't help you to do that' thought Alison wearily, 'unless you give me the ammunition'. She pulled out the staff schedule she wanted to discuss today (see Figure 8.2).

Alison continued. 'Perhaps if you can explain to me exactly what each of these people is responsible for, we could think about how to meet the savings targets. I know your two SCMOs would be happy to take early retirement, so how could we reallocate their load? Could you let me have job descriptions and weekly work programmes for the senior registrars and CMOs. And talking of work programmes, do you have one for Lydia Wright too?'

'Alison you are talking about a number of independent professionals; I would not dream of asking them for work programmes. They are all

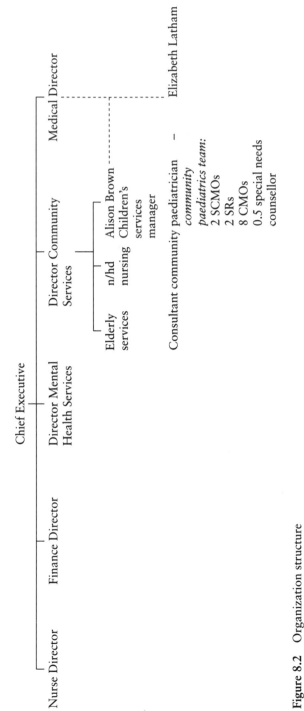

Figure 8.2 Organization structure

extremely busy with education panels (assessing educational needs for the education statement) and adoption and fostering panels. One works very hard on the child health information system, so important now that the GPs are doing more and more immunization and vaccination; one runs a very successful school counselling session every week; another an enuresis clinic; yet another specializes in audiology. I'm pleased to say that they have all developed their own interests. As for Lydia, she really is excellent you know, what we would all do without her I do not know, I really would like to see her upgraded.'

As she reflected on the conversation later, Elizabeth wondered whether she'd been a bit hard on Alison. As managers went she was quite helpful. Of course, she didn't understand the nature of their work, how emotionally draining it was having to try and meet so many needs with so few resources, how burned out everyone became. That's where Lydia Wright had been so very valuable, in providing support to the staff. She so hoped that they would be able to give her the upgrading she was asking for. If it wasn't for Lydia, Elizabeth thought, she would feel almost completely isolated. When first appointed, she had retained her professional and friendship links with her colleagues in acute paediatrics. As time had passed, however, their interests had increasingly diverged. She recalled a recent conversation in which she had tried to justify a programme screening children for a condition that was as yet untreatable. Her acute counterparts lambasted the idea, on the basis that if nothing medically could be done for these children, there was little point in the parents knowing the prognosis. Elizabeth's argument that they had a right to know, to help plan their working arrangements and their lives, cut no ice. If her peers in the acute services were unsupportive, what about her colleagues in the community? On the whole, they were a good team, each with their own specialist interest. Yvonne was a bit of a problem still, coming in late and not really carrying a fair load. Elizabeth suspected that she saw community paediatrics as a soft option and had tried to explain to her that they all needed her to take on rather more, but to no avail. She would like to raise the matter again but wasn't sure exactly how. She had been peripherally involved with a case that had ended up at an industrial tribunal a few years previously and she wanted to avoid anything like that again.

Alison, replaying the same meeting in her mind, fumed at Elizabeth's incompetence as a manager. 'She hasn't got a clue what her staff are doing' she thought, 'yet she wants one of them upgraded at a time when she's being asked to *save* money. I could help her if only she would stop seeing me as the enemy. If only she would ask me.' Alison had given up offering assistance. She had tried on several occasions but Elizabeth had expressed her resentment of this 'interference' as she had put it.

Geraldine and Anna were old friends who happened to work for the same Trust. Geraldine as a speech and language therapist and Anna as a health visitor. They met for lunch once a fortnight.

'No it hasn't got any better, since you ask' said Anna, 'I still feel as though I'm being pulled in five directions at once. I've just had a good look at my caseload and I've got 260 families, 22 of them families with children with special needs. All of my patch qualifies for deprivation payments and yet I met a health visitor from a much more affluent part of London last week who reckons that their average caseload is 200. It's ridiculous.'

'Yes it's all historical accident isn't it' said Geraldine. 'This Trust has far more chiropodists than X and Y Trusts but fewer community physios and SLTs. X have a designated special needs service too.'

'Oh that would be wonderful' said Anna, 'I really despair sometimes. If I had the *time* to spend with those families I still wouldn't have the skills to offer real help.'

'And yet lots of them tell *me* that they don't know what they would do without the health visitor' said Geraldine, 'you must be helping somehow'.

'Just by being there I think; being the easiest person to get hold of. When I refer them on to specialist services, like yours, or the physio, it takes so long for them to be seen and *then* not much seems to happen. But there's such a wide range of needs: Downs, diabetes, physically disabled, partially sighted; I couldn't be an expert in all of them anyway.'

'Yes I know our waiting list is long – we just don't have enough staff' said Geraldine. 'It causes real problems; a lot of the parents who have to wait 6 months for an appointment don't turn up, so you can spend a day in clinic and have 25 per cent of your appointments DNA. And because there is such pressure on us, I never know whether it's best to assess all the children on our list and offer a very small number of them help, or to assess a small number and offer all of *them* treatment.'

'Yes. Ian, the physio, was saying much the same about wheelchairs last week' said Anna, 'apparently there are four children needing wheelchairs and the budget will provide four of those ordinary ones that don't help very much, or two super duper ones that really make a difference. He says he wishes he'd been taught some ethics at college!'

'Be more useful if the managers and purchasers were interested in ethics' said Geraldine. 'We know from research that speech and language therapy is best offered intensively – three to four times a week – but we just can't offer that, so we constantly know what we're doing isn't good enough. When I look back at the care plans I used to write when I'd just qualified and compare them with the ones I write now . . . I used to think the care plan should say what was needed, now I write down what we can realistically provide, so that it doesn't raise the hopes of the parents so much.'

'I heard Mrs A having a go at you the other day' said Anna, 'what was all that about?'

'Oh, she just wanted more than I could offer. They always take it out on us because we're there. They don't see the managers who allocate the budgets' replied Geraldine. 'But I don't blame her, she has terrific problems with her son and it's having a huge effect on her older daughter. She's only 8 but she's having to take on such burdens. I think the marriage is cracking up. What a real shame it all is. To tell you the truth it's a relief to talk to you about it, I've been waking in the night and fretting over it and that's just stupid, I'm not making it any better that way.'

'Why don't you talk to Lydia Wright about it?' asked Anna, 'everyone says she's really good on family therapy'.

'Oh would she see them?' Geraldine seemed relieved.

'Oh no I don't think so, but she would teach you about family therapy – she runs weekly sessions – so *you* could use it.'

Geraldine was silent, thinking that she couldn't cope with all the speech and language therapy that was needed without adding another skill she wouldn't have time to use. She sighed.

'How is Jane getting on?' Jane was a newly qualified therapist based in Anna's centre. Jane, she knew, had a caseload particularly heavy with special needs cases. She remembered back to her own early days when she felt so alone and unsupported, with people so dependent on her. With that in mind she asked Anna to keep an eye on her.

'By the way, how did that complaint about your CMO get dealt with?' she asked. Anna had told her of the complaint about a CMO who had been late for a child health clinic. When the mother, who had deliberately booked the first appointment in order to get to work on time, was told by an over-helpful receptionist that it was best not to book the first two appointments of the day because the doctor was always late ('she has a long way to come'), the mother had written in to complain about lax management. 'Oh the woman who complained was sent lots of letters about it, but this particular CMO is still usually late. Not that she's much use when she's there, she's so out-of-date. I don't think she's read a journal for years, I know she hasn't been to any conferences ever since I've been around. I think she just wants a soft option and checking kid's hearing and hips is just that.'

'What a depressing conversation this has been' said Anna, 'next time let's be more cheerful, we'll ban "work" as a subject'.

Caroline and Ben Green arrived home exhausted. Ben was now 7-years-old and had been diagnosed when 6-months-old as having cerebral palsy. This meant that he and Caroline, his mother, were regular visitors at the local general hospital, at a health clinic (for speech therapy), the GP surgery, a nearby health centre which housed the physio, and twice a year they visited a specialist at a teaching hospital in town. In addition, they saw a social worker and a benefits advice helper at a drop-in centre after school. Ben attended the local school but received some special teaching. Caroline wasn't sure that this was the best arrangement, but she didn't think she had the strength to fight the education department as well as everyone else.

'Because that's what it feels like' she thought, 'as though I'm always fighting'. She thought back to this afternoon's performance. The two of them had arrived at the hospital in good time for a 1.30 appointment with the ophthalmologist. She liked to arrive early to settle Ben so that he wasn't difficult when it came to the assessment. By 2.00 Ben hadn't been called but she hadn't worried as they often had to wait quite a while. She kept Ben amused and occupied. At 2.30 she made enquiries and discovered that no-one could find Ben's notes. He wasn't seen until 5.30. Four hours! He had become more and more restless, so when it came to his turn he wouldn't cooperate at all. She knew he could see more than he had pretended to. She wondered what the point of the whole thing was. To make matters worse, there was no-one on the desk when they came out, so she couldn't make the appointment that the doctor had asked for in 2 months' time. Now the hospital would send her one and the chances were it would clash with something else.

'What an effect this has on families' she thought. 'I wonder if any of the people in power, real power, prime ministers and so on, have any idea what it's like for us. They say they're spending more on the NHS, more on education, but whenever we need anything *everyone* tells us there's no money in their budget. Perhaps there aren't any votes in children like Ben.' She knew that if Ben had been born 20 years earlier he would have spent most of his life in a home. She was glad that there was now support for people in their own homes. She had a fear though, that never really left her, of what would happen to Ben when she went, now that all the homes had been closed.

Neil Andrew, director of development at the HA, reconsidered the papers in front of him about the Green Glades centre. £X00,000 for a course of therapy that by no means all professionals considered efficacious.

When extra-contractual referrals were made, the HA had very limited grounds for turning them down. If it was a GP referral, two questions would be asked: (1) Is there a contract with a local provider that deals with these cases? (2) If so, what is so special about this case? For consultant-to-consultant referrals, the HA would only be notified; their permission would not have to be sought.

The Green Glades referral, from a multidisciplinary, multi-agency team to a centre about which professional opinions differed, was not straightforward. He would ask the other agencies, education and social services, whether they would help fund it, but he was fairly sure of their response. Everyone was defining their boundaries much more carefully and was unwilling to step over them for fear of creating precedents.

He looked further down his in-tray. The request from the Community Trust, for additional funding to pay for an artificial voice box, irritated him. Frankly he agreed with the education and social services departments that it was a health responsibility and the HA gave the Trust £50 million a year to meet community health needs, yet they were always coming back for more to meet these one-off requests. The HA had to budget for unexpected cases, why couldn't the Trust?

He knew they were upset about the 12 per cent savings the health authority would be taking out over the next year, but he was sure it was more than possible to do so *and* maintain activity levels. There were two reasons for his certainty; first, that the Trust was still measuring activity for most of its staff in 'patient contacts', so they never had any sensible information to discuss with the HA. And neither, presumably, to manage the services themselves. Second, the new GP contract had made a big difference to the number of GPs involved in child development work, yet there had been no change at all in the pattern of working of community medical staff. This suggested that many staffing levels and working practices were set by historical factors, rather than current needs, and that an overhaul was urgently needed.

The third in-tray item was the draft of his paper to the next health authority meeting on paediatric in-patient services, spelling out the reasons why changes needed to be made. They were a major concern because of the national problem with paediatric medical manpower, which had been highlighted in the regional specialty review. The paper was the result of discussions with the Institute of Child Health and a number of provider Trusts. Of course there were several mutually exclusive objectives in all the guidance that existed about provision of such services. For example, the recommendations on paediatric cover to A&E and obstetrics couldn't be met unless services were centralized, which conflicted with those on local provision. Still, Neil had come to realize that purchasing was about pleasing hardly any of the people hardly any of the time. At base this was because, as survey after survey had shown, people did not believe that, where health was concerned, money should enter into the decision-making process at all.

He couldn't afford the luxury of such moral high ground. He would need to make some decisions.

Discussion

In many parts of the country, professionals working in this area feel that their service is desperately underfunded. If this is the case, it is all the more important that resources devoted to children with special needs are used wisely, to optimal effect, with maximum efficiency.

Are the resources referred to in the case being used wisely? What changes need to be made if the Trust's child clients and their carers are to receive effective, efficient services?

On the contrary, the resources described (people mostly) are being used with great profligacy. Examples include:

• The child mental health liaison meeting wastes 12 person hours on the discussion of an issue outside their remit. Given the salaries of the participants the Trust could employ another half-time counsellor instead. There is an indication in Lydia's letter that different kinds of such multidisciplinary meetings are regular and frequent.
• Admission to the family therapy workshop appears to be at the discretion of individual staff members themselves. It seems to be an *ad hoc*

arrangement with no wider policy discussion about whether family therapy is best provided by specialists or generalists, no arrangements for supervision, etc.

- The special needs counsellor is completely disregarding her job description and pursuing her own interests.
- Speech and Language Therapists (SLTs) are wasting 25 per cent of their appointments.
- The SLTs, and everyone else involved, are re-assessing children previously assessed. Parents and carers of children with special needs regularly express weariness and cynicism over the number of assessments when what they need is therapy.
- An enuresis clinic is provided but its existence, purpose and referral arrangements are not publicized to possible referrers.
- Elizabeth Latham is trying to have her special needs counsellor upgraded without much idea, because she does not know how she is spending her time, of how effective she is being.
- New practitioners (e.g. the new SLT) are not given adequate formal (as opposed to informal) support and supervision.
- One of the CMOs is not pulling her weight but is drawing her salary.
- As a result of a system failure in the out-patients' department, Ben's consultation is of little value. This does not fall within the remit of the Trust except in so far as the special needs counsellor could (if she had any time) take on an advocacy role and challenge those out-patient operational systems.

All this waste and yet the individuals described are all passionately concerned about their work. How does this happen? It is the result of reactivity, when people and organizations are in 'reactive' or 'victim' mode.

In the case study, we see Lydia Wright reacting to requests from other staff, rather than determining what are her own priorities if she is to deliver the services required. Elizabeth Latham sees herself and her services as a victim of the cuts; of GPs not referring appropriately; of SLTs who waste their time; of the Trust not providing money for the voicebox; of the purchasers over Green Glades; about collecting numbers and the prospect of being held accountable. Alison Brown feels helpless about the number of meetings, does not challenge Elizabeth about her view of the data, has not insisted on work programmes, and when her offers of help are declined decides not to offer again.

As both cause and result of this individual reactivity, the organization is also in reactive mode. Unexpected extras are not budgeted for, so the Trust is always running, cap in hand, to the purchasers. Its staffing mix is based on historical accident. It is not taking opportunities to influence purchaser priorities; it has not made sure, for example, that the regional review of paediatrics included community-based services. More seriously still, it is allowing, indeed requiring, that major *ethical* decisions are made by frontline practitioners rather than by the resource allocators. It is also allowing people rights without corresponding responsibilities. The Green Glades decision, for example, was taken by people who are not accountable for any budget for such care.

Underlying this reactivity is a profound lack of information. Without information you cannot take responsibility and charting your course is impossible. You can only react to your immediate circumstances. Persuading staff used to wielding emotional assertion as their argument to collect and present hard evidence requires all the skills of a *real* manager. It will require all their generosity and discipline to avoid writing these 'victims' off, especially as they, the managers, will be on the receiving end of considerable hostility. If they are to 'turn' these staff round and revitalize them, they will need to develop significant personal credibility based on an insightful understanding of the issues, genuine commitment to meeting the needs of clients and empathy for the professionals involved.

When people are deeply into being a victim, challenges to their thinking and behaviour have to be gentle. Reflecting back to them their own arguments can help: 'So you don't know exactly what Lydia does but she's well qualified and you like her; so you want to give her more money although you are desperately short of it. Why don't we discuss it next week when you've had time to prepare a more convincing case. Yes I know you don't have much time, that's why you might find it useful to discuss it with Alison or to look at this example of a case for additional funding which I have recently approved.'

Rendering the staff proactive again is essential, but the organization must also be turned around. It, too, needs a clear idea of what it is doing (what needs it can meet, the services it must offer) and how. It needs to agree on its priorities, both internally and with purchasers, and set up systems to ensure that it can work to them. In doing so, it must address the ethical issues that are currently left to frontline practitioners to resolve. It must support its staff, recognizing the danger of 'burn-out' in this emotionally draining area, with formal supervision and support mechanisms rather than allowing meetings to proliferate and degenerate into informal and ineffective group therapy. It must require all staff to be appraised and be given constructive feedback on their performance, and their performance must be assessed in terms of the agreed priorities. When deciding on the services to be offered and the means of doing so (e.g. whether to use specialists or to develop another skill in their generalists), suitable arrangements for supervision, monitoring and evaluation must be determined. The agreed priorities must drive the budget-setting and budgets should be devolved to the groups and individuals whose responsibility it is to make decisions about clients. Until staff have lost their aggressive 'victim' attitudes, this will be difficult, but without it they will never lose them; they need to feel in control.

However, before the organization can even take the first step towards proactivity (i.e. discussion on priorities), it must search for the wherewithal to fill the current information void at strategic (organizational) levels. Services of this kind tend to be awash with both data and information but do not bring it together in a way that enables strategic decisions to be made. Every assessment generates useful information, so a means of capturing it needs to be introduced. Doing so requires intent rather than money as long as the perfect (an all-singing, all-dancing, hi-tech solution that collects *all* relevant information on a continuous basis) is not allowed to become the enemy of the good (something *ad hoc* that works for these purposes, i.e. the determining of priorities). Staff in victim mode will tend to feel helpless and defeatist when faced with the organization's inability to offer the 'perfect'. They must be reminded constantly of the purpose of the exercise and encouraged (by the offer of short-term clerical input perhaps) to devise ways of contributing their own hard evidence to the debate.

The frustration of a *real* manager trying to transform the effectiveness and efficiency of these services will be very great. He will need to remind himself, probably hourly, that 'it is systems that fail, not people'; that these passionate clinicians have been badly let down by being unmanaged, by being thwarted in their attempts to provide more and better services, by not being forced to think clearly or to work together productively, by not being supported. He needs to feel compassion rather than anger for the individuals concerned, while remaining strongly opposed to their behaviours, attitudes and practices. No this is not easy, it's hard. Simple but hard. That's what *real* management is.

Community care

'Well, *I* can't do anything about Mrs Field' reflected Jane Morris angrily. Twice today Mrs Field had been brought to her attention, by Dr Pendle the orthopaedic consultant whose bed she was 'blocking' and by the directorate business manager who was worried about 'the impact on the cost per case of these outliers'.

Jane had agreed with them both that Mrs Field's broken ankle was now securely encased in a plaster cast and there was no need for further hospital-based medical care. She had also pointed out to both of them that Mrs Field could not cope at home yet and that no discharge could take place until a comprehensive needs assessment (CNA) had been done by a care manager from the local authority. In response to Sam Pendle's angry (and largely, she thought, rhetorical) question, 'Well, how long is that going to take?', Jane could only shrug her shoulders and say that the request had been made when Mrs Field had arrived 2 weeks earlier.

She had heard that the local quality target for assessment response times was 2–10 days. 'So much for quality targets' she thought, 'the reality is a month and sometimes much longer'.

Grace Field was no stranger to the assessments either. She had been discharged from the same hospital 3 months ago, back to her own home, with a complex package of care involving the local authority, district nurses and Cross Roads. 'Not as complex as some' she thought. She had heard of someone who had 27 different people coming into her house. 'Enough to drive you barmy if you aren't already' she smiled to herself. She did so hope she would be able to go home again and soon. She knew she was getting slower and she did forget things at times (Could she *really* have turned on the gas cooker and forgotten to light it? That's what her daughter told her).

She had lived in that house for 50 years; she and Mr Field had moved in not long after their daughter Marjorie was born. When Marjorie had moved out to get married, Mr Field's brother Tom had moved in. The timing had been quite good really. Tom had always been a bit simple and had lived with his mother, who died just about the time Marjorie moved out. Since Mr Field died 10 years ago, Grace had been pleased to have Tom's company. Marjorie lived nearby of course and popped in frequently, but that was not the same as having company all the time. She hoped Tom was coping without her.

Yes, they were all very nice to her in the hospital but she couldn't wait to get home again.

A week later the name Grace Field was at the top of Mercia Koenig's action list. As care manager, she would need a number of contributory assessments and there were two she simply could not put in motion. Another occupational therapist (OT) had just left the authority and not been replaced. Not for the usual financial reasons, Mercia knew, but because OTs were like hens teeth, they simply were not able to recruit to the post. The home assessment would have to wait.

She needed a psychiatric assessment too, but that needed the right piece of paper to be signed by one of the junior doctors, and could she get it signed? She had been trying for 3 days. 'I know I should feel sorry for them, all those horrendous hours, but they are so obnoxious that it's difficult to be. And I do wonder whether, if they were a bit more organized, they wouldn't have so much work to do. After all, it must be quicker to look in the notes and sign the form than to read 'phone messages from me three times a day.'

What a difference between the way various wards in the same hospital approached things. On the rehabilitation wards Mercia felt part of the team, she attended the ward round when she needed to, and knew all the other professionals involved – physios, speech and language therapists, the continence adviser. On the orthopaedic ward the team saw her as an irritant. 'Bloody social workers' she had heard one of the nurses say a few months ago, 'we get a sensible multidisciplinary decision on how the patient should be managed and then they come in and mess it all up'. 'You may get their bodies fixed again' Mercia had thought, 'but not their lives'.

Still, at least all the ward staff now knew that they should be thinking about discharge at the time of admission. Well, nearly all of them; there was still the odd dinosaur who expected (and told the patient and family) that they would be able to 'just 'phone home care'. A few more were not aware of the proper procedures – how to make a referral, who should make it, the lead time needed. But mostly the problem was that these staff, based on wards, simply did not realize that the hospital admission was part of a fundamental change for the client. The ward staff expected to rehabilitate them to their status prior to admission, or as close as they could get to it, but often physically and/or psychologically the client was sufficiently different to make their previous living arrangements inappropriate.

Mercia chuckled to herself as she remembered the case of Mr X, admitted with a broken leg after he'd slipped on the ice. Sam Pendle was all for discharging him home when the plaster cast was on and his face, when told that his patient's address was a cardboard box under the motorway extension, had been a picture!

Last time Mercia had calculated her average response time for a CNA it was 3 weeks (3 weeks from referral that was; if the ward didn't refer until the patient had been in 4 weeks that was *their* problem, not hers). Not the target, but not bad. Of course putting the care package in place took time too.

'Be careful' Jane Morris had warned her yesterday about Grace Field, 'Sam is getting so fed up that he may be tempted to do a decibel discharge'. They had laughed. Mercia didn't think Jane was serious but she had experienced the 'decibel discharge'. A previous client had needed a care package involving a voluntary organization which, after 3 weeks of putting a package into place around their service offer, suddenly withdrew the offer. They had had no choice and Mercia understood that, but it had left her back at square one. Sam Pendle had been furious, and told one of the ward nurses to 'phone and book an ambulance and had himself 'phoned the relatives to say he was discharging the patient the next day. Of course she had had to make temporary arrangements immediately, but in doing so she knew she was rewarding this atrocious behaviour.

Marjorie sat back stunned, anger fighting fear and disappointment.

'So as your mother has assets of over £16,000 she will be responsible for paying the nursing home fees of £250 per week. Of course it will mean selling her house. Fortunately we've found a lovely nursing home for her.' Mercia paused.

Grace Field's case had become more complicated when she had a stroke while in hospital. That had solved Sam Pendle's problem because she had been transferred to the rehabilitation wards, but Mrs Field's condition was now such that moving back home was out of the question and the Eligibility Panel had agreed that a nursing home place was the answer.

The placements team had had difficulty finding a place, but had eventually tracked one down, some miles away but in a very well run home. There was a perfect place much nearer, the community care centre, but Mrs Field was not a patient of one of the GPs with admitting rights.

Now Mercia was explaining to Mrs Field's daughter Marjorie that the placements team had also assessed Mrs Field's financial situation and discovered that she owned her own home.

'But what will happen to Tom?' Marjorie asked.

'I'm terribly sorry but that's not my responsibility' said Mercia, 'he'll have to apply to the Housing Department if he can't stay with you'.

'He can't possibly stay with us, we're falling over ourselves as it is. Three children in a small flat. We were reckoning on the money from Mum's house to buy something bigger one day. Now that's never going to happen. Not that I want Mum to go of course. I've always thought of her as my best friend. Although she's getting less and less like her real self now.'

Mercia asked gently, 'Did no-one every suggest to you, when your Mum was in hospital before, that she transfer the house into your name? If she had done that 6 months or more before the financial assessment she wouldn't be having to pay for her care.'

'Someone did say something about it, yes, but it's always been Mum's house. I couldn't ask her to just give it away to me, and I didn't really understand why they said it, they were a bit secretive in the way they said it.' Marjorie tried to absorb the new situation, the different life prospects now facing her. '*Couldn't* she stay at home? Suppose I were to go there every day, Tom would help too, and my eldest can do her homework there every evening. If you could get nurses to come in and help, we could manage and you know how desperate she is to be back in her own home. At least let us try', Marjorie pleaded.

'Oh the joys of being a care manager' Mercia fumed as she walked the dog that evening. 'It was all supposed to be much better than it used to be. Money to spend on new, imaginative packages of care to meet all sorts` of needs and keep people functioning well in their own homes instead of going into residential care. Instead it's far worse; instead of creative packages I can't meet basic needs, the gap between what I need to provide and what I can provide is enormous. I really thought that I could achieve more as a care manager than as a social worker, but whereas before I was counselling individuals and families, sorting things out with welfare rights, etc., now I'm doing no case work at all, I'm just filling in forms. Some of the forms take hours to complete. And now I'm getting it in the neck because I'm saving some precious time by not filling in the ones about the services clients need, only those recording the services they can actually have. Well I used to fill in the others but it was a complete waste of time. Nobody ever did anything with them.

'With a caseload of 60 clients at any one time (and some of my colleagues have up to 100), the majority needing intensive packages, how can I really *manage* their care? When I first started I had a placement in a part III home for a while. With 40 beds it had a manager, a deputy manager, three shift leaders, plus care staff, cleaners, cooks. Now I'm supposed to manage 60 people of about the same dependency. What a comparison. Of course I can't come up with creative solutions. I take off the peg solutions whenever I can.

'And where do I go from here? I used to think I wanted to be a principal social worker leading a team. We used to get such good support from our team leaders. They used to supervise us on a case by case basis, modelling their skills in listening, counselling, directed reading, etc. Now we report to team managers (20 of us to one team manager) who are more concerned with bringing back the latest edict, and information on how budgets are being cut and eligibility criteria being tightened. I don't want to be a team manager now, but where else can I go? I'm really stuck. I wonder whether kids at school who used to say "I want to be a social worker" will say "I want to be a care manager"? I can't imagine so. Where is it all going?

'Just look at how ineffectual I've been with Mrs Field. She's going to end up miles away when there's the community care centre much nearer; if only those GPs would see sense and stop trying to limit it to their own patients. Take that client last week, Mrs A. She doesn't meet any of the eligibility criteria for a residential place let along a nursing home place, but Dr Smith kept saying I wasn't taking her health needs into consideration. No I hadn't assessed them, I had a contributory assessor do that, the CPN was very clear about what was needed and it didn't qualify Mrs A for a place. Of course it would be lovely if she could have a place, it would do her a lot of good I can see that, but when there are so many people so much worse off it simply can't be justified.

'If I'd had a nursing background it would be different, they'd believe me then, the GPs, even if I said exactly the same things. If only they'd listen. You can't ever get more than 5 minutes of a GP's time. They never come to case conferences or liaison meetings and if you can get hold of them on the 'phone they never remember who you are; and just when you've started to explain the situation to them they interrupt with "so what you're trying to tell me is you can't do X, Y or Z" and that's that. People's lives are so complicated; you can't describe them as quickly as you can a temperature or a rash.

'They're always complaining about the number of care managers they have to deal with. But I have to deal with up to 50 GPs and I take the trouble to remember who they are. They also complain that we're difficult to get hold of, but there's *always* a duty officer on call who passes messages on; try getting hold of a GP between noon and 4 or after 7 p.m. The patients all think they're marvellous of course, they stay with the same practice all their lives most of them. That's partly why it's so frustrating when GPs don't match up to their image.

'Oh being a care manager is the worst of all possible worlds!' Mercia burst out laughing at this melodramatic thought and started to jog round the park, putting care management behind her for the night.

Victoria Smith read the letter from the local director of social services with mounting anger. The final paragraph caused her to throw it onto the table in despair. 'So what they are proposing', she confirmed to the rest of the community care centre committee, 'is that they fund four of our six beds but that they nominate who is placed in them!'

She reminded the committee of the history of the centre, of the way she, as the local GP, had established it in the late 1980s with the support of local volunteers, to provide health and social care for local residents; of the way they had applied for registration for six beds so that they could offer nursing and respite care; of the way funding had initially been provided by the Department of Social Security if the patients were eligible; and of the way things had changed now that the local social service department held the purse-strings.

In the early years the GPs had made all the admission decisions and it had worked very well. The implementation of the Community Care Act in 1993, which transferred funding responsibility to the local social services, had changed all that. Now the GPs had to undertake joint assessments with assessors from social services, often people in whom they had little confidence, and with whom they frequently disagreed. The committee knew of these disagreements. As local people they represented the volunteers who helped staff the centre, and they knew of all the local residents who could benefit from the overnight care but would not be deemed a priority by the social services care managers. They felt they really could not accept that all the admission rights would be held by social services, and voted to reject the proposal.

Victoria mulled it over as she drove home. Without that assured funding they may lose the registration. How demoralizing. All of the local GPs supported the concept of overnight beds and there were so many people in need of them. The respite care they could offer made all the difference to carers, who could then go on supporting people in their own homes indefinitely.

It was all very well saying, as the care managers always seemed to, that there were people who were much worse off who needed the places more, but if people were well supported early on they needn't get to such a desperate state. Anyway, they didn't seem to take into account all the relevant factors. Not their fault, they didn't have the skills or knowledge, but take Mr C for example. Sure he wasn't cooking his meals, but meals-on-wheels was not the answer. It was because he was so depressed that he wasn't getting up, that he wasn't cooking his meals. What he needed was care from a GP and a CPN. Anyway, people who need long-term nursing care should really be cared for by the NHS, not social services. Since when had nursing stopped being a healthcare profession?

She had another patient she wanted to admit to the centre but the thought of the referral process was depressing. She would 'phone social services and speak to someone she had never come across before, who would take no notice of the fact she said she wanted a response *urgently*, who would pass the message on to someone else, who may or may not 'phone back, probably right in the middle of surgery, some time within the next 3 weeks. And then, once the referral was in the system, she would be lucky to get any feedback on it thereafter. What she wanted was a named contact person in social services, feedback on all referrals, with a care manager based in or attached to the practice.

She knew of one large practice in which their practice nurse was their care manager. That must be marvellous. A nurse (especially one you had recruited and trained) could really be trusted to have the insight to refer on to you the people with physical needs. They would be so much more, well, professional, too. Yes that summed up her feelings about the care managers, they were unprofessional. They had an inconsistent approach to dealing with referrals, their meetings (oh, so many meetings) were unstructured and went on for hours, they were always late and their reports were verbose to the point of rambling. And didn't they understand the meaning of a simple word such as 'urgent'?

What a mess, and all because of money. Nobody could do anything for nothing these days. Their district nurse had told her the other day that she had been forbidden to make coffee or lunch for her patients. Ridiculous, it must be cheaper for the nurse to rustle up a nutritious sandwich than for meals-on-wheels to be driven to a house not otherwise on their rounds. The nurse had been upset because she saw it as the opposite of good practice, the loss of an opportunity for observation. So it would be cheaper and better for the nurse to do it. Ah, but meals-on-wheels came from a different budget. So it might cost the country more but the local NHS Trust less. Ridiculous.

This was the same Trust proposing a Hospital at Home scheme where the medical care was expected to be provided, free of charge, by the local GPs. GPs were the backbone of the NHS; for patients they were the focus, the one unchanging part of the service, but they were taken for granted by everyone.

And now this, the end of a wonderful service that was badly needed.

'Well I'm pleased that social services have asked for our views on the funding of the community care centre' thought Angela Mead, manager of the elderly service for the Community Services Trust. 'It's the first time we've been consulted, although I know our district nurses are often asked to help out.'

Angela knew the centre committee felt very aggrieved at the authority social services could now exercise. Angela felt more ambivalent. Communication between the two organizations had improved considerably and, with it, confidence. She understood their dilemma. That didn't mean she condoned all their decisions. Take the 'One Stop Home Care Scheme', for instance. The idea had been to provide all the health and social care needs for clients needing nursing care at home. After 6 months, a detailed evaluation showed that of all the care provided 30 per cent was social care, 40 per cent personal care (i.e. debatable whether social or health) and 30 per cent health care. Yet the Trust was funding it all.

After much discussion, the officers of the local authority had finally agreed to contribute financially. The local councillors, however, had vetoed the proposal. There was, they said, no way they could let money raised by a democratically elected council be spent by an unaccountable quango. Naturally, the One-Stop service no longer existed, with clients being referred to a care manager instead.

About the centre, the question that had prompted this train of thought, Angela was not sure what to recommend. In her view, the nurses funded at the centre undoubtedly provided nursing care to people who benefited from it. If the centre were not funded, would it mean more work for the Trust's community nurses? Almost certainly. Were the patients who received treatment those who most needed that kind of care? Probably not. She started to compose her response.

Discussion

Community care is possibly the area in which more professionals from more agencies are forced to interact with each other than anywhere else; resources are finite and tensions run high. It is therefore important, if misunderstandings are to be avoided, for both generosity and discipline to be displayed. We saw in earlier chapters that the likelihood of this is enhanced when individuals and groups are clear about what it is they are trying to achieve.

Are the individuals in the case study demonstrating generosity and discipline? Does Victoria Smith's personal vision help her in dealing with a difficult situation?

Individual generosity and discipline

Sam Pendle either knows, or should know, how long a comprehensive needs assessment takes. What's more, he should understand why it takes so long and appreciate the skills and integrity of the other professionals involved. Getting angry is an inappropriate response unless he is going to direct that anger into energizing his attempts to improve the systems that cause it.

When asked to undertake a piece of work, especially by someone entitled to ask, the disciplined response is either to do it immediately, or to discuss its degree of urgency and agree when it can be expected. Ignoring messages is selfish, arrogant and undisciplined. In doing so, the junior doctors in the case study are assuming that their own assessment of priorities is the correct one and that the reasoning of other people, other professionals, is inferior to their own.

The staff on the orthopaedic ward exhibit a similar lack of faith in colleagues from another profession when they complain about social workers messing up the discharge arrangements agreed by the ward-based staff. Whenever one individual or profession stands out in opposition to the views of a number of others, there is an understandable tendency for the group to dismiss or decry the position of the one. But just as individuals need to accept challenges to their perceptions of reality, groups also need to work on the avoidance of stereotyping, by testing their views, by welcoming (rather than cold-shouldering) contrary opinions.

When Mercia Koenig stops completing one set of forms – those keeping track of what care is needed by clients – choosing to fill in only those recording the care that is actually planned, she denies her organization the evidence with which arguments for greater resources can be fought. While she can be disappointed at not being told of the use to which these are put, it is her responsibility to find out the consequences before taking such action. The principle of delaying gratification often requires us to undertake tasks from which our successors and their clients will benefit, rather than ourselves.

Mercia contrasts her caseload now with the kind of care arrangements available 15–20 years previously and of course finds that the resources per client were then very much greater. That kind of comparison is interesting; it must not, though, lead her to feel hard done by. Rather, she must use it to remind herself of the way the world changes, of the constancy of change and of the need to be prepared for, and be able to, change. This is difficult without a sense of personal mission rooted in what we want our life (our living) to have contributed. If we find meaning in our involvement with processes rather than outcomes, then whenever those processes alter we will feel threatened, defensive and angry. We will not be able to embrace the inevitable – change, change and more change.

Mercia's attitude to GPs is not helping her or them. Similar attitudes are often expressed by members of professions working closely with GPs, while at the same time very many GPs feel put upon, overloaded, taken for granted and misunderstood.

General practice is characterized by small businesses operating in isolation from each other. Relationships in small businesses are often fraught and medical practices are certainly no exception. Pressures upon general practice have increased, as indeed they have on every part of the health system. However, other health professionals have drawn succour and support from working in larger groups and from access to the professional support systems provided within larger organizations. This has not been available, generally, to GPs. Those working with them must accept, therefore, that it is unsurprising that many GPs are at the reactive end of the maturity continuum, and they must include this knowledge when planning their conversations and other interactions. People in the greatest need of our help along the maturity continuum are also the most aggressive and 'difficult'. Choosing to see the need rather than the behaviour is hard work, but whenever we respond in anger, whinge to others, take an easy way out by agreeing with someone that the world is against them, then we are part of the problem rather than its solution.

The distrust of the care managers and their competence, as expressed by Victoria Smith on behalf of the GPs, is understandable, but her anger must not be directed at individuals but at the system. Disagreement on the assessments must not be left to fester. They can be welcomed by the GPs as a challenge to their perception of patients' problems. Alternatively, they can be documented and fed back into the system to support an argument for better training for care managers. Better still, both.

Similarly, Victoria's anger over the Community Trust's decision to forbid their district nurses to prepare sandwiches for their clients must either be used to good effect (lobbying the right people in the right way) or lost. Unless she can do one of these, it diminishes her ability to be effective and she becomes a victim.

The centre committee rejects the offer from social services to fund their beds because the committee would lose admission rights and thus 'their' patients/residents would lose out to others deemed by social services to be in greater need. The centre only exists because of the vision, energy and enthusiasm of its founders *and* the finance provided by the FHSA and (now) social services. Rights accompany responsibilities and if the centre committee is prepared to shoulder the responsibility for financing its work, it can retain all the rights to make decisions about whom to admit.

As a result of the considerable voluntary input to the centre, services provided here will be cheaper than those offered elsewhere, and unless they accept responsibility for providing additional funding to pay this difference then social services cannot insist on all the admission rights.

It is always disappointing when a scheme with practical benefits is vetoed on ideological grounds and the councillors mentioned in the case would certainly benefit from questioning their own motives and goals. If this ideology was unknown to the Community Trust and could not have been ascertained, then they have reason for disappointment. If, however, these political principles could have been guessed at and prepared for, then they should recognize their mistake in not doing so and learn from it, so that they do not jeopardize promising schemes in the future.

How does an individual caught up in this situation identify their best course of action? What should Victoria Smith do next?

Victoria Smith has a problem. Indeed she has two. First, she cannot persuade the relevant care managers to approve admission for the patients she feels will benefit from respite care. Second, the future of 'her' centre is in jeopardy unless the committee agree to most of the beds being utilized by people who are not local residents.

As Victoria has these problems it is up to her to solve them; before she does anything else she must accept this responsibility. The fact that a problem is caused by the actions of others does not make it their problem. Even if they are experiencing a problem it will be of a different nature.

Once she has accepted that these problems are her's, Victoria's next step must be to understand them fully. Both the problems are the outcome of a system (a set of interrelationships) of which she is a part. Victoria must therefore identify all the other elements in both systems and find out as much about them as she can. She must ascertain the role and responsibilities of care managers, the pressures they are under, the constraints they must work within, the ways in which they determine priorities, the way they see GPs, the way they feel about her. She must also consider them individually. What is Mercia Koenig's relationship style? (see Chapter 1). What does this suggest her response will be to the way Victoria behaves?

When Victoria has fully understood the dynamics of her first problem she can apply similar questioning to her second. This time it will be more difficult because she does not know the decision-makers within social services. She will have to find out.

Armed with these insights Victoria is in a position to plan her role in the negotiations. She will know what relationship style to adopt, what arguments are likely to succeed and, because she will now (in all likelihood) have considerable sympathy for her 'opponent's' point of view, she can adopt a collaborative approach in place of her previous competitive one. This means that she will try and find a solution that meets their needs as well as her own. That may not be possible. A compromise may be the best she can achieve, and it is only possible where there is generosity on the part of the problem holder.

If Victoria Smith were to articulate her 'mission' she would probably say: 'to enable my patients to be as healthy as possible [purpose], by ensuring that they have access to a full range of diagnostic, therapeutic, rehabilitative and preventive services, locally where possible, so that existing support networks can be maintained [primary aims]'.

She has become angry with care managers and social services because she is fearful, and the reason for her fear is: 'If I lose my admission rights to the centre then a number of the services my patients need to maximize their health will be unavailable and I will be unable to achieve my "mission".'

Identifying the fear at the root of this anger and hostility would help Mercia Koenig to interact with her more effectively.

If Victoria is to achieve her purpose then she must become more proactively involved in decisions about resource allocation. She must therefore expand her mission statement to include a further primary aim:

• To secure the necessary resources for these services.

To meet this aim will require her to interact with very different groups, organizations and individuals than do her other aims. Only if she accepts that this aim also is primary will she feel able to do so, without begrudging time taken away from clinical activities. Her alternative, if she feels that she cannot do this – if she does not want to take the time necessary to be effective in gaining additional resources for her patients (and others) – is to amend her mission. To accept that she cannot ensure that her patients have access to all the services she would like. Either path is justifiable. In one she remains a full-time clinician, in the other she accepts a *real* management role as well. The hybrid of leaving her mission unchanged, but also refusing to accept the need to make time available to influence resource allocators, is the 'victim's' choice. This would be a recipe for stress, anger and helplessness.

Newtown Mental Health Trust

'Well it has certainly upset the apple cart' thought Mark Colbet, chief executive of Newtown Mental Health Trust, as he considered how his staff had received the recent report of purchasing intentions from Newtown and Swanning Health Authority.

When he had first seen the report, the result of a series of consultations to which Mark had been a party, he had welcomed many of the principles contained in it. He had found it much easier to work with the new authority than he had with the old DHA, whose members and senior managers had, he felt, paid only lip-service to the needs of his clients. He knew he was lucky, several of his peers were fighting an uphill battle trying to educate purchasers about new models of mental health care. Mark had found the chief executive and mental health project manager at Newtown and Swanning well informed, responsive to well thought through schemes and proposals and, above all, genuinely interested in the needs of people who were mentally ill.

He flipped through the document and thought back to the reaction the key points had provoked within the Trust. There had been some resentment at its tone. Some mutterings that the health authority was trying to take the credit for services that other people would be providing. Mark had spent 20 years working in mental health, training as a Registered Mental Nurse (RMN), moving up the nursing hierarchy, becoming Unit General Manager (UGM) and then chief executive. He knew that providing good care to people who are mentally ill is very much easier said than done, so he had some sympathy with these feelings.

The phrase 'current services can create as many problems as they solve' had caused frustration, even anger, among professionals who had long argued for better resourcing to ensure that this was not the case. Many of them pointed out that they had been trying to close the long-stay hospital for 10 years. Mark did wonder privately whether, had it not been for the health authority's adamant refusal to pay for services there after 1997, they would have been 'trying to close it' for another 10 years.

His staff had, as the report suggested, been divided over the plans for 24-hour crisis help. Broadly, the community staff had welcomed it, the staff on the acute wards seeing no relief from their current over-stretched position had argued strongly for more acute beds instead. Mark knew the pressure their acute beds were under and the daily decisions not to admit people who clearly needed the service. He knew that people could wait for hours in casualty while staff tried to find them a bed, that a major part of the junior doctors' day was spent on the 'phone trying to locate beds, and that patients out on weekend leave would often return to find that 'their' bed had been given to someone else and that they had been moved. He had just had a conversation with one carer, Mrs Jones, who had pleaded with Mark for him to admit her husband Rob. Mark knew Rob Jones from his own time on the wards and from the description Mrs Jones gave of his behaviour and mood he felt admission was appropriate. However, the psychiatrists had decided that there were others in greater need.

Nearly everyone had supported the report's recognition that individual needs differ greatly and that services need to be flexible in order to meet those needs. The greatest difficulty that the unit had encountered when part of the old DHA had been the assumption, of many of those involved in the provision of general acute services, that mental illness could be classified as neatly as physical complaints, into clearly defined diagnoses for which a standard package of care was appropriate.

Mark thought again about the community mental health teams. These would be locally based teams which included CPNs, psychologists, psychiatrists, OTs and GPs. The CPNs had welcomed the proposals wholeheartedly; Mark wondered whether he was being overly cynical when he thought that the CPNs saw these teams declaring UDI, operating autonomously without any management 'interference'. The psychiatrists had raised objections, that they were in danger of becoming deskilled and they would be unable to maintain their specialized interests. Mark believed that that problem could be overcome but he had strong reservations mainly about the role the report envisaged for GPs.

Mark's experiences of working with GPs had not always been happy and he was left with a view that, with some exceptions, they were not interested in mental illness, not sympathetic to mentally ill patients (particularly when at their most needy) and very willing to offload all responsibility onto specialists. He could see that the CMHTs could assist GPs in being more effective, but he wondered whether there were any sticks or carrots to encourage the GPs to play their part.

There was undoubtedly a gap in the services provided by GPs and by the Trust. This gap had become obvious as a result of the open access clinic which had been running for about a year now. This was a clinic to which GPs could refer any mentally ill patient, who would be seen that day without appointment. At least half of the people presenting did not have a mental illness severe enough for the Trust to treat them, but had conditions such as phobia, depression, anxiety, or mild somatic illnesses with which GPs were not trained to cope. When working more closely with the GPs, the CMHTs would be under a lot of pressure to meet these needs rather than some of the higher priority cases. This would require very skilful management.

Making the gap explicit had not helped relationships with the GPs. But it was not only the GPs. There was a general lack of understanding in other organizations about the role of the Trust. Take housing. Yet again Mark had had to explain to the local authority chair of housing that he could not section people just because they were behaving peculiarly and upsetting their neighbours.

The section on accommodation, Mark remembered, had caused great amusement at the meeting of the management team at which the report was first discussed. The fact that the health authority appeared to be rejecting the results of consultation when it suited them to do so had led one member to say, 'the words righteous and self come to mind'. The users and carers consulted requested a 'halfway' hostel, accommodation with a preventive and/or respite role. The health authority rejected this saying that more support in the community would reduce the need for it, that the CMHT was the answer. 'In an ideal world maybe' thought Mark, 'but we're a long way away from that yet, and in the meantime its the carers who pick up the pieces'.

The Trust might well have to rethink its structures and processes in light of the purchasers' requirements. The care group directorates no longer seemed so appropriate with the increased emphasis on community-based services. This would be an opportunity to rethink the role of the clinical directors and the management capabilities of the directors themselves. There had been a lot of disappointment in the other professions when all four posts went to psychiatrists 18 months ago, and although two had proved strong managers, meeting savings targets and producing coherent business plans, the other two had abdicated their responsibilities, exhibiting little leadership and leaving their staff to set their own priorities. No wonder those two directorates were projecting such a heavy overspend. A restructuring would give him the opportunity to replace those individuals with people more capable.

There had been a good deal of suspicion, as the report indicated, about where the money was coming from for all the changes proposed. Mark did not doubt the sincerity of the health authority's chief executive and mental health project manager, but he had heard that they were considerably overspent on their ECR budget and he wondered whether, as always in the past, mental health funding would suffer as a result. He believed the chief executive when he said it would take a 'major catastrophe' to throw them off course. But then major catastrophes sometimes seemed to be the order of the day.

Joy Redlan, a consultant psychiatrist at Waybourne Hospital for over 7 years and clinical director for the last 18 months, tried to keep calm as her registrar reported that Rob Jones' wife had complained to the chief executive about Joy's decision not to admit Rob to an acute ward. 'Well that really takes the biscuit' she fumed. 'We can already be overruled by the tribunal over detention decisions and by approved social workers over admission, and now managers are getting involved in clinical decisions – this is just ridiculous.' She paused. 'Yes it *would* be ridiculous' she thought, 'and Mark Colbet will know that too'. But she did wonder for a moment whether she would have been happier in a branch of medicine that had not seen its autonomy so undermined.

She thought back to Rob Jones. He would certainly benefit from an in-patient stay and if she brought him in now, his stay could well be shorter than if she delayed his admission. But she simply did not have a bed to offer him, because there were so many people in a more acute phase of their illness. She hated having to tell Mrs Jones 'I am so sorry but Rob isn't ill enough yet', but she had to.

She felt constantly uneasy about their admission policy. In common with most other acute mental health facilities, they gave priority to people suffering from schizophrenia, at the expense of those suffering from other disorders, for example obsessive compulsive disorders (OCD). And yet there was an argument that their intervention was more likely to be successful in the latter case than the former. By changing their policy they could bring far more people back to leading productive lives with fruitful relationships. They ought to be able to care for both groups but there just were not enough resources. The more she thought about it, the more she thought that this was an area where she wished managers would take more of a role. They left admission decisions to the consultants on the basis that this was a matter for clinical judgement. But her clinical judgement was that they all required care. Surely this took the decision out of the clinical and into the managerial (or even political) domain?

She opened her mail and found a note from the finance department advising her that her drug budget for January was again overspent and asking what she proposed to do about it. She assumed that the increase in expenditure must be due to respiradone. They had started using it for patients with fixed delusional states just over 18 months ago and had achieved some very promising results. Several patients had managed in the community for far longer than was the norm without requiring re-admission. She had decided to ignore previous warnings from the finance department, reasoning that although much more expensive than the alternative drugs, respiradone was much cheaper than a hospital bed and that what they lost on the swings they would gain on the roundabouts. They needed to discuss it again. But when would they find the time? They were under more and more pressure. GP referrals were higher than ever, and when they were forced to have two acute facilities instead of the current one, because the health authority had asked users what they wanted, things would be even more hectic. It was all very well asking users what they wanted, but by virtue of their illness they were not always the best judge.

This, together with the move to locality-based community mental health teams, was a source of real worry. In the past, consultant psychiatrists had been able to specialize in particular conditions, which was very much to the benefit of patients. The introduction of care group directorates had changed this somewhat, particularly as some of them had had to take on a managerial role which severely reduced the time they could devote to research. However, the locality focus would require them all to carry a completely generic caseload; as individuals they would become deskilled and the specialist resource currently available to patients would be very much diminished. Joy sighed. She recognized the importance of generalists and she had actively supported the principle that when the long-stay hospital finally closed, decamping its last residents into the community, the hospital clinicians would be a resource to primary care teams to help the latter to care for mental illness. But didn't they realize that her load had to be reduced, in order for her to provide that secondary support? With so many referrals she was on a treadmill, and she couldn't lengthen her waiting list any further because she was the gatekeeper to all the other hospital-based services. Until patients saw a consultant, they had no access to these other services. Other members of staff, particularly the OTs, questioned whether all referrals needed to be seen by the consultant first; but the GPs referred to a consultant and wouldn't be happy with anyone else. If only GPs would take more of an interest in mental health. There were a few good ones of course, but some of them operated to the most appalling standards, offloading anyone they found difficult. It wasn't all their fault though. Their psychiatric training was almost totally irrelevant to their needs in general practice. Mark had recently asked about the possibility of developing 'shared-care', but it was just not possible.

Talking of OTs, she must speak to someone soon about Maria Springstein. Maria had been openly angry yesterday when Tony Sherrard (a fellow consultant psychiatrist) had rejected her advice about a patient. These tensions didn't help the team to function properly. Team members needed to feel their advice was taken seriously. She would have a word with Tony perhaps about how he had conveyed the fact that he disagreed with Maria over the patient's discharge. She did wonder sometimes whether Maria was fully aware of the legal responsibilities of doctors. At the end of the day, the buck stopped with them. They were the ones who got sued if there was any trouble.

The other professions in mental health had, over the years, become more and more dominant, constantly lambasting what they described as 'the medical model'. Joy had begun to wonder whether the 'medical model' referred to everything a doctor did, said or even thought, the term was used so glibly and so often (and with such aggression). It was ironic really that mental health services were becoming more and more *de*medicalized just when the neuroendocrine basis of schizophrenia, depression and OCD

was at last being understood. That may not help the cause of the consultant psychiatrist she reflected; we shall then have to fight off incursions into
our territory from neurologists as well. Still the other professions had an
enormous amount to offer and she had actively tried to engage them in the
development of the business plan. It was taking a long time, however, and
she knew Mark was fretting at the delay. Surely he would realize though
that it would be a much better document, and be a useful team-building
process, if everyone was involved. Joy glanced at her watch, all this intro-
spection had delayed her. She sighed as she made her way up to Ward X.

Alex Ludlow, ward manager at Waybury Park, sighed as she heard two
vistors talk of making a complaint. They were furious that their son had
found 'his' bed occupied by somebody else when he returned from a weekend at home. It had taken several hours to locate another bed for him and
then it was on another ward.

Alex sympathized but felt helpless. Only the day before she had been
involved in a heated exchange with a senior house officer. He had telephoned
to ask if there was a bed available for a patient requiring urgent admission
and Alex had responded in the negative. When he visited the ward later
he had been furious to find that there were three beds empty. Alex had
explained that they were so short-staffed that these beds could not be
covered; that the beds were only empty until patients returned from home-
leave, but in vain.

'How can they expect us to provide *care*. When the wards are so grotty,
the patients are so ill and so resentful. Half of them are detained against
their will, medicated against their will and just when they reach a state
when we could start to help them they are discharged. The managers say
we have 115 per cent occupancy' she thought, 'but its only numbers to
them. This is what it feels like.'

Alex was due to meet tomorrow with one of the contracts managers
and the directorate business manager. They were to discuss the feasibility
of running one central clinic for depot medication instead of providing
the service in GP surgeries. Alex had suggested that one of the CPNs be
invited, but had been assured that this was only a preliminary meeting
and that the members of the community staff would be included when it
was more appropriate. Alex wondered if the two managers were trying to
avoid the wrath of the CPNs or whether they simply did not know how
upset they would be at yet another impediment to the development of
good working relationships with GPs. Of course they would achieve their
contracted numbers more cheaply. That's what it was all about these days
wasn't it?

How depressing, after pushing so hard for so long to develop new ways
of working, models of care that recognized psychosocial factors as well as
the biomedical, that it all seemed to have been thrown out of the window
with Trust status. Previously the nurses and therapists had had strong professional managers who had fought for those new care models; now they

were in clinical directorates headed by psychiatrists and they were moving backwards again to a model of illness rather than of health.

They had all been hopeful initially that Jane, the old DNS, would be influential as the board nurse director, but in practice her power base had gone and she could only fight a rearguard action. She had, for example, objected to the use of re-admission rates as an outcome measure when it was proposed by the purchasers. She had been seen as old-fashioned at the time but now, as a result of the consultation, people were realizing that re-admission should not be seen as a failure but as appropriate treatment for people in a particular condition or at a particular time.

Perhaps the new arrangements proposed by the purchasers would help change things for the better. She certainly hoped so.

Maria Springstein, an occupational therapist, and Phil Brown, an art therapist, reviewed the hospital's day centre therapy schedule. Phil mentioned how upset some of the patients had been when four of the ten sessions had been cancelled last week: 'And it hasn't been much better for the last 5 or 6 weeks' he said. 'Why don't we publicize a schedule we know we can keep to? Then at least people wouldn't be looking forward to something that doesn't happen.' It was an old conversation and Maria had previously suggested this to the day centre manager, but he hadn't been at all keen, saying he would discuss it with the clinical director. 'After all' he had said, 'it's only because you're acting up as business manager while Mike is away on sick leave and he could be back any day'.

That was partly true thought Maria, but not entirely. They were desperately short of OTs right across the Trust, with one on maternity leave, one on long-term sick leave and two vacant posts they hadn't been able to fill.

Maria had been pleased to be asked to 'act up'. Now that OT career structures had been so foreshortened, she could see she would need to move into general management at some point. It had meant lots of meetings though, that always seemed to take place in prime morning and afternoon slots, so that she had to cancel clinics and centre sessions.

She contrasted this with her husband's experience. He was sales manager with a confectionary company. This week one of his reps was away and he was covering his client list for him. When she had joked that he was acting down while she was acting up, he had muttered something unrepeatable about the public sector!

She thought back to the changes she had seen in her profession since she joined it 7 years ago. They had always been short-staffed she remembered, social services always paid more for their OTs, and it was difficult to recruit. But they hadn't realized then how lucky they were, or how much worse things could become. It wasn't just the loss of the district OT posts, she had never really seen what the district OT *did* anyway, apart from filling in the holiday rotas. But they had had a really dynamic head of the old unit OT service, a head I who had enthused the old unit management team with the potential of OT; and they had worked so hard to develop their services in the community and to prepare for the move of long-stay patients into community homes.

Now the whole service had been dismantled and put into directorates, the head I had become head of therapy services at another Trust and things were falling apart. No-one seemed to value the skills of the OT any more. She thought back to her altercation with Tony Sherrard. She was still cross. What right had he to dismiss her observations and recommendations? If they were both part of a multidisciplinary team, then the team should make decisions. They should strive for consensus. Instead, Tony acted as though decisions were for him to make and the others were only there to advise him.

With such an attitude there was little hope that he would agree to her suggestion that when GPs made referrals, the patient could be seen by any member of the team, who would only refer to a consultant if necessary. She knew it worked well elsewhere and had investigated the assessment skills and procedures of the professionals in the team. There was considerable overlap and it would be straightforward to identify a core assessment, with each profession specifying prompts which should alert the assessor to the need to refer on to another profession or service. She had described the system to Phil before and she mentioned it again. 'Some hope' he said. They agreed to post up a schedule that once again would probably not materialize.

Frances Donovan helped her sister Cathy to gather her things together. Cathy had been told she was well enough to leave and Frances had come to collect her. She recognized the difference in her sister since her admission 10 days ago, and was thankful for it. 'So it's alright 'till the next time' she thought. 'Perhaps now the divorce is through she can accept it.' But she didn't mention Cathy's ex-husband, just in case.

Cathy had had several stays in hospital over the last 15 years. Cathy had been married for 10 years and her husband Tom had been a saint. Eventually though he had had enough. The family had not been surprised when he sought a divorce. Cathy, however, had been devastated, and while the divorce proceedings were taking place, she'd had to be admitted three times in 12 months.

Now that she was well again, Frances could feel sorry for Cathy, for when she was ill anger often took over. She knew Cathy had quite a stormy relationship with her GP and she could understand why. 'What a pity that when she is most in need of help she is at her most aggressive', she thought.

When well Cathy was an articulate, passionate critic of the system and had once been invited to represent users on a planning forum. She had been delighted until she found that she was the only member of the forum expected to turn up for free. She hadn't minded so much about the hospital staff on salaries, but when she found that the GP was being paid to attend, she asked to be paid as well. She had also asked to hold meetings of users, so she could be sure she did represent their views, but had been told this would be too difficult to organize. Eventually, feeling frustrated at her inability to change things for the better, Cathy had resigned. A lot had changed in the health service since then though, and the local branch of the National Schizophrenia Fellowship, to which Cathy's parents belonged, had been consulted over local plans for mental health services.

One of the pleas they had made was for some 'halfway' accommodation, somewhere for people to go when they were not well enough to cope with their own home situation but not ill enough to need admission to hospital. Frances reflected wistfully that perhaps if such accommodation had been available Tom could have managed. The last they had heard was that the health authority didn't think halfway hostels were the answer, that more support in the community was what was needed. 'So much for consultation' the family had said. 'The trouble is that people providing services for people with mental illness don't know what its really like trying to live with them.'

Apparently, there was support for an advocacy scheme though. Frances was glad of that, Cathy had a supportive family but others didn't. Besides, the family couldn't always get staff to explain things to them in terms they understood; perhaps an advocate could. But she had been disappointed when she had mentioned advocacy to one of the ward nurses, whose response was not encouraging: 'Oh someone else telling us how to do our jobs I suppose'.

They were ready to go now, perhaps they wouldn't need to trek to the hospital again for a while. Cathy could have her injection and her blood tests done at the local surgery. The doctors there were a real source of continuity; on the wards there was someone different almost every time, but the GPs were there year in, year out.

At Newtown and Swanning Health Authority, Nigel Hooper, the chief executive, and Brenda Dean, the mental health manager, were having their regular bi-monthly meeting to review progress.

'It's all very well them complaining' said Brenda, 'but people in the Trust have been talking about closing down the long-stay hospital for years and years. It is only our deadline which has prompted any real action. Even now they keep talking about an "evolutionary process"! And I know they don't think our specifications should go into such detail, but if they can't or won't show convincing detail themselves, then they'll have to accept ours.'

'I have heard some mutterings about teaching grandmothers to suck eggs' said Nigel, 'is it because you have asked them to go and look at what Glasgow and Nottingham are doing? Or is it because they resent our use of external consultants to advise us on professional and skill-mix issues?'

'Oh they're very peeved at the latter' replied Brenda, 'but a lot of them were very interested to see the alternative care models we asked them to look at. The psychiatrists are still hopping mad at the decision to commission two acute in-patient facilities, one in each locality. The fact that this was so strongly supported by users and carers cuts no ice with them. They claim that they won't have the access they need to clinical colleagues and they won't be able to work as efficiently. Personally I think they don't like the though of being based in the community and part of the community mental health teams.

'Sometimes I think our major role has been to force the providers to hear what the users are saying to them. It's been difficult to get from the centre of Newtown to the long-stay hospital for at least 15 years. The transport we laid on three times a week has been enormously popular and it costs twopence ha'penny. Why didn't someone think of it before?'

'Are you still having problems convincing them we're serious about mental health?' asked Nigel. 'Although I'm not sure quite what else we could do to convince them.'

'I think they are beginning to believe us' said Brenda. 'What really helped us was when the non-executives all turned up at the consultation meetings. That was really useful, it helped convince the providers we were serious, and the non-execs of the need for improvement. You haven't had any difficulty getting the money ringfenced have you? That must have helped when you met Mark Colbet last week.'

'The trouble is we have such a lot of "living down" to do' replied Nigel. 'I told him it would take a major catastrophe to prevent us spending the extra £1.2 million on mental health again this year and he said he'd met major catastrophes before, the old DHA had one every year in the acute unit just before the end of the financial year!'

Nigel wondered aloud how they could persuade the GPs to take more of an interest. They had both met all the GPs in one locality the day before. When asked what kind of services they wanted, most had insisted on 24-hour crisis support and much more counselling. Of course, most of the mental health problems *they* saw could be helped by counselling. All the difficult cases became the clinical responsibility of the clinicians in the Trust. When Nigel had asked Mark about shared-care possibilities, Mark had been very unenthusiastic about the GPs' lack of interest. 'Chicken and egg of course' mused Nigel. 'With proper discharge planning and meaningful dialogue, they'd become interested; it's only when people are powerless they switch off.'

'Well the CMHTs will help there' said Brenda. 'I don't want to build shared care into the specification. We were over-detailed with the first one and had to admit our mistake and start again; I don't want to make the same mistake twice.'

'Yes, I know we have made mistakes', mused Nigel. 'There are some things we would do differently if we had our time again, but then we were very much feeling our way. Somehow, though, I would have liked us to gain more ownership within the Trust; I wonder how we can try and achieve that now?'

Discussion

Here we have a familiar tale of mistrust and acrimony: between purchasers and providers, between Trust staff and GPs, between professionals and patients, and between staff within the Trust. The purchasers want to gain commitment to their programme of investment and improvement. Instead they have reluctant compliance. *How can the DHA achieve ownership of their change programme within the Trust? How can the acrimony between players be replaced by harmony?*

We came across the contrast between commitment and compliance in Chapter 7, where we saw that imposing a vision results in the latter, whereas finding a vision (developing a shared vision from the personal visions of individuals in the system) is necessary to achieve the former. Can we accuse the health authority in this case of imposing their vision? Is that why they are unable to gain commitment to it?

Surely not. The health authority has gone out of its way to consult with all the relevant individuals and agencies and has held a number of stake-holder conferences to discuss and explain the results of these consultations. In the course of their research, they changed their own views and increased their determination to support mental health. We can hardly accuse them of imposing their vision. Or can we? We also saw in Chapters 6 and 7 that the role of a real manager is to sell problems, not to solve them. Let's think about what that means in a case like this.

The health authority has perceived that there is a problem with mental health services. They want to do something about it and recognize (and that in itself takes maturity and confidence) that other people will know better than they what are the options, and what constitutes best practice. They have therefore consulted all the individuals and agencies involved, and only when they have gathered together this information have they decided what to do. *They* have decided what to do; they have solved the problem. To ensure that they have solved the problem correctly, they have consulted, again before finalizing their plans. Wherever possible they have built into their proposals the wishes of those concerned, but naturally, as these sometimes conflict and finances are limited, they have not been able to accommodate everyone's views. This is as open and genuinely intentioned a problem-solving process as it could possibly be. At the end of the day, however, *they* have solved the problem and they are imposing that solution. They can therefore expect only compliance not commitment.

What would a problem selling approach have looked like? The first stages may have appeared very similar. In these the health authority would start to flesh out, from discussions, what the nature of the problem was. It is a complex problem, however, and this process would have been an iterative one. One in which individuals and groups engaged with the health authority project manager over a period of time, contributing thoughts and experiences, responding to challenges to their own perceptions, seeing the situation from others' perspectives, and gradually building an awareness of the complexity of the system which is achieving such sub-optimal results.

Once the problem has been sold in this way to the participants in the system, then the health authority can use the same methods to encourage them to generate approaches that will help to solve it. Again, engaging with those participants will be necessary, encouraging them to construct solutions, sounding out these ideas with other stakeholders and gradually, iteratively, gaining consensus on a number of changes which contribute to, and together form, a solution. To this course of action there will be genuine commitment.

Now let us consider the second question, the acrimony between professions. There are many reasons for this, including all those causes of misunderstanding and disharmony discussed in Chapter 2. But perhaps the greatest factor here is that no-one is implementing the three fundamental rules for managing people that were described in Chapter 1. Almost no-one in the case study has a clear idea of what is expected of them, certainly not one that has been agreed with others and with the resource allocators. Similarly, most of them feel that they do not have the skills and resources to achieve what they would like, and there are many instances where feedback on performance is simply not given. The results are predictable.

It is possible, as we saw in Chapter 1, for individuals to implement the three rules even in a context where their seniors lack clarity of purpose, but it is very much easier where the organization as a whole has agreed on what is expected of it and has confirmed this remit with other agencies in the local health system. We can see that in this case this has not happened. There is a gap between what the Trust provides and the services offered by GPs that has never been made explicit. The Trust's remit is therefore ambiguous. Within the Trust there has been no formal discussion to develop an admissions policy that is known to all parties. Admission is left to the 'clinical judgement' of the consultant psychiatrists and yet their clinical judgement is that many more clients require in-patient care than there are beds available. Ambiguity again, because the resources available do not match the expectations.

As the restructuring takes place, specialist psychiatric skills will be lost. Is this being harmonized with a change in the requirements of the psychiatric service? The role of clinical director is being interpreted differently by the various post-holders, a sign that it has been inadequately explained. There is also evidence of a lack of the necessary skills (e.g. financial) and that Mark Colbet has given no feedback on her business planning performance to Joy Redlan. Instead he is about to 'restructure' her out of these responsibilities.

On a more operational level, individuals in the multidisciplinary team disagree as to its role and appear to receive no feedback on their performance as a team. Without accord on the former, it is not surprising that they can reach no agreement on how best to use the skills they have, some insisting on a gatekeeping role for the psychiatrists, others wanting a common core assessment.

Maria Springstein's experience of 'acting up' is interesting in that it indicates that in Newtown Trust the managers do not see their role as supporting their frontline staff (as they should), but rather the opposite. Clarifying with Maria her priorities in this temporary role would surely have exposed this topsy-turvy thinking and restored clinical care to where it belonged – that is, as the top priority.

There is a suggestion that one group of staff, the ward nurses, is attempting to introduce reasonable limits, such that within their resources they can provide a satisfactory service. They are closing beds when they do not have the staff to cover them. They fail, however, to negotiate this with other groups (and with the Trust management) and thus make life even more difficult for Trust colleagues.

It looks as though Mark Colbet is proposing to remedy part of this situation by restructuring the organization to put people he favours in the top positions. Among the winners will be the clinical directors who are imposing business plans on their staff. The losers include those who are engaging their staff in the business planning process. We can therefore expect the dissonance and poor performance in this Trust to continue or even worsen.

What could he do instead? First, he needs to clarify the remit of the Trust. He needs to articulate the Trust's vision. In order to do so, he needs to spend time with his staff encouraging them to look beyond the day-to-day difficulties and revisit the ideals that initially drew them into health care, albeit tempering this idealism with an appreciation of certain constraints. When he understands the personal visions of his staff, he will be able to start to engender a Trust-wide sense of purpose that encompasses these. One of the outcomes of such an approach will be that ethical decisions about who should receive treatment, when it is not possible to meet all needs, are based on evidence and are taken by managers and clinicians working together instead of being left, inappropriately, to clinicians alone.

When the Trust's direction is clear, Mark needs to consider all the seven Ss explored in Chapter 4. The numbers, qualifications, motivation and abilities of his *staff*; their clinical, interpersonal, managerial and evaluative *skills*; the *systems* which make the Trust work; the management *style*; the planned actions which constitute a *strategy*; the organization's *cultures*; and the *structure*, which describes who is accountable to whom for what. Moreover, he should probably consider them in that order, decisions about structures coming last. By the time he is ready to announce decisions about structures, he will have been reminded that, as we saw in Chapter 4, there *is* no perfect organizational structure, that all of them have advantages and disadvantages. In this case, a locality structure has a major drawback – the potential loss of specialist skills on the part of the consultant psychiatrists. Ignoring this, or ascribing the opposition of the individuals concerned to base motives, would be irresponsible. Rather, Mark needs to explore with them ways in which this can be avoided or minimized. Similarly, a structure based around professional specialties can introduce difficulties with access and with seamless care across boundaries. Here again these disadvantages need to be recognized and means devised of overcoming them. All the solutions to these problems rest on the existence of goodwill and trust. Given their presence, almost any structure can be made to work. Mark may therefore realize that his energies will be more valuably directed to engendering that goodwill and trust than to poring over alternative organization charts.

The healthcare manager has to balance a triad of needs: those of the patient (people in need of health care), those of the organization (so that the greatest number of healthcare needs can be met) and those of the professionals (whose skills must be developed and maintained if those needs are to be met). In the past, the needs of the professionals and their patients predominated. Since 1990, in the UK, the needs of the organization have taken precedence. Combined with the increasing emphasis on the healthcare needs of populations, which sometimes conflict with those of the individual being seen by a clinician, this has left many HCPs feeling undervalued and undermined. We cannot expect people to be proactive, to behave with generosity and discipline if they are discounted, disbelieved and left out of the decision-making processes.

St. Marks

This case study is rather different from the others in that it describes what many readers will recognize as a particular series of events concerning one hospital. As in the previous cases, however, the people described in it are fictional.

Simon Jones could still hear the protesters as he walked through the arched gateway of St. Marks Hospital, across the courtyard and into the East Wing. The 'Save Marks' campaign team was highly active and mobilized supporters to demonstrate at every opportunity. Simon, a consultant, was, like most of his colleagues, appalled at the suggestion that after several hundreds of years on the same site St. Marks should close. St. Marks! With their reputation and history? Incredulity was the emotion expressed most often when Marks people discussed the possibility, either at work or socially. 'Because that is one of the joys of St. Marks' thought Simon, 'we do all know each other so well, both in the hospital and outside. Oh there are feuds between some individuals but there is a sense, almost of family, of belonging here.' He put that down to the fact that St. Marks normally appointed to senior clinical posts people who were already familiar with the St. Marks way, having spent some time there earlier in their careers. It worked well. St. Marks was able to select from the brightest candidates for the training grades, so the pool from which these senior appointments were made was a highly talented one.

In normal times, dinner parties of senior Marks clinicians were very enjoyable affairs with wide-ranging discussions encompassing the many and varied interests of the diners. Now, however, there was only one topic of conversation. The absurdity of government proposals to close the hospital and merge it with St. Matthews. Generally, the opinion seemed to be that no government would dare to incur the wrath of the country by closing one of its oldest and best-loved institutions. Some individuals remembered patients, famous for one reason or another, who could be expected to have fond memories of St. Marks and lend their support to any anti-closure campaign. Others speculated on the tenacity and courage of the Health Secretary. It was most unlikely, once she realized the strength of feeling against her proposals, that she would stand firm. After all, Marks had a reputation for excellence all over the world. It would be political suicide.

Others reminisced about the number of times the capital's leading teaching hospitals had seen off rationalization threats in the past. Committee after committee had recommended closures or mergers as a result of the capital's declining population base and changing residential and transport patterns. Yet all the hospitals were still there, centres of excellence, a resource for the nation as a whole. As a result, there were Marks people in consultant positions all around the country; and in nursing, and the PAMs too, there was a pattern of employment in the capital in the early years, followed by career grade posts elsewhere.

There was a responsibility, then, which St. Marks felt acutely, to maintain excellence, to develop and promote best practice. Yes it meant that their costs were higher than in the DGHs in the suburbs, but it was ridiculous to think only in financial terms. It was like comparing apples with pears. The quality of care at St. Marks was so superior to that of the standard DGH that if, in the new 'market', money really followed patients, then the hospital would do very well as a result of its popularity.

On the whole, the St. Marks management had, over the years, been supportive of its clinicians and of their striving for excellence. Most of the time they had had a doctor in the top job and that had ensured that decisions about expenditure were taken on their clinical merit. Indeed, when Simon compared St. Marks' facilities with those at St. Matthews, the former were, in most cases, much superior. There were problems of course. As the hospital had grown it had taken over all sorts of proximal buildings, so both staff and patients had to manoeuvre in and out of doors, along corridors (used as waiting areas often) and into the open air between buildings as they made their way from one department to another.

Simon had never had a great deal to do with his colleagues at St. Matthews. Yet now, if Marks were really to close, he would be moving in with them. Goodness knows where. There had been meetings to discuss things like office space but never at times when he could easily attend. Anyway, the important priority was his patients, not some hypothetical argument about rooms.

On opening his post, Simon was irritated to find yet another request for activity information from the contracts department. Didn't they realize how busy he was? Surely that was their job. He hadn't come into medicine to collect statistics. They were always talking about inefficiency and waste, and surely it was highly inefficient to use expensive clinical time for number crunching exercises like this. Besides, he wouldn't be as skilled at it as they were. Far better for everyone to do what they do best. He noted the threat contained in the letter that without this information the contracting team would find it even more difficult to negotiate contracts. 'They do cry wolf' he thought, 'they've been saying for months that they can't persuade out-of-London purchasers to commit to contracts, because the prices are cheaper locally; but that's ridiculous. Oh, the managers and the accountants may not understand the clinical arguments, but the GPs (and the public) won't let them take away their right to refer to us.'

Ever since Simon could remember, St. Marks had been told it must cut its costs, that there was a financial crisis, that there would have to be emergency cutbacks (vacancy freezes, etc.) to get them through to the end of the financial year. And yet it had never come to that. The money had always been found from somewhere. Still, if they did want him to cut costs he could always cut out the work he did over at North End Hospital. North End was a newly built hospital, about 10-years-old with further building phases yet to be completed. Medical staff at St. Marks provided services there, ensuring high-calibre input into a hospital in a deprived area without a reputation of its own, that would otherwise find it difficult to attract good staff. It took time getting there, meant he wasn't available for Marks patients and he wouldn't be sorry to give it up.

Some of his colleagues had tentatively suggested, when North End was built, that Marks should move. They proposed making a case for designing North End as a teaching hospital and following the example of the Royal Free, which had moved from outdated premises on a cramped site in Grays Inn Road to purpose-built accommodation in Hampstead. Naturally the suggestion had been withdrawn. St. Marks had been on this site for nearly a millennium. 'And no doubt it will be for another millennium' thought Simon. 'That's the pity of all this, that it takes time away from patient care. That's what we all care about. We just want to continue to provide the best care possible for our patients and this closure debate takes our time and energy and deflects us from why we are here.'

If Simon had used the analytical process described in Chapter 4, he would have reasoned as follows:

St. Marks' mission

To continue the very long tradition of St. Marks being a national and international centre of clinical excellence.

Internal analysis

Strategy

To invest in the resources (people and technology) which will allow St. Marks to offer the high-quality services needed by its national and international patients, and to take service decisions independently of those concerning finance.

Staff and skills

High-calibre, highly motivated staff, attracted by the hospital's reputation. Senior appointments usually made from a pool of candidates who have significant experience of working at St. Marks. In this way, standards are consistently maintained.

Management structure and management style

The management team is medically led and the organizational structure is one of clinical directorates led by consultant staff. Nursing, although nominally decentralized into these directorates, remains professionally centred on a charismatic and clinically sound director of nursing who has worked at St. Marks for many years and has known many of the consultants from when they were juniors. In this way, clinical issues receive the priority required at all levels within the hospital, including the top management team.

Premises are a problem. St. Marks has grown and grown and added and converted buildings wherever it can. This does mean that both patients and staff have complicated journeys between buildings, which is obviously not ideal.

Systems

A plethora of new systems is now in place to deal with the 'internal market'. Fortunately, individuals running these are kept separate from the clinical focus of the hospital. However, they do request more and more information about activity levels, which puts pressure on clinical staff already hard-pressed with patient commitments.

Culture

The St. Marks historical tradition of service to the suffering strongly influences current day clinicians who share a belief in the importance of their work to the health of patients across the country and throughout the world.

External analysis

Political factors

The government wants to save money and the NHS is being hit. There is even the possibility that the Secretary of State for Health wants to close one or more London teaching hospitals. Let her try. We have seen off numbers of her predecessors. She won't want to be seen to take such a decision, the voters of the country wouldn't stand for it, not a hospital that has been here as long as we have.

The purchaser–provider split has been a nuisance; we have to waste a lot of time collecting information. Some purchaser health authorities are threatening to give contracts to their local DGHs but their GPs and local populations will not let them do so. They will want to come to a national centre of excellence. Although individual purchaser health authorities may want to buy secondary care locally, they will realize that unless they support us they will have nowhere to send those complex tertiary care cases.

Economic factors

Public sector finances are being squeezed, and to the extent that it affects us we must fight back; we cannot jeopardize the clinical care of our patients. On the whole, though, it affects other people and organizations much more than us. You cannot provide care of this quality without it costing money and people come to St. Marks to receive this quality of care.

Sociological factors

Our local resident population base has been steadily declining for nearly 100 years now; however, our patients come from all over the country (and indeed the world) and so that is not particularly relevant.

Technology

New developments have enabled us to be so much more effective clinically. We are fortunate here in having managers who understand the need for investing in technological solutions to clinical problems.

Preserving and developing St. Marks as a resource to the nation:

Its strengths

St. Marks is recognized nationally and internationally as a London teaching hospital of great clinical skill. It recruits and develops the brightest clinical staff and supports them with appropriate technology. The culture is of insisting on the highest clinical quality. Its reputation and its hundreds of years of history make it invulnerable. It will continue to make a major contribution to teaching and to the development of best clinical practice well into the next millennium.

Its weaknesses

- Premises are a problem, space is limited.
- Our contracting staff are not succeeding in bringing in all the contracts

we ought to have, but this is a short-term problem while the new purchaser health authorities are flexing their muscles.
• Other services and other local hospitals keep making demands on our
  resources. We may have to stop providing medical cover if our own services become further squeezed.

Opportunities

If the reforms do mean that 'money will follow patients', then ultimately
St. Marks will be even more successful as a result of our popularity.

Threats

The new purchasers are hostile to St. Marks but they will have to listen
to GPs, the public and politicians. Politicians want to save money and
close a London hospital, but they are dependent on voter goodwill and the
public will support us.

The critical issue that we need to address is therefore

St. Marks has an excellent reputation nationally and internationally, which
in the longer term will ensure its continued success. There is a short-term
problem about contract income being insufficient, but no politician could
be seen to allow the closure of such a renowned institution as St. Marks,
so we will have to be bailed out somehow.

Objective

St. Marks overcomes its temporary financial shortfall.

Options

1 Ask Region to 'manage the market' and require purchasers to purchase
  from St. Marks.
2 Remind purchasers of the reputation and prestige of St. Marks.
3 Make sure prices to captive purchasers are high enough to cover all our
  costs.
4 Make sure politicians ensure we are supported financially by mounting
  a national campaign to save St. Marks, using as many high-profile ex-
  patients as we can.
5 Reduce costs where possible by removing our staff from other local hospitals and services.

Themes

Devote our energies (in the short term) to a campaign, using whatever
means at our disposal, to make it impossible for any individual or group

to allow St. Marks to close because of the damage it would do to their reputation(s).

Helen Murphy encountered the same group of protestors. On previous occasions she had tried to debate with them the issues, asking them if they didn't want the good community services that could be provided if St. Marks was not leeching money out of the rest of the local health system. Today though she just walked past.

As chief executive of the Central Capital Health Authority, she was responsible for purchasing health care to meet the needs of a million residents. Many of her residents were among the most socio-economically deprived in the country; on many measures, the boroughs comprising Central's 'patch' demonstrated this: lowest per capita income; lowest car ownership; highest number of occupants per dwelling. Many of her residents had lived in England for only one, two or three generations. For many, English was not their first language and their sense of history encompassed other continents, traditions and philosophies. And yet, Helen chuckled to herself, the Marks campaigners were trying to influence her decision by appealing to that sense of history, emphasizing the centuries of health care and healing on the site of St. Marks. 'In any other field' thought Helen, 'we would be extremely suspicious of any argument that was based on the fact that a facility happened to have remained on the same site for nearly a millennium. There is absolutely no comparison between the way of life, the ways of thinking, the kinds or patterns of health and health care, *anything*, between then and now. Is that really the best they can do?'

She tried to master her irritation at the campaign and ensure that her decisions were based on logic rather than emotion. They aren't helping their cause though, she reflected, by insulting and offending (as they do) the people in whose hands decisions lie. They just don't get it. They don't understand that its not the government that's endangering St. Marks, its the market. At the moment the government is protecting St. Marks. Without that protection it would have gone under by now. The people they should be appealing to (not insulting) are me and my colleagues, the purchasers. Instead, whenever we ask for information to justify their inflated prices, we are met with unquantified, unsubstantiated assertions about case mix and quality of care. And their track record on keeping within a budget is so dreadful that it is difficult to have any confidence in their ability to deliver to contract anyway.

Helen didn't doubt that there were many talented clinicians at St. Marks: 'perhaps not as good as they think they are (they didn't score very highly in that research ratings exercise for example, in spite of claiming to be a centre of research excellence), but still a very able bunch whom the NHS cannot afford to lose'. Inevitably, some would go rather than merge their services with St. Matthews, but she hoped most would stay. 'They might even find being part of a well-managed organization congenial. If they had become familiar with making a fully thought-through case for every investment they made in clinical technology, or new clinical staff, then they would be much better prepared for the post-reform world. Instead, they've never really had to account for their use of resources and, not surprisingly, they are now finding it an anathema. They've been so protected and isol-ated in their Marks time warp they haven't realized the world has moved on. We don't accept any more that "doctor knows best", either as indi-vidual patients or as taxpayers.'

There were other factors in Central's wish to merge St. Marks and St. Matthews and eventually to locate them both on the Matthews site. Ac-commodation was a major one. The Marks site was tiny and with its listed buildings any large-scale redevelopment programme was so constrained as to be virtually impossible. St. Matthews, on the other hand, although cur-rently very run-down, had a large site, which lent itself to redevelopment schemes.

Access was another. With low levels of car ownership among Central's residents, services must be provided as locally as possible. Marks was right at the edge of Central's patch, surrounded by businesses, whereas St. Matthews was in a densely populated area and much closer to the heart of Central's area.

North End was well placed and its future was secure; indeed, Helen was optimistic that it could be considerably enhanced, both in size and reputa-tion. What an exciting place that could be, Helen thought. But what was the latest she had heard? The Marks consultants were proposing to sever links with it? Yet more evidence of their inability to avoid cutting off a nose to spite the face.

Central's share of the Marks activity had risen since the introduction of the internal market from 30–40 to 50 per cent. This was a result of the decisions made by purchasers further afield to commission services locally. Helen sympathized. There were excellent clinicians in the 'outer ring' hos-pitals, many of them Marks-trained, who could offer services just as good for many patients. Yet there were patients who still needed the tertiary care expertise of the big teaching hospitals and, knowing this, many of those purchasers may have supported Marks if only they had been asked to do so. But instead of a request for help, they had been on the receiving end of arrogance, complacency, hostility and aggression. 'Oh well, what do you expect?' Helen had asked them, 'you know the old joke: How can you tell a Marks man? You can't tell him anything'. But its even worse than that, she thought, its not just that they won't be told, they don't *notice* what is going on around them. I have never come across a place where the outside world has so little impact. They keep up with clinical developments but little else. They really believe that they are invulnerable. They are wrong.

The mission of the Central Capital Health Authority (CCHA) is: to meet as many of the health needs of our culturally diverse residents as is pos-sible within the resources provided. The CCHA has to decide where to purchase the secondary and tertiary care its residents will need, but within a context of improving primary and community services which have historically been underdeveloped, partly as a result of the heavy resource use of St. Marks. They perceive the situation very differently from their colleagues at St. Marks. It is not in their remit to offer strategic advice to St. Marks but had they done so their recommendations would have been based on the following analysis.

Internal analysis

Strategy

To invest in high-quality services to retain its reputation as a national centre of excellence. To take service decisions independently of decisions concerning finance and of those concerned with meeting the health needs of a local population.

Staff and skills

High-calibre staff, with good (and in some cases excellent) clinical skills but a tendency towards arrogance and complacency.

Structure and management style

The medical leadership and 'group-think' of the decision-makers mitigates against financial control and St. Marks is a constant drain on other local providers who frequently bail it out at the end of the financial year.

Systems

St. Marks simply has not grasped the importance of the purchaser–provider split. They assume that money (in whatever quantities they choose to seek) will follow 'their' patients as though they have proprietary rights on these people. What is more, they respond aggressively to any requests for information and cannot justify the price differential between their services and those of other local providers.

Culture

'How can you tell a St. Marks man? You can't tell him anything!' Arrogance, complacency, self-congratulation.

External analysis

Politics

The London teaching hospitals have seen off many governmental attempts to rationalize them over the years. However, there is now a difference, and a monumental one at that. It is no longer a government decision about whether hospitals remain open or close but a market one. Alright it is a quasi-market, but such a decision will now be taken by purchaser health authorities and unless they can be convinced of the value of services offered, they will not purchase. A secretary of state may choose to step in to *save* a hospital, but it would not be *her* decision if one were to close.

This dramatically changes the nature of the audience to whom St. Marks must appeal. It must now justify its high costs to us and other local purchasers who will want evidence rather than rhetoric and will rely on information rather than tradition.

Economics

Many DGHs now have highly skilled consultants (some of them Marks-trained) who have chosen to leave behind the hidebound complacency of the major teaching hospitals. They are offering services very similar to those at St. Marks but very much cheaper. Purchasers do need to support excellent tertiary care centres but not necessarily as many as there are inner-London teaching hospitals. Many would welcome the opportunity to develop supra-district specialties locally.

Social factors

The people living within the district are culturally diverse, many have lived in the UK for only one or two generations. The hundreds of years of tradition at St. Marks is of little interest to them. Very many are economically deprived and do not own their own means of transport, so they do not wish to travel long distances to attend a hospital.

To help compensate for their socio-economic deprivation, they need better primary health care and community-based services. Only if these are available can the hospital length-of-stay figures fall to national norms. Instead of being better than the national average, these community-based services are worse and completely inadequate for the task. One of the reasons they are so poor is that they have frequently had to support St. Marks. St. Marks is right at one edge of this district, with another major teaching hospital (St. Matthews) more centrally located.

When St. Marks comes to contract for funding from DHAs:

Its strengths

Expertise in complex cases, although they are unable to provide evidence of outcomes or other aspects of quality of care.

Its weaknesses

- High costs.
- 'Take it or leave it' attitude to purchasers.

- A history of poor financial control leading to a lack of credibility about financial and activity data, and to a lack of support from other local health services.
- A reliance on politicking and outdated assumptions of invulnerability, offending decision-makers.
- Cutting back services to local hospitals with lower prices again reduces local support.
- Small, protected site unsuitable for development.

Opportunities

- Many DHAs would welcome the opportunity to develop excellent services locally. The local DGH St. Marks is withdrawing from (North End) would make a good base for such a development.
- Purchasers do not yet have the skills to make purchasing decisions that cannot be challenged. While they do not (as yet) have confidence in their role, approaches demonstrating that providers understand their problems and would like to work with them to help achieve it are much more likely to be successful than aggressive or hostile responses.
- If we, the purchasers, do decide that we will not support an independent St. Marks, but will only purchase from a merged Trust combining St. Matthews and St. Marks, then we will not intervene any further to say how the merger is managed. In such a scenario, if the Marks people really are as clinically superior as they claim, they will be able to negotiate favourable terms and conditions. If they chose to see it that way, they could 'take over' St. Matthews.

Threats

DHAs are looking for good prices, short travelling distances and evidence of quality. Where we do not find them, we will not purchase. No hospital can any longer rest on history and tradition if it cannot persuade us and other DHAs to buy its services.

The critical issues it needs to address

St. Marks is further away, more expensive and more aggressive than its competitors. It is therefore failing to persuade DHAs to purchase its services.

Options

1 Eat humble pie and ask DHAs for help.
2 Find out what DHAs want and focus efforts on trying to provide that.
3 Seek support from other local health organizations.
4 Learn from what St. Matthews and North End are doing – they *are* securing contracts.

5 Accept that St. Marks will have to do things differently.
6 Read the writing on the wall.
7 See any change short of closure as a reprieve and an opportunity, something to work positively towards.

Theme

Challenge your own thinking. Accept that the world has changed. Ask for help in directing your talents to creating an organization which meets needs that are defined elsewhere.

Discussion

Imagine you have just taken over as chief executive of St. Marks. What would your priorities be? What part should non-executive directors play in enabling you to be effective?

In order to answer these questions, we must re-analyse the situation from the perspective of an enlightened but searching chief executive, one whose *aim* is to maintain and develop St. Marks' ability to contribute to the health care of the nation, thus perpetuating its long tradition.

The strengths of St. Marks

1 *The calibre of clinical staff* (i.e. gifted staff are recruited and retained)

So *what?*   Good clinical care offered.
So *what?*   Good clinical outcomes.*
So *what?*   Patients and their medical advisers want to use St. Marks rather than local DGHs.
So *what?*   St. Marks will have no difficulty persuading DHAs to place contracts.

Why?   Reputation and ethos.

Until the purchaser–provider split, the 'so what?' questioning need have continued no further than the asterisk. As soon as the answer related to improved outcomes or to decreased costs, the feature could have been accepted as indeed a strength. This is no longer the case, and the questioning now needs to yield an answer that refers to contracts. This highlights one of the reasons for the disparate views of St. Marks. The staff at St. Marks have not appreciated the need to continue beyond the asterisk. If they had, they would have been able to perform a simple 'reality check' by looking at the number of contracts placed and using the answer to challenge their thinking.

The cause of this feature is St. Marks' reputation. This is distinct from premises, site or organizational bureaucracy and must not be confused with them.

2 *Culture of clinical excellence*

So what?	(a)	Clinical priorities have taken precedence over financial considerations.
So what?		The thinking of clinicians has not been challenged by the need to present a 'business case'.
So what?		The 'excellence' may not be being maintained.
So what?	(b)	Costs have not been contained.
So what?		Prices are high.
So what?		Where purchasers have a choice they are placing contracts elsewhere.
Why?		A particular set of beliefs have gone unchallenged.
Why?		Group-think.
Why?		Lack of new blood; senior appointments always to people with St. Marks experience.
Why?		Pride (arrogance?), a belief in the superiority of St. Marks and its ways.

To many HCPs feeling beleaguered and embattled, the idea of an organization which puts clinical excellence before all else will seem attractive. It must surely be a strength, something that will help the organization achieve its mission. And yet it is not, as we can see when we continue the 'so what?' questioning. This is an example of a 'system' in which a laudable aim itself limits its achievement.[1] As a result of aiming for clinical excellence, the excellence initially fostered will eventually be decreased because of the lack of challenge to the thinking of the clinicians.

This feature is a result of the group-think engaged in by the staff at St. Marks. Group-think and its causes are described in Chapter 2, as are the measures that can be taken to prevent it. Seeking the views of outsiders is one of them. Actively recruiting new blood is another. St. Marks has done the opposite. How can you tell a group-think victim? You can't tell him anything.

So far, the only strength is the reputation of St. Marks to encourage talented clinicians to join and stay; and this in itself is not enough, as the contract picture demonstrates.

Weaknesses

1 *The premises are inappropriate for a hi-tech specialist hospital*

So what?	(a)	Staff and patients waste time making their way between buildings.
So what?		Adverse impact on cost and quality.
So what?		If purchasers have a choice they will place contracts elsewhere.

So what? (b) Future growth or changes in response to technological or other innovations seriously impeded.

So what? Ability to offer quality care in the future will be constrained.

Why? Adherence to one particular site in an expensive and architecturally protected area.

HCPs are innovative and dedicated and will use every nook and cranny available if it is necessary. Sometimes this prevents them from stopping to consider whether it *is* necessary, whether a move to another site would overcome many of their problems. An emotional attachment to a tradition on a particular piece of ground should not get in the way of the commitment of HCPs to provide excellent health care to those who need it. Articulating this vision and keeping it in mind will help prevent people confusing one possible set of means with the ends.

2 *Contracting staff not delivering contracts*

So what? St. Marks loses its right to take responsibility for its own destiny.

Why? (1) High prices, limited information, lack of ability to justify price differentials, take it or leave it attitude.

Why? Failure to recognize realities of market, and failure to identify decision-makers and their priorities and concerns.

Why? Belief in invulnerability, complacency, self-congratulation.

Why? (2) Lack of credibility over financial control, leading to lack of confidence in ability to deliver to contract.

Why? Financial and clinical decisions kept separate.

Why? Belief in invulnerability and one law for St. Marks and another for the rest.

Why? Group-think, belief in moral superiority.

Why? Lack of challenge to thinking.

Opportunities

1 *Purchasing, at the time of the case study, is a new activity and purchasers have not yet developed the relevant skills or confidence*

So what? While they will respond defensively to hostility (a generous response requires confidence), purchasers are likely to respond favourably to providers who admit to finding the post-reform world difficult, and who ask for help or for a collaborative approach.

Therefore? St. Marks must find out a lot more about its major purchasers, their concerns, interests, priorities and expectations.

2 *North End and St. Matthews are both succeeding in negotiating contracts*

So what? Both are on sites suitable for development.

Therefore? St. Marks should investigate the feasibility of relocating, or of becoming the dominant force within a new merged organization.

3 *National concern about the future of St. Marks*

So what?   If harnessed to a cause that *can be supported* by major players (even if it is not their preferred option), then this concern may well carry the day.

Therefore?   Major players must be identified and their positions ascertained, while campaigns are carefully planned and kept in control.

Threats

1 *The world really has changed. The government no longer makes decisions about the shape of healthcare provision locally; it is the purchaser health authorities*

So what?   They want to make their resources stretch as far as possible and to know just what they are getting for their money. They are also concerned about quality, one aspect of which is access.

Therefore?   St. Marks must be able to justify its prices, provide reliable activity information and deliver to contract.

2 *The resident population surrounding St. Marks has decreased to the point where it is almost non-existent*

So what?   Only a small group of residents has easy access. The access of other Londoners to St. Marks is more difficult (or at any rate no easier) than that to neighbouring hospitals, including North End and St. Matthews.

Therefore?   The feasibility of relocation must be considered.

3 *Other hospitals (North End) increasing their demands on clinical staff*

So what?   Shift in clinical time from St. Marks to North End.

So what?   North End has the contracts and can offer security to clinical staff that they will lose at St. Marks.

Why?   North End have different case mix and much cheaper site and can offer lower prices.

Therefore?   There is an *opportunity* for relocation, but St. Marks must repair its relationship with North End.

The critical issues if St. Marks is to 'maintain and develop its ability to contribute to the health care of the nation' are, therefore:

1 *Contracts.* St. Marks is not securing the contracts it needs to stay in business. Expressing this more fully and precisely:

Who: For whom is this a problem? For *all* St. Marks staff (and not just a small contracting department).

When: When is it a problem? *Now.*

Where: Where is it a problem? With a large number of purchaser health authorities.

What: Exactly what is the problem? That purchasers are refusing to buy at current Marks prices and information levels.

How: How is it a problem? Unless purchasers buy, St. Marks will lose its right to self-determination.

Why: Why has the problem arisen? The staff at St. Marks do not realize that they must *sell* themselves and their services to purchasers in order to secure contracts.

2 *Location.* The Marks site is suboptimal now and, more importantly, offers no scope for expansion; there is no resident population for whom access is easy and therefore the major purchaser is favouring other providers. Other sites (North End, St. Matthews) have potential.

Who: Staff, patients, purchasers and Central's residents.

When: Already, but even more so in the future.

What: The site is the wrong size, has the wrong buildings and is in the wrong place.

How: Both access and expansion are difficult.

Why: Historical accident combined with sentiment and nostalgia.

3 *Group-think.* At the heart of many of St. Marks' problems is the mindset of its staff. This is limiting their ability to excel clinically, determining their hostile, offensive stance with purchasers, preventing them from identifying the needs of their customers and rendering their national campaign counterproductive.

Who: Senior clinical staff as opinion-formers, but all-pervasive.

When: Now and for some considerable time past.

Where: Throughout St. Marks.

What: Staff are self-congratulatory and place the blame for any difficulties elsewhere.

How: The St. Marks mental model of the world differs from reality in crucial respects.

Why: Lack of challenge to prevailing beliefs.

4 *Reputation.* Both the cause and effect of St. Marks' ability to recruit talented staff is its reputation as a centre of excellence with a venerable historical tradition. This reputation must be maintained.

Who: Actual and potential staff.

When: In the future.

Where: Wherever St. Marks is sited.

What: The tradition of selfless and excellent care must be maintained and developed and associated with the St. Marks name even if the location of the care is moved.

How: The tradition is a potent motivator and symbol of the best in professional care. Its loss would diminish the NHS.

Why: The tradition has been associated with one particular site, and site and tradition are now confused in the minds of some staff and supporters.

Objectives

As discussed in Chapter 4, objectives can now be set for each of these criteria. If St. Marks were to address these issues effectively, it would:

1 Work harmoniously with purchaser health authorities and secure the contracts it needs.
2 Operate from a site(s) that allows excellent service and future development.
3 Be staffed by people who are proactive, generous and disciplined.
4 Deserve a reputation as prestigious for the next X00 years as it has earned over the last.

Options

To make progress towards these four objectives the chief executive could pursue a number of options:

Objective 1: Work harmoniously with the purchaser health authorities and secure the contracts needed
1.1 Identify interests, concerns, expectations and priorities of purchasers – personally, but encourage staff to do the same.
1.2 Ask purchasers for help, preferably nicely (persuade staff that if they cannot say something nice, they must not say anything at all).
1.3 Behave generously towards purchasers, recognize their lack of confidence in their role and the behaviours this may give rise to.
1.4 *Sell* the problem to opinion-formers among the staff (certainly to senior clinical staff). Persuade them of the scale and nature of the problem but also of its validity. In other words, do not stand behind a bogeyman and place the blame with others.
1.5 Persuade staff to turn their enormous talents to solving the problem. Resist the temptation to solve it for them; in spite of the need for speed this is essential, given that the problem is rooted in shared beliefs.
1.6 Restrain the language of supporters and ensure it does not offend key decision-makers.

Objective 2: Operate from a site that allows excellent service and future development
2.1 Explore the possibility of support from Central Capital Health Authority for relocation.

2.2 Along with opinion-formers on the staff, investigate the implications of relocation to the North End or St. Matthews sites, keeping minds open by tailoring arguments to meet individual concerns.

2.3 Ascertain views of region and Department of Health.

2.4 Discuss relocation with North End and St. Matthews and encourage staff to do the same.

2.5 Explore existence of other possible locations with other purchasers.

2.6 Understand the ethos and tradition of St. Marks and persuade staff that it is this which must be perpetuated, not its site.

2.7 Find out from staff, ex-staff and patients which parts of the current site are most dear to the St. Marks tradition and investigate ways in which these could be retained.

Objective 3: Be staffed by people who are proactive, generous and disciplined

3.1 Challenge any victim language, any placing of blame, any ungenerous or undisciplined behaviour whenever it occurs.

3.2 Assess the maturity of staff members and devise individual development programmes for all opinion-formers.

3.3 Debate widely within St. Marks the phenomenon of group-think, so that people have a common understanding and vocabulary even if they reject its relevance.

3.4 Recruit new blood at all levels and support the individuals recruited.

3.5 Expose staff to the views of outsiders: invite outsiders to debate their views and encourage staff to develop links with colleagues in other parts of the health system.

3.6 Identify individuals able and willing to adopt devils advocacy roles within decision-making teams. Brief and support them.

3.7 Model the behaviours and attitudes you want to see in your staff.

3.8 Recognize the enormous personal effort required of you in mastering your own feelings and being able to 'expect the best' of your staff, especially in the early stages while they are still immature, blaming and vitriolic.

Objective 4: Deserve a reputation as prestigious for the next X00 years as St. Marks has earned over the last

4.1 Persuade staff to clarify and articulate the nature of the St. Marks tradition.

4.2 With key staff explore aspects of health care for which a centre of excellence is needed.

4.3 Assess realistically the talents of the staff of St. Marks and their potential to contribute to health care.

4.4 Work with trustees, staff and ex-staff around the country to develop a vision of St. Marks' contribution to the nation's health care to take it into the next millennium.

4.5 Foster an enthusiasm for the spirit rather than the site of St. Marks.

4.6 Expose St. Marks' staff to the views of other players in the health system.

Themes

These actions can be grouped into three major themes, which should be the priorities of the chief executive:

1 Work with other players and not against them.
2 Understand St. Marks' staff well enough to be able to sell them the problems.
3 Personal mastery – bring to bear the work and courage needed to behave with generosity and discipline.

---

1   Work with other players

1.1 Identify interests, concerns, expectations and priorities of purchasers – personally, but encourage staff to do the same.
1.2 Ask purchasers for help, preferably nicely (persuade staff that if they cannot say something nice, they must not say anything at all).
1.3 Behave generously towards purchasers, recognize their lack of confidence in their role and the behaviours this may give rise to.
1.6 Restrain the language of supporters and ensure it does not offend key decision-makers.
2.1 Explore the possibility of support from Central Capital Health Authority for relocation.
2.3 Ascertain views of region and Department of Health.
2.4 Discuss relocation with North End and St. Matthews and encourage staff to do the same.
2.5 Explore existence of other possible locations with other purchasers.
3.5 Expose staff to the views of outsiders: invite outsiders to debate their views and encourage staff to develop links with colleagues in other parts of the health system.
4.2 With key staff explore aspects of health care for which a centre of excellence is needed.
4.4 Work with trustees, staff and ex-staff around the country to develop a vision of St. Marks' contribution to the nation's health care to take it into the next millennium.
4.6 Expose St. Marks' staff to the views of other players in the health system.

---

2   Understand and sell

1.4 *Sell* the problem to opinion-formers among the staff (certainly to senior clinical staff). Persuade them of the scale and nature of the problem but also of its validity. In other words, do not stand behind a bogeyman and place the blame with others.
1.5 Persuade staff to turn their enormous talents to solving the problem. Resist the temptation to solve it for them.

2.2 Along with opinion-formers on the staff, investigate the implications of relocation to the North End or St. Matthews sites, keeping minds open by tailoring arguments to meet individual concerns.

2.6 Understand the ethos and tradition of St. Marks and persuade staff that it is this which must be perpetuated, not its site.

2.7 Find out from staff, ex-staff and patients which parts of the current site are most dear to the St. Marks tradition and investigate ways in which these could be retained.

3.2 Assess the maturity of staff members and devise individual development programmes for all opinion-formers.

3.3 Debate widely within St. Marks the phenomenon of group-think, so that people have a common understanding and vocabulary even if they reject its relevance.

3.4 Recruit new blood at all levels and support the individuals recruited.

3.6 Identify individuals able and willing to adopt devils advocacy roles within decision-making teams. Brief and support them.

4.1 Persuade staff to clarify and articulate the nature of the St. Marks tradition.

4.2 With key staff explore aspects of health care for which a centre of excellence is needed.

4.3 Assess realistically the talents of the staff of St. Marks and their potential to contribute to health care.

4.5 Foster an enthusiasm for the spirit rather than the site of St. Marks.

---

3 Mastery

1.3 Behave generously towards purchasers, recognize their lack of confidence in their role and the behaviours this may give rise to.

1.5 Persuade staff to turn their enormous talents to solving the problem. Resist the temptation to solve it for them.

2.6 Understand the ethos and tradition of St. Marks and persuade staff that it is this which must be perpetuated, not its site.

3.1 Challenge any victim language, any placing of blame, any ungenerous or undisciplined behaviour whenever it occurs.

3.2 Assess the maturity of staff members and devise individual development programmes for all opinion-formers.

3.3 Debate widely within St. Marks the phenomenon of group-think, so that people have a common understanding and vocabulary even if they reject its relevance.

3.7 Model the behaviours and attitudes you want to see in your staff.

3.8 Recognize the enormous personal effort required of you in mastering your own feelings and being able to 'expect the best' of your staff, especially in the early stages while they are still immature, blaming, and vitriolic.

4.1 Persuade staff to clarify and articulate the nature of the St. Marks tradition.

4.3 Assess realistically the talents of the staff of St. Marks and their potential to contribute to health care.

These three themes must now drive the day-to-day actions of the chief executive. They must be the criteria against which he makes all major decisions. They must guide how he spends his own time and the direction he gives to others.

The generosity and discipline needed by the chief executive will not be easy to sustain, especially in the face of the childish or malicious behaviour that can be expected until some of the measures have borne fruit. It can be superficially attractive in such circumstances to 'go native' and adopt the mindset of reactive victim in which his staff are so comfortably ensconced. One of the most important roles of non-executive chairs and directors is to prevent this happening. To offer the supportive challenge and challenging support that allows the *real manager* to refuel their reserves of generosity and discipline.

Generosity

- Choosing to care (to engage in acts of work and/or courage to nurture another's growth – Chapter 1).
- Choosing to meet hostility, aggression and self-congratulation with compassion rather than fear (it is fear which leads to our own anger – Chapter 6).
- Choosing to include and value rather than exclude and compare (Chapter 2).
- Choosing to expect the best (Chapter 2).
- Choosing not to allow self-image to be shaped by the ungenerous (Chapter 6).

Discipline

- Acceptance of responsibility (if I have a problem only I can solve it – Chapter 6).
- Dedication to reality (my model of the world must be constantly challenged if it is to be a useful representation of reality – Chapter 6).
- Delaying of gratification (undertake unpleasant activities first, in the widest sense – Chapter 6).
- Balancing (in order to strike the many balances required of us our judgement must be deployed more frequently than our emotions – Chapter 6).

The story of St. Marks shows what happens when generosity and discipline are absent. It is an extreme case, but their absence must be addressed whenever it becomes evident. Generosity is inclusive not exclusive; discipline includes a preparedness to challenge mental models. So whenever nurses demand that nurses can only properly be trained by other nurses, when doctors taking on management roles patronize an association exclusively for 'medical managers', when managers gravitate towards managerial networks and join organizations dominated by ex-administrators, they must be questioned. Not dictated to, not pandered to, but challenged to examine the reasoning and feelings which lead them to want to do so.

Every time we fail to challenge we collude. Yet when confronted with ungenerous or undisciplined behaviour, we find it easier (although more complicated) to analyse it, or to introduce a new communications strategy, or to restructure certain people out of the organization (or out of reporting to us!), or to design a different reward system, than to care for them enough to say 'that response doesn't help, I expect better from you'. Simple, but very hard.

What I hope these case studies have shown more than anything else is that when staff and organizations are not *really* managed, then people get badly hurt. When, at the university, we run sessions around case studies like these and invite patients, carers and professionals to describe and discuss their own experiences, their stories can be heart-rending. Sometimes the problem is a lack of resources. Mostly it is not. Mostly it is the attitudes and behaviours of HCPs. Thoughtlessness resulting from a greater concern for their own needs than for those of their patients. Failure to take responsibility because they are being reactive and dependent. Professional preciousness or group-think where they see only the tag someone is wearing and cannot hear their arguments, their suggestions for other ways of doing things.

Of course HCPs hurt patients only because they are themselves hurting. Highly skilled, committed people feel angry, frustrated and helpless. They don't have to. Not if they are *really* managed. Not if they (you) become *real* managers. Introducing *real* management matters, and it is up to you to do it.

9 Conclusions

In this book I have tried to persuade you of the importance of the 'simple hard' aspects of management and to differentiate between these and the 'complicated easy'. Both are necessary, neither alone is sufficient. This parallels good clinical practice where the complicated easy encompasses technical skills and reasoning, and the simple hard the processes of interacting with patients, carers and other professionals. Indeed the simple hard aspects of clinical care and those of *real* management are very similar; it is in the complicated easy that they all differ.

The following comparison will illustrate this.

Simple hard aspects of:

Clinical practice

- The interaction is seen by both parties as a meeting between experts. One expert has a detailed knowledge of the relevant abnormality and of prognosis, treatments and risks. The other has expert knowledge of his or her lifestyle, personal priorities, hopes and fears. These two kinds of expertise must be brought together; this requires an openness to the other and to what he or she is saying that is unencumbered by stereotype and prejudgement.

Real management

- *Real* managers engage similarly with their 'clients', who are their staff. We saw in Chapter 7 that *real* managers do not solve problems, they sell them; so they deal openly with their staff, recognizing that unless the two kinds of expert knowledge (strategic and operational) are brought together, no satisfactory solution will be devised. They listen to their HCPs unhindered by stereotyping in their judgements.

- The transparency standard[1] requires that a clinician's reasoning is made transparent to the patient. Such transparency requires clinicians to engage in ongoing consideration of their own reasoning. They need to note and challenge any 'leaps of abstraction'.[2] They must also be aware of their own feelings, conscious of the causes of unpleasant emotions and the ensuing behaviours.

- Real managers also make their reasoning transparent to their staff. They too reflect upon any leaps of abstraction and try to be aware of the impact their feelings have on their behaviour.

- Where bad news must be given, in this ideal interaction it is given with genuine care; the clinician empathizes (brackets themselves)[3] with the patient and does not allow his or her own feelings of discomfort to impede effectiveness or empathy.

- When bad news must be given they do not delegate its telling to a minion nor send it in writing: they give it personally, in full understanding of its implications for the receiver.

- When asked to make a difficult decision, the good clinician agonizes but retains the ability to act.

- When asked to make a difficult decision, real managers act decisively, but they are also fully and passionately aware of the negative consequences of each option.

- The course of action recommended (or agreed with the patient) may differ for different patients with the same clinical condition since their circumstances and personalities differ.

- Real managers select different approaches with different staff according to their perception of personalities and preferences.

- Good clinicians gracefully accept challenges to their way of seeing, or thinking, from patients, carers, colleagues and members of other professions. They incorporate such new information into a review of the evidence on which decisions about diagnosis and treatment are based.

- Real managers similarly encourage challenges to their thinking and actively seek dissidents and devil's advocates.

Thus real managers and good clinicians alike spend time and energy on the simple hard, and HCPs who develop their real management skills become better clinicians too. They recognize that the ways in which they work with others require attention, time and energy in their own right. They adopt behaviours which are generous and disciplined, and gently but firmly challenge behaviours which are not.

The trouble with the simple hard is that it is unattractive on two counts. First, it is simple. There are no interesting new facts, no new applications of logic, no satisfying analyses and calculations. Second, it is hard. Try it only once and it will fail; it requires constant practice. Naturally therefore the ungenerous and undisciplined will dismiss it as trivial and impractical. They will claim that the problems are all caused by others and blame lack of resources and increasing expectations. Of course resources may be an issue. They may not: ungenerosity and indiscipline are so very expensive that we cannot know. However, it is only by working together in generosity and discipline that we can adduce the evidence that will enable the taxpayer to make a sensible choice.

Ultimately we may need to recast the education processes for many of the healthcare professions, using the engendering of generosity and discipline as the criterion for selection of teaching methods and philosophies. This could accompany changes to the complicated easy that must take place as needs for new and different skill combinations emerge. However, we must not wait for that to happen. Indeed it will not happen unless opinion-formers within the professions experience the benefits of real management themselves.

So real management is not something to wait for. It starts today with your next decision, or not at all.

Notes

Introduction

1 Batten, J. (1991). *Tough Minded Leadership*. Amacom, New York. In this book, Batten contrasts the complex easy with the simple tough and draws a further distinction between tough and hard – the former resilient, the latter brittle. However, for a British audience, the terms 'hard' and 'complicated' more accurately convey the sense he intends.

Chapter 1

1 I employ the term 'healthcare professional', abbreviated to HCP, throughout the book. It is used to refer to members of all the clinical and clinical support professions.

2 I am referring here to the feedback that is an ongoing part of a manager's or leader's role. The formal feedback that forms part of a disciplinary procedure is different and requires local specialist advice from the personnel department.

3 Batten, J. (1991). *Tough Minded Leadership*. Amacom, New York.

4 Peters, T. and Austin, N. (1986). *Passion for Excellence*. Fontana, London.

5 Maslow, A. (1954). *Motivation and Personality*. Harper and Row, London.

6 Hunt, J. (1986). *Managing People at Work*. McGraw-Hill, London. This book provides a readable, research-based, wide-ranging discussion of individual motivation, group processes and organizational structures.

7 Belbin, R.M. (1996) *Team Roles at Work*. Butterworth Heinemann, Oxford. The original research is described in Belbin, R.M. (1981). *Management Teams: Why They Succeed or Fail*. Butterworth Heinemann, Oxford. The concepts are now widely disseminated, but it is worth reading about the research on which they are based.

8 Honey, P. and Mumford, A. (1986). *A Manual of Learning Styles*. Peter Honey, Maidenhead.

9 Jung, C.G. (1990). *Collected Works*. Routledge, London.
10 Alessandra, T. and Cathcart, J. (1985). *Relationship Strategies*. Nightingale Conant, Chicago. Only available on audio-cassette.
11 de Pree, M. (1989). *Leadership is an Art*. Arrow Business Books, London. A simple, heart-felt book that needs to be read carefully and repeatedly.

Chapter 2

1 Janis, I.L. (1971). Group think. *Psychology Today*. Reprinted in Hackman, J.R., Lawler, E.E. and Porter, L.W. (eds) (1983). *Perspectives on Behaviour in Organizations*, pp. 378–84. McGraw-Hill, New York. This classic text is well worth tracking down.
2 Blois, M. (1984). *Information and Medicine: The Nature of Medical Descriptions*. University of California Press, Stanford, CA. Hierarchical levels of medical descriptions, page 113.
3 From Blois (1984). See note 2. Descriptions of natural objects allocated to appropriate hierarchical levels to produce a knowledge network, page 47.
4 Tuggett, D., Boulton, M., Olson, C. and Williams, A. (1985). *Meetings Between Experts*. Tavistock, London. A fascinating description of qualitative research into the nature of doctor–patient conversations and the factors which influence recall.
5 Succintly described by Marsden Blois (1984). See note 2.
6 See note 2.
7 Quoted in Wulff, H.R., Audut Pedersen, S. and Rosenberg, R. (1990). *The Philosophy of Medicine*, pp. 2–7. Blackwell Scientific, Oxford.
8 Simply described in Popkin, R.H., Stroll, A. and Kelly, A.V. (1969). *Philosophy Made Simple*. W.H. Allen, London.
9 Ibid., p. 41.
10 Ibid., p. 41.
11 See Jones, S. (1994). *The Language of Genes*. Flamingo, London.
12 Peck, M.S. (1979). *The Road Less Travelled*. Arrow Books, London. Many people I have worked with have found this book to be profoundly helpful.
13 Ibid.
14 Seedhouse, D. (1991). *Liberating Medicine*. John Wiley, New York. Seedhouse applied this definition to the role of the doctor, I have amended it to apply to all HCPs.
15 See note 12.
16 See, for example, Smith, R. (1994). Medicine's core values. *British Medical Journal, 309*, 1247–8.
17 This is covered in Covey, S. (1990). *The Seven Habits of Highly Effective People*. Simon and Schuster, New York. Covey uses the terms 'win' and 'lose'. Two psychologists, Kenneth Thomas and Ralph Kilmann, have devised a questionnaire, The Thomas-Kilmann Conflict Mode Instrument (XICOM, New York, 1992), to help assess individuals' preferred conflict mode, and use the terms 'competing', 'accommodating', etc.
18 Smith, M.J. (1981). *When I Say No I Feel Guilty*. Bantam Books, New York.
19 Dickson, A. (1987). *A Woman in Your Own Right*. Quartet Books, London.
20 Gaunt, R. (1991). *Personal and Group Development for Managers*. Longman, London. This book is highly recommended to anyone wishing to develop skills in action learning or in mentoring.
21 'Bracketing' is the phrase used by Peck to describe this activity (see note 12).

Chapter 3

1 Covey, S. (1990). *The Seven Habits of Highly Effective People*. Simon and Schuster, New York. A number of people I have worked with have found this book to live up to its title; namely, it has helped them to become more effective. It has also helped them to assess the development inputs required by others in their organization. I find this book complements Peck, M.S. (1979). *The Road Less Travelled*. Arrow Books, London. Peck's book introduces the territory, whereas Covey's book is a 'how to' manual.
2 Taken from Covey (1990). See note 1.
3 de Pree, M. (1989). *Leadership is an Art*. Arrow Business Books, London.
4 Quoted in Peck (1979). See note 1.

Chapter 4

1 See, for example, Bradley, W. (1993). *Disease Diagnosis and Decisions*. John Wiley, New York.
2 Peters, T. and Waterman, R. (1980). Structure is not organization. Business horizons, Indiana University. In *The Strategy Process* (edited by J.B. Quinn and H. Mintzberg), pp. 309–14. Prentice-Hall, Englewood Cliffs, NJ. Figure 4.1 is taken from this paper.
3 Porter, M. (1980). *Competitive Strategy*. The Free Press, New York. Porter means by this that in order to compete successfully products must either be significantly different from others in the same market or they must be produced in the most efficient way allowing the price to be lower. We can argue about whether healthcare is, or should be, a proper market; but whether it is or not, the discipline of testing out bland assumptions/assertions about the value of a service against these two competitive stances is worthwhile.
4 See Gaunt, R. (1991). *Personal and Group Development for Managers*. Longman, London.
5 See Glaser, R. (1988). *The Force Field: Problem Solving Model Exercise*. Organization Design and Development Inc., Pennsylvania.
6 de Pree, M. (1989). *Leadership is an Art*. Arrow Business Books, London.
7 Russell Ackoff takes this distinction further and talks of 'problems' and 'messes'. A group of changing problems which interact with each other is a mess. Ackoff suggests that the role of the manager is to manage messes. Quoted in Schön, D.A. (1983). *The Reflective Practitioner*. Temple Smith, London.

Chapter 5

1 From a survey conducted by Drury and co-workers. Reported in Drury, C. (1994). *Costing: An Introduction*. Chapman and Hall, London. This book is an accessible introduction to management accounting.
2 See note 1.
3 Because healthcare services are so complex, you may find it easier to familiarize yourself with the concepts of management accounting by visualizing widget production.
4 See note 1.

Chapter 6

1 Covey, S. (1990). *The Seven Habits of Highly Effective People.* Simon and Schuster, New York.
2 Peck, M.S. (1979). *The Road Less Travelled.* Arrow Books, London.
3 Taken from Peck (1979). See note 2.
4 Ibid.
5 Ibid.
6 Quoted in Senge, P. (1990). *The Fifth Discipline.* Century Business, London. This book is about how to help organizations to learn. It contains valuable information on how to encourage team learning, develop shared visions and challenge mental models. It is also a good introduction to systems thinking.
7 Taken from Peck (1979). See note 2.
8 See Stewart, I. and Joines, V. (1987). T.A. Today: An Introduction to Transactional Analysis. Lifespace, Nottingham.
9 See note 1.
10 For many people, and women in particular, the advice of a good colour consultant can be very liberating as well as fun. Feeling confident that you look your best means that you never have to think about it and you can concentrate on the task at hand. House of Colour and Colour Me Beautiful are both reputable companies.
11 See Batten, J. (1989). *Tough Minded Leadership.* Amacom, New York.
12 This view was expressed by Berwick at a conference on 'Quality Management' run by the British Medical Association in 1993. The application of total quality management to health care is described in: Enthoven, A. and Bunker, J.P. (1992a). Quality management in the NHS: The doctor's role I. *British Medical Journal, 304,* pp. 235–9; Enthoven, A. and Bunker, J.P. (1992b). Quality management in the NHS: The doctor's role II. *British Medical Journal, 304,* pp. 304–8.
13 Toffler, A. (1973). *Future Shock.* Pan, London.
14 See note 1.

Chapter 7

1 Donabedian, A. (1980). *Explorations in Quality Assessment and Monitoring Vol. II: The Definition of Quality and Approaches to Its Assessment.* Health Administration Press, Ann Arbor, MI.
2 Seedhouse, D. (1991). *Liberating Medicine.* John Wiley, New York.
3 de Pree, M. (1989). *Leadership is an Art.* Arrow Business Books, London.
4 See, for example, Walton, M. (1991). *Deming Management at Work.* Mercury, London. This book includes a study which introduces Deming's principles to the Hospital Corporation of America.
5 Senge, P. (1990). *The Fifth Discipline.* Century Business, London.
6 Highlighted by Berwick at a conference on 'Quality Management' run by the British Medical Association in 1993.
7 See note 3.
8 This is a quote from one of Tom Peters' videos, entitled 'Excellence in the public sector', Melrose, 1989.
9 Hamel expressed this view at a seminar at the London Business School in 1994. See Hamel, G. and Prahalad, C.K. (1994). *Competing for the Future.* HBS Press, Boston, MA.

10 Hampton Turner, C. and Trompenaars, F. (1994). *The Seven Cultures of Capitalism*. Piatkus, London.
11 See note 5.
12 See note 9.

Chapter 8

1 See the systems templates in Senge, P. (1990). *The Fifth Discipline*. Century Business, London.

Chapter 9

1 Quoted in Seedhouse, D. (1991). *Liberating Medicine*. John Wiley, New York. The 'transparency standard' is advocated by American ethicist Howard Brody. According to this standard, adequate informed consent is obtained when a reasonably informed patient is allowed to participate in the medical decision to the extent that the patient wishes. In turn 'reasonably informed' consists of two features
   (i) the physician discloses the basis on which the proposed treatment or alternative possible treatments, have been chosen; and
   (ii) the patient is allowed to ask questions suggested by the disclosure of the physician's reasoning and those questions are answered to the patient's satisfaction.
   According to the transparency model . . . disclosure is adequate when a physician's basic thinking has been rendered transparent to the patient.
2 'Leaps of abstraction' is the term Senge uses in *The Fifth Discipline*, Century Business, London (1990) for the unsound conclusions we make from limited evidence which then form a dangerously faulty platform for further reasoning. He suggests noting them but also voicing them to allow the subject of the abstraction (usually the person we are talking to or about) to comment on their validity.
3 See Peck, M.S. (1979). *The Road Less Travelled*. Arrow Books, London. Bracketing is the term Peck uses for the empathic listening described in Chapter 2.